Lesley Ash not only used to read Jackie, she used to appear on the cover! See the back pages and cover from 1977!

"Girls don't realise it, but most fourteen-year-old boys read Jackie. I used to read Cathy and Claire every week." — Rik Mayall.

"I used to buy Jackie when I was younger — and I loved it!" — Hazell Dean.

"I read Jackie . . ." and so say all of us! Kim Wilde, Bananarama, Limahl, Paula Yates, Shirley Holliman, Wham!, Clare Grogan, Joan Armatrading, Tracey Ullman, Billy McKenzie, Dee C Lee, Nick Heyward, Janice Long, Cheryl Baker . . . we could go on, but we don't like to boast!

AND take a wander down Memory ne! Turn to the back pages for the ntinuing saga of 'Jackie through e ages' . . .

YOU SAID IT!
YOU SAID IT!
YOU SAID IT!
YOU SAID IT!
YOU SAID IT!
YOU SAID

Paul Weller has done his fair share of talking in the past few years. Not noted for being one of the least outspoken people around, here're a few of the controversial and not so controversial things he's said in his time . . .

Paul Weller on himself:
"I've got on well with everyone I've met."
"I don't eat meat or fish."
"I don't see myself as British any more."
"I don't care any more; I'm just going to do what I want to do and say what I want to say. I don't care if people think I've cracked or changed or whatever. I'm an angry young man."
"I'm a bit like Oscar Wilde."

Paul Weller on The Jam:
"It wasn't really a hard decision to split because I realised that The Jam was getting limited and it would become meaningless to carry on with it."

Paul Weller on The Style Council:
"It sums up something more than just music — it refers to culture more widely."
"This Europe thing is us trying to broaden our horizons and look further than our own lifestyles."
"We're a bit of a culture club, quite honestly."

Paul Weller on politics:
"The problem with England is that it's so tied up with America."
"The women at Greenham Common are the real patriots, the people who really care about England, and yet they are being slagged off."

Paul Weller on music:
"I really like Culture Club, George has got a brilliant voice."
"The British music scene is absolute rubbish. There are all these guitar-based bands churning out the same stuff, and it's meaningless, it doesn't do anything, it doesn't achieve anything, and it's just boring."
"Record companies call records 'product,' and sales 'units.' They might just as well be selling baked beans or dog food!"

Paul Weller on Nick Heyward's lyrics:
"Where's your head, Nick?"

and on the most fanciable human being . . .
"Mick Talbot."

Jackie

ACKNOWLEDGEMENTS

The Publishers would like to thank the team at DC Thomson & Co. Ltd for
all their help in compiling this book, particularly Martin Lindsay.

THIS IS A PRION BOOK

First published in the UK in 2007 by Prion
An imprint of the Carlton Publishing Group
20 Mortimer Street
London W1T 3JW

ISBN: 978-1-85375-626-9

Edited and compiled by Lara Maiklem and Lorna Russell

Art director: Lucy Coley
Production: Janette Burgin

PR**I**ON

Jackie
ALL YOUR FAVOURITES!

More of The Best of The Annual

CONTENTS

POP

FEATURES

Living

BEAUTY

FUN

QUIZZES

Fashion

FICTION

FOREWORD

Hello!

Looking through the pages of this collection brings back so many happy memories. I remember tearing the wrapping paper off my first *Jackie Annual* on Christmas Day as if it were yesterday. Over the years I've collected old copies of *Jackie* from its first issue in 1964 to the last in 1993, but it wasn't until the 1980s that I finally persuaded Mum that I was old enough to buy it!

Those were the days, when all we ever wanted was curls like Farah Fawcett, eye makeup like Kim Wilde and to be dating John Travolta. The *Jackie* of the 1980s was so different from the *Jackie* my older sister read in the 1970s. We had Shakin' Stevens, Limahl, Captain Sensible, Adam Ant and Boy George; music was both New and Romantic, the two things we really loved, and we listened in every Sunday to see if Duran Duran or Spandau Ballet would top the week's charts.

Fashion was hugely important because trends were changing so quickly. One week tartan was in (even after the Bay City Rollers) and the next everyone was wearing boys' waistcoats, fingerless gloves and legwarmers – for a while I even had a snood! *Jackie* would tell me who my fashion sense was going to attract: bad boys, shy boys, sports fans or the boy next door. You could even tell what type of boy he was from the shape of his face or the shape of his thumbs! And there were, of course, a hundred different ways to tell what kind of girl you were, from the way your bedroom looked to the way you wrote your diary.

More importantly, once you got the boy you were after, what did you do with him? What if he was useless and you had to take the lead? Where did you lead him? Or what if he was all wandering hands? What could you do about that? Cathy and Claire were all well and good for some down-to-earth advice, but the annuals also gave you handy, one-page features on everything from first date nerves to break-up blues.

Boys read the annuals too; it gave them inside knowledge into what made teenage girls tick, which gave them a distinct advantage when it came to finding out what girls really liked. But what could you say to a girl whose obsession was spots, or blushing, or oily hair, especially if you didn't look like Leif Garrett? Once again it was

Jackie to the rescue, with guides on how to keep a conversation going and working out if you were making a good impression through body language – invaluable to both genders, I'm sure!

But it wasn't all boys and fashion. For a while the magazine went mad for white Toblerones when they first appeared, and I remember, when Sarah Ferguson was about to marry Prince Andrew in 1986, *Jackie* ran features on beauty tips for redheads. Then there were the crafty articles that showed how to make jewellery, knitted legwarmers, customized T-shirts and gifts – vital when having to rely on pocket money and Saturday job earnings! This was also the era of the Brat Pack, when our heroes were Emilio Estevez, Molly Ringwald, Demi Moore and Rob Lowe. *Jackie,* of course, was there with the inside scoop on movies such as *The Breakfast Club, St. Elmo's Fire* and *Pretty in Pink* (and to this day, I *still* believe Andie should have chosen devoted Duckie over feeble rich-boy Blane).

For many, the 1980s is now a source cringing shame, from over-sized T-shirts

to the puffball skirt, which surfaced again briefly in more recent years only to, thankfully, die another swift death. Yet I still have a great fondness for many of that era's trends; the music, the fashions, television shows and films, many of which have now made a comeback or influenced the popular culture of today.

One of the *Jackie* articles featured in this collection, 'A Time for Love', looks back over what life was like for teen girls during Medieval, Puritan and Victorian times, and asks, 'Do you wish you'd been there? Or does it make you realise just how lucky you are to live in our pulsating, punky, plastic, dare we say perfect age?' Re-reading that now, I can honestly say this: with *Jackie* on hand, I wouldn't have missed the 1980s for the world!

Melissa Hyland

(Journalist and diehard *Jackie* fan)

For your delight this year, ladies and gentlemen (because we just *know* that there are some gentlemen out there who read Jackie), we have pleasure in introducing The Jackie Christmas Show! Everyone you could hope for — and a few you probably haven't thought of — are here! So settle down and *ENJOY* yourselves!

FIRSTLY, let us introduce the one who'll be doing most of our introducing for us, none other than that well-known compere, that little green Master of Ceremonies, yes, Kermit the Frog.

"OK, OK, get in line for The Muppet . . . on no, The Jackie Show! And first to step on to the stage are Elton John and the Watford Football Team just to kick things off — take it awayyyyy, Elton."

It's probably dawned on you by now that part of the reason we asked Kermit to come along to MC for us was so that we could all have a good time with him in the wings between acts. And talking of Wings, Paul and Linda are getting a bit annoyed at us standing between them having fun.

"All right, you people, quiet for our next guest, or should I say guests? Yes, I suppose I should, because even though they move as one body (and what a body that is!) there are quite a few of them — let me introduce to you — Hot Gossip . . ."

This is the point where everyone in the audience starts crowding the stage front to get their paws on Floyd, or Donna Fielding, or any other member of the group they can reach. Fortunately we Jackie people are quite prepared for this kind of thing and we've got a couple of bouncers along to hold the crowds back — The Incredible Hulk and Dolly Parton — just try getting past them!

But wait! Someone from the audience *has* managed to fight his way past them . . . it's Sid Snot, thinly disguised

as Kenny Everett, and he wants Hot Gossip all to himself . . .

"Now, folks, let's have a big hand for someone who's bound to make this a Billericay Dickie of a show — Ian Dury and the Blockheads — ayyy!"

WELL, that was really great, Ian, and now for something a little lighter, we've got a few stand-up comics waiting in the wings for you. There's Tony Blackburn–you mean you *don't* think his jokes are wonderful? Oh well, you can always throw (Johnny) rotten tomatoes at him. Then there's Demis Roussos, we laugh at him every time he stands up — it's something to do with those dresses he wears; and then, wait for it, the cast of "Crossroads", just being themselves . . .

And it looks as if those acts have gone down very well indeed because Alison has just spotted a very regal wave from the royal box (we thought we'd better invite Her Majesty along to make sure we pulled in the crowds) and what's this? YES! It's that right royal prince, Andrew. This is the moment where the bouncers have to stop all the Jackie staff from climbing up to the box!

Meanwhile, another big hand for our compere extardinaire, Kermit . . .

"And next in this star-studded cast we give you the

CHRISTMAS SHOW!

delightful, the lovely, the blond and beautiful — no, not you, Farrah dear — Rod Stewart! And we've got him along specially so that he can come to our end of show party, then we can show him that brunettes, redheads, mousey browns — and grassy greens even — can have *just* as much fun as blondes.

"Thank-you, Rod. And we're really boxing clever now, folks, because we're going to have Bob's Big Box Game set up on stage for you. Yes, they're all here to pit their wits against questions from us, the rest of the cast, but mainly YOURSELVES."

And Lesley takes the lead by asking Sylvester Stallone if she can rub him down between rounds in "Rocky II" (not the kind of questions we'd expected . . .) but he's saying no to that one and Lesley's fainted and is getting a quick rub-down from Kermit. Rod's just asked David Bowie if he can have a few make-up tips and David's now busy with pen and paper making a list . . .

PAULA'S next and she's asking Magnus Pyke why it is that her best pal Marjie's toes curl up every time anyone so much as mentions Edward Fox, and Magnus has fallen out of his box trying to explain it — not to worry, he's landed on Dolly Parton.

An R.S.P.C.A. inspector has just demanded to know why we have six Rats all squashed into one little box and none of us has had a chance to answer because Modest Bob won't shut up!

Anne's just asked Madge and Beryl if they really do argue all the time and Beryl's said of course they don't, Madge has interrupted and said they do sometimes, Beryl's hit Madge . . .

And we'll just carry on with the next question which comes from Fiona, and she wanted to ask Fred Astaire and Ginger Rogers how they manage to trip the light fantastic so fantastically but they seem to have paso dobled out of their box and far, far away!

And what's happening here? One of the people in the boxes is asking Kermit a question, it's Miss Piggy, and she wants to know when they're getting married! Kermit's fainted and Lesley's giving him a rub-down now.

We've got Muhammad Ali here too but he's pulling no punches at all by speaking so loudly and fast that no-one has a chance to ask him anything. And last, but certainly not least, we've got Martin Shaw and Lewis Collins adding a certain amount of professionalism to the whole show. I would've liked to ask them something but I couldn't stop drooling!

And so, as all good things come to an end so does The Jackie Show. For our big finish a word from our Ed.

"Thank-you all so much for coming along to my little show. I'd just like to say how happy I am . . ." CURTAIN.

BOY CALENDAR 1980

WHERE THEY'LL THEY'LL BE —AND HOW TO

SPRING

THE DAFFODILS are out, there's a spring in your step, the birds are pairing off and every boy's fancy is turning to love . . .

WHERE THEY'LL BE

Down by the riverbank, enjoying the last of the fishing season. Packed like sardines on the football terraces, throwing all sort of things at the ref. Learning Martial Arts at an Evening Class, so they'll be ready for the Bully on the Beach next summer. Or just dozing in the back row of the cinema as they watch "Enter The Dragon" for the 120th time . . .

WHAT THEY'LL BE WEARING

Spring's still a pretty cold time of year nowadays, so boys everywhere will be wrapped up warm in fraying sweaters, moth-eaten Parkas, football scarves and even woolly bobble hats (groan!). But don't despair, because just as a gorgeous butterfly will emerge from a crummy-looking chrysalis, a moth-eaten Parka can give way to better things . . .

SPRING SMALL TALK

Right, now you're about to stroll along to where you know the boys will be . . . Stuck for something to say to them? You mean you don't know the kind of small talk that's suitable for spring? Well, here are a few openers that ought to come in handy!

To the boy in the cinema:
"Excuse me, can I borrow your (sniff!) hankie?"

"Is that Bruce Lee or the Dragon?"

"I'm scared! Mind if I hold on to you?"

To the boy on the riverbank:
"What's the biggest fish you've ever caught?"

"What's the biggest lie you've ever told?"

"Are those really maggots?"

To the boy on the football terraces:
"Who's winning?"

"Why's that one dressed all in black? Has someone died?"

"Who's that one in the cage down the far end?"

SPRING THINGS TO DO

Once you and your boy are going steady, you'll need some ideas for things to do — public places to go to have fun, and private places for whispers and tender moments . . .

PUBLIC FUN

Spring can be cold or mild. So indoor and outdoor things are both needed. Fancy learning judo together? Or swimming? Or gymnastics? Weight-training? Or something gentler, such as jewellery-making or pottery? Why not enrol together at night school? It's great fun, and courses are in full swing in the spring.

As for the great outdoors, wrap up warm and go out in search of the first ducklings (parks and riverbanks), daffodils (council flowerbeds) and cowslips and harebells (the wild, wild woods). Go and see the animals in the zoo (you're bound to find one that looks just like him).

PRIVATE MOMENTS

It's hard to find places to be private in, unless the weather's very mild (in which case, wander along to the wild, wild woods again). A city's best, really, as there are lots of steamy, cosy little cafes you can cuddle up together in.

HOW TO END IT

If it all starts to go wrong, and he begins to say things like "Cowslips remind me of you . . ." **(Cow's lips — how dare he!)**, then it's obviously time to Spring Away in the other direction. But how? Tell him you're giving him up for Lent.

If you're the gentle, lying type, tell him you're going to Switzerland on a long Easter holiday, and he mustn't ring you up for at least three weeks. Then when he phones again, tell him you met a wonderful Swiss boy called Hans Kneesanboompsadaisy or Heinz Fiftisevenvarieteez, and that you're terribly in love!

BE——WHAT WEARING CATCH THEM!

As the year wheels round and the seasons change, boys change too. They look different, they do different things, and if you want to catch one of them and turn him into a super boyfriend, *you'll* have to adapt *your* technique to the time of year too! Study our special Boy Calendar for all you need to know about boys and their habits — all year round!

SUMMER

BIRDS, bees, flowers and cricket umpires are blossoming all over the country. Summer's a lovely, idyllic time of year . . . but are all those boys ready for their idyll?

WHERE THEY'LL BE

Playing football or cricket in the park, lying in the sun outside the pub, lying in the dust under their motor-bikes or lying in a puddle of chlorine by the swimming pool. Gathering on the beach for a game of Frisbee, going for long hikes along the Pennine Way . . . Or even, if they're studious, in the library, 'cos it's exam time, too, you know!

WHAT THEY'LL BE WEARING

Summer's the only time most boys look good. You can't go wrong with a T-shirt and jeans, can you? A stripey T-shirt shows he's a sporty type. A T-shirt with a rude message on shows he's a rude boy (but some rude boys are in disguise!). A T-shirt with arrows on it shows that he's escaped from jail.

SUMMER SMALL TALK

OK, so you're all togged up in your prettiest summer clothes! If you teeter over to his motor-bike and he *still* doesn't look up, you'll need some summer small talk—

To the bike boy:
"What does two-stroke mean?"
"What a beautiful bike!"
"What's the fastest you've ever gone on that thing?"

To the studious boy swotting for his exams:
"Would you like an iced Coke?"
"Can I sharpen your Biro for you?"
"Shall I test you on Julius Caesar?"

To the boy lying in the sun:
"Gosh, you're really brown! What suntan oil do you use?"
"Excuse me, would you mind rubbing oil on my back?"
"Are you asleep?"
"Do you mind if I join you?"

SUMMER THINGS TO DO

Once the exams are over and everyone's gloriously *free*, you

and your boyfriend will have the long summer days to get to know each other, in all sorts of different places!

PUBLIC FUN

Now's your chance to get out and enjoy the sun (or cloud). Go swimming, walking, sailing, boating, biking. (You can hire boats, bikes and even boots.) Take crazy photos of each other paddling in streams and falling off haystacks. Have a picnic with your mates out in the country. Collect wild flowers (and tame ones). Make him a daisy chain. Get a tan together. Go to London or the nearest big city for the day and wander about sight-seeing.

At night try the disco, and if it's too steamy for that, have an open-air barbecue! Go to an open-air play — there are masses of them on all over the country. Go to a pop festival if you can afford it. Try camping with some friends, if you've never tried it before. Britain's full of beautiful places. Or go abroad (a day trip to France if you're broke — bring back some smelly cheese for Dad).

PRIVATE MOMENTS

Well, you've got the whole of the countryside for your private moments. Walking around a rose garden at twilight is glorious — the scents are perfect.

And if you're on holiday, meet on the beach at 6 a.m. when everyone else is still asleep . . .

HOW TO END IT

Summer romances are notorious for being short and sweet. If a sour note begins to creep in, take action! If you met him on holiday, tell him you've got a steady boyfriend at home. If he *is* the steady boyfriend at home, tell him that you met someone on holiday (even if you didn't)! If he keeps phoning you, tell him you've got sunstroke (*especially* if it's cloudy). If he keeps writing to you, return the letter unopened, marked "GONE OFF." Well, you may not have gone *away*, but you've certainly gone *off* him!

➤

♥

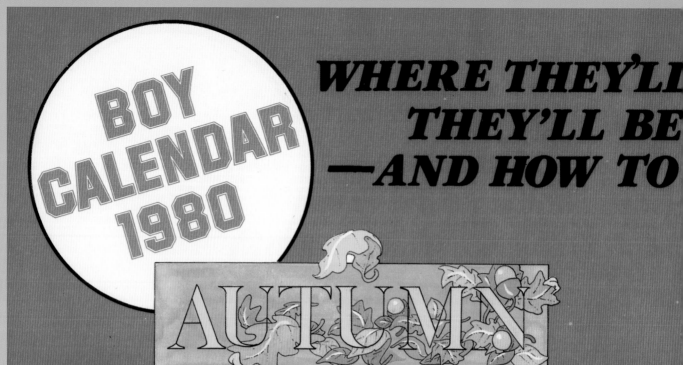

AUTUMN

AH, autumn, the "season of mists and mellow fruitfulness," as someone once wrote . . . The season of going back to school, college, or work. Of new beginnings. And maybe new boys!

WHERE THEY'LL BE

It's the start of the football season (enough said). And the fishing season. Plays and concerts really get going in the autumn, so he could be rehearsing. Or you might find him sweeping up dead leaves and building a bonfire. Or jogging. Or taking his dog for a walk. Or writing poems about mists and mellow fruitfulness.

WHAT THEY'll BE WEARING

If they've got protective mums, they'll be wearing their winter vests (not that you'll be able to tell, thank goodness). Now's the time when cuddly, brushed-cotton tartan shirts, Fair Isle pullovers, boots instead of sneakers, and last year's bomber jackets (some of them look as if the bomb's already dropped) begin to appear.

AUTUMN SMALL TALK

As you saunter about looking stunning, don't forget you'll need some juicy pieces of small talk to get him well and truly hooked. Try . . .

To the boy walking his dog:
"What a beautiful dog! What's his breed/age/name?"
"Can I throw a stick for him?"
"Does he do tricks?"
To the boy building a bonfire:
"Is this for Guy Fawkes Night?"
"Can I help?"
"Need any potato-bakers?"

To the boy jogging:
"Are you training (puff, pant)?"
"Tell me, where did you get your lovely — gasp — track-suit?"
"You're not Brendan Foster's brother, are you?"

AUTUMN THINGS TO DO

Once you've joined your jogger, hooked your fisherman or prised your poet away from his pen, what can you do to make life lively in autumn? Well, there's . . .

PUBLIC FUN

Autumn's full of celebrations. Most places have Michaelmas Fairs in October. So eat candy floss together. Go on the Big Dipper together (and be sick behind the Rifle Range together). Then, there's Hallowe'en. You could have a ghoulish party, or do "Trick or Treat" with the neighbours. And then there's Guy Fawkes Night,

when you can cling to him (*your Guy*) as the rockets take off, and share a baked potato in the glow of the bonfire.

Autumn's when evening classes start, too, and if you're interested in drama, most local groups start rehearsing for their pantos now. How about you as Cinderella and him as an Ugly Sister? Sell poppies together on Remembrance Day. Go apple-picking together. Make sure you go to the disco regularly — jogging's not the only way to keep fit, you know!

PRIVATE MOMENTS

Why not meet in the churchyard on All Hallows' Eve (you might not be alone, though!)? Wandering around the country lanes is lovely at this time of year, too — there are haystacks to sit behind, and the fields are all warm from the summer sun. If you're stuck in the town, find a sheltered corner of the park and whisper sweet nothings as the leaves fall all around you . . .

HOW TO END IT

If, as the weather cools, so does your passion, you'll have to do something about it! Tell him you've got to concentrate on some work and you'll see him again at Easter! Make a Guy Fawkes who looks just like him and see if he twigs! Ask him to pose as a model for your turnip-lantern on Hallowe'en . . .

If none of these delicate hints gets through his turnip-head, tell him that you've got an evening job and can't see him any more. If he suggests weekends, tell him you've got a weekend job, too. And if he asks what the job is, tell him it's as a Boy Disposal Officer!

BE — WHAT WEARING CATCH THEM!

BOY CALENDAR 1980

WINTER

WHEN icicles hang by the wall in winter-time, the problem is to find a nice warm boy to cuddle up to. So . . .

WHERE THEY'LL BE

Wherever it's warm! Herded together at pop concerts, discos, record shops and cafés. Christmas is a great time for meeting boys, as there are lots of parties, and plenty of mistletoe about. New Year's Eve is great, too — once you join hands for "Auld Lang Syne," hold on tight and don't let him go! If it snows, you'll find lots of boys out in the park, throwing snowballs and making snow-women . . .

WHAT THEY'LL BE WEARING

Long coms, if they've got any sense! Luckily, most boys don't have much sense, so you'll find them in their usual winter gear or lumberjack shirts, cowboy boots, soldiers' jerseys and donkey jackets (which, unfortunately, all look better on lumberjacks, cowboys, soldiers and donkeys).

WINTER SMALL TALK

As you bear down on him in your winter woollies, try some winter small talk . . .

To the boy in the record shop:
"Excuse me, what's the difference between the Four Tops and the Three Degrees?"
"May I look while you flip?"
or even, "Is this a record?"

To the boy standing alone at a party:
"Haven't I seen you somewhere before?"
"I don't know anybody here — do you?"

"You're not quite under the mistletoe — move a step to the right!"

To the boy at the pop concert:
"You're standing on my toe!"
"May I sit on your shoulders to get a better view?"
and, when the band starts,
"----- -- ----- --- ------?"
(these bands are really LOUD!).

WINTER THINGS TO DO

The world can be a winter wonderland with the right boy at your side. Here's how to get yourselves organised and enjoy it!

PUBLIC FUN

Go carol-singing together for a chance to hold hands in the dark and sing in close harmony (you don't get that sort of chance often!). Then, go to all the Christmas parties, even if you have to gatecrash! Carol Services are pretty nice if you fancy a serious evening. And put the decorations up together. He can hold the ladder steady and catch you if you fall!

If it snows, chuck snowballs at each other. Make a snowboy and snowgirl. Go sliding on the ice. Cook potatoes in their jackets and hot soup when you get back. If there's a blizzard outside — play Monopoly, or Mastermind, or even a game of Snap!

PRIVATE MOMENTS

The occasional moment behind the Christmas tree (with your own bit of mistletoe) isn't going to last very long. For a real bit of privacy, go to the public library and hide behind the stacks. Or take a round trip in a country bus (on the back seat!). Or find one of those cosy cafés with seats in alcoves . . .

HOW TO END IT

If you want to ring out the old and ring in the new, it's not difficult to think of an excuse. Tell him you're making a New Year's Resolution to give up boys altogether. Send him a Christmas stocking filled with all his old letters and presents to you. Tell him you haven't got a fairy for the tree so will he volunteer instead? Give him a Monster Plant with a card that says, "This plant reminds me of you." If that doesn't do the trick, tell him you're more interested in an Older Man at the moment (Father Christmas, to be exact!).

CATCH THE PARTY FEVER!

THE best party always turns out to be somebody else's. All *you* have to do is turn up looking ravishing (and feeling ravenous), while the poor mug who organised it is standing around perspiring like mad and feeling totally shattered after spending the whole day preparing the food and drink.

Sooner or later, though, someone will notice that you've never held a party and sooner or later they're going to suggest that you change the situation. When this happens you've got two choices . . .

1. Leave town, find a new group of friends somewhere else and start going to their parties. Or —

2. Have one!

Those of you who haven't left town, read on:

There are five things to consider before you start wildly scribbling invitations, and they are: *Why, What, Where, When and Who.*

WHY are you having a party? You must have an excuse.

WHAT kind of party will it be?
WHERE is it going to be held?
WHEN is it taking place?
WHO are you going to invite?

WHY? It's not essential to have a reason to throw a party. You

could just say, "I've got a great idea! Let's have a party!" But having a reason does help to explain why you're doing it in the first place and also stops anyone wondering if you're only giving it to make up for something awful you've done that they haven't discovered yet.

If it s near Christmas, call it a Christmas party. If it's Midsummer, make it a Midsummer party. Almost anything will do, from Guy Fawkes to the anniversary of the day you gave up your grottiest boyfriend.

Birthdays, though, are always the best reason. That way you may even get a few presents as well.

WHAT KIND OF PARTY? You could make it fancy dress except that boys are always more embarrassed about dressing up than girls are. Tramp parties are quite popular, as no-one seems to mind "dressing up" as a tramp.

If you're feeling really extravagant you could splash out and hire a disco for the night. If, however, like most of us you're not exactly loaded with spare cash, you could solve the problem by having a Bringalong party! Ask everyone to bring something for the party, salads, cheese, sandwiches, crisps, (caviare?), cans of Coke or anything else.

Then all you have to do is set out some plates and glasses and sit back — leave the rest to the guests.

IF you're having your party at home and you live in a flat, you'd be better off without the disco — unless your neighbours above and below are disco fanatics, in which case you could even invite them along.

Even if you don't live in a flat you're still likely to have a few problems. Like not waking up your kid brother or sister or both.

Try to persuade your parents to have a night out, too — you'll feel a lot more relaxed and so will your friends if you don't have them breathing down your neck. If, however, they insist on being around because they've nowhere to go or they don't trust you, or your guests, try to manoeuvre them into another room or the wardrobe or even outside to the garden shed.

Get them to take the furniture with them if and when they go, so you've got room to dance and less things to wreck!

WHEN? It's not much good holding a Christmas party in July or a Hallowe'en party in February. Parties for occasions like these ought to be held at more or less the right times.

There's no law about it,

though. If you want to hold a New Year party in October, go right ahead. Though don't be surprised if you get laughed at.

Spring always seems to be a popular time to have a party as it cheers everyone up after the long, cold Winter, and when Summer's over and there's nothing to look forward to until Christmas, an Autumn party is great fun and everyone will enjoy it all the more because there's nothing else going on.

NOW that you've sorted out why, where and when you're going to have your party you can get down to the serious business of *who* you are going to invite. The success of your party depends a lot on who your guests are and it's up to you to make sure you get it right.

If some of your friends aren't going out with anyone try to invite plenty of unattached boys along so you don't end up with a room full of wallflowers. If you *really* want to enjoy yourself don't, whatever you do, invite too much competition.

Your friend who looks like Debbie Harry's twin sister might be good fun but her presence could spoil your whole evening!

When it comes to boys, the same thing applies! If you invite

the local Casanova, even if you fancy him yourself, you're asking for trouble.

If he starts his romantic antics with some of your friends there's always the possibility that their boyfriends won't like it too much. Punch-ups at parties — especially yours — are no fun!

If this hasn't put you off the idea of having a party, then — what's stopping you? There's probably no reason why you shouldn't go ahead and throw a really great party. Being prepared means *you* should be able to enjoy yourself as well as your guests. So next time you're complaining that there are no parties to go to, take the plunge and have one yourself!

Take a very close look at your thumb. Did you know that its shape reveals a lot about the kind of person you are?

The shape of your thumb — whether it's small, large, fat or thin — tells you what makes you tick! So get to know your thumbs and gain an insight, not only into your own personality, but into those of everyone around — including the boy in your life!

THUMBS UP!

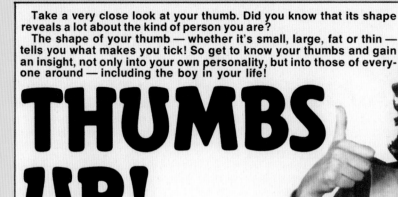

SIZE

If your thumb is Small

A small thumb means you're a romantic at heart. You love watching soppy old films on TV and you often let your heart rule your head — so watch out!

Long

Long thumbs show an interest in the mysterious, sinister things of life. You too tend to be a bit mysterious and don't like giving away much of yourself. You're highly sensitive to those around you and will defend or protect your friends no matter what the cost.

Large

If you have a large thumb you have a strong will. You believe in yourself and won't let anything or anyone stand in your way. Try not to be so ruthless, and you'll find you'll make a lot more friends!

Short

Short thumbs mean a quick temper. You're always ready for action and don't have time for those with less enthusiasm for life than you have. Try to control your temper a bit and you'll be lots happier!

SHAPE

If your thumb is Pointed

You have an ability to make people do what you want — and as a result, you usually get your own way! As you're a sympathetic listener, you're very popular with others, and you never have too little time to advise or help someone in trouble.

Straight

Persistence and stubbornness are two of your most noticeable traits. Once you've made up your mind, there's no changing it! Life might sometimes be a bit dull for you — but that's what you want. Anything unusual scares you.

Square-tipped

Square-tipped thumbs are a sign of ambition and intuition. You know instinctively which is the right path to follow, and you'll keep going till you get there. Everything you plan is carefully thought out before you decide what to do!

Waisted

Waisted thumbs — those which narrow in the middle — show a strong will and unending mounts of patience. You lead a very active life and have a love of all sports and out-of-doors activities. You're a romantic — but no-one is ever likely to have you under their thumb!

Almond shaped

You're full of energy and your whole life is spent in a state of disorganised chaos! Your impulsiveness often lands you in trouble and you're never quite sure how to get out again.

Your thumb is divided into three parts called phalanges. The first — the bottom one — shows willpower, the second reason and determination and the third, love and affection.

If your first phalange is the longest you have a bossy streak and tend to take the lead in any relationships. If it's short, you're the type who keeps your emotions to yourself and enjoys the air of mystery this creates.

The second phalange — if long, means you're obstinate — if short, it shows lack of judgment which can lead you into trouble.

The third phalange, at the top of your thumb, if long, means you have a romantic streak and you're always falling in and out of love. A short one, though, shows you're quiet, reserved and very fussy when it comes to choosing your friends.

Now that you've thumbed through our special feature, you should be an expert in thumbonology! So take another look at everyone you know, especially those you're close to, and find out thumbthing about them!

★ Do you wish upon wish that you could lose weight every time you bite into yet another cream doughtnut?

★ Do you wish upon wish you could put on just a few more pounds every time you pick and fiddle with your food?

★ Do you feel really guilty each time you gorge your way through yet another packet of chocolate biscuits?

Do You Know When To

If you answered yes to just one of these questions, then you're a foodaholic — you eat *not* because you're hungry, or because you physically *need* to, but because something's wrong with your life . . . In short, the way you eat, and the amount you eat — far too much, or far too little — is saying much more about the state of your mind and your emotions than words could ever say.

So just why do *you* nibble or gorge yourself when there's no need for it? Here's exactly what your eating habits tell about you — and how to eat your way back to health and happiness, the *right* way . . .

WHEN you were little, your mum probably gave you a sweet for being a good girl, or to comfort you when you fell over and grazed your knee. So it's natural that you should associate food with reward and pleasure, and with love and security.

At the other extreme, although you probably don't realise it, eating too little is a subconscious way of *punishing* yourself. This again goes back to childhood when Mum said, "No, you naughty girl, you don't deserve a sweet/doughnut/toffee-apple/strawberry!" So denying yourself the pleasure of enjoying your food can be a sign that you're angry with yourself, and are in fact trying to punish yourself because you feel guilty about something.

Any kind of emotional stress is likely to make you change your eating habits too — either by over-indulging yourself, or depriving yourself.

Are You Feeling Sad And Lonely?

YOU can see exactly how food is related to your emotions if you follow this girl's thoughts as she absently-mindedly works her way through a load of sweet treats!

Her name's Julie. She's going through a bad patch right now — it's Saturday night, and she's stuck at home with nowhere to go and nothing to look forward to. Her mum's out. She feels really sad and lonely . . .

"I feel rotten," she's thinking. "Nothing seems to have gone right lately. I'll have a cup of tea and a biscuit to cheer myself up . . ."

Then she thinks about school, about how badly she's doing in her Maths class and

how she thinks the teacher hates her. She's getting more and more depressed.

"I'm still hungry, I'll just have another biscuit, and some of that cake left over from tea yesterday . . ."

Next, Julie thinks about her best friend, Jenny: "She promised to ring me and she hasn't. Perhaps she doesn't like me any more, and I haven't seen Rita for *ages*, either. She's probably avoiding me, too. No-one seems to like me any more . . ."

Then she remembers a box of chocolates her mum got from an aunt. "Well, she won't mind if I just have one or two . . . Strawberry cream, my favourite!"

Now Julie starts to worry about Dave, the boy she fancies. "I really thought he was interested in me, he was always chatting me up, but then he did have to go and take that creep Linda Smith out, didn't he. Just my luck. I can't understand what's *wrong* with me . . .

"Oh God, I've eaten all the strawberry creams, plus two hazel whirls, two toffee crisps and a peppermint crunch — Mum'll be *furious*!"

Do you recognise yourself when, like Julie, you're going through a bad patch emotionally, and compensating yourself with food? The trouble is, though, the comforting effect doesn't last for long, and it's an easy temptation to eat more, and more, and more . . .

Are You A Greedy-Guts?

EMOTIONAL over-eating can become a habit which can be very hard to break . . . Take Sue, for instance. She's fifteen and very self-conscious about being overweight, even though she admits she's a bit of a pig with her food.

"The trouble is, the more I worry about

being fat the more I seem to eat," she told us.

"The funny thing is, that when I go away on holiday it's completely different — I don't think about eating at all. We went to Cornwall last summer and it was smashing — I came back all lovely and slim. But as soon as I came back home, I put it all on again . . ."

You can understand Sue's food problem if you look at it from an emotional point of view. Sue's become dependent on food as a way of coping with stress, because eating has a soothing effect on the body and emotions.

The point is, when Sue goes on holiday she's relaxed and free from stress anyway, so she doesn't need the calming-down effect of compulsive eating.

So if *you've* got into the habit of over-eating, the best cure is an interesting life! Try rushing round being energetic and doing things, being interested in things, enjoying yourself.

Are You Lovesick?

EMOTIONAL stress can also make people go to the other extreme of under-eating. If you're nervous and anxious, you'll feel too wound up to bother to eat anything.

An extreme emotion like being lovesick for someone can change you from a happy, bouncing girl to a mere shadow of your former self. That's what happened to Pam, who fell in love with a fantastic boy — but he, unfortunately, didn't feel the same way about her . . .

"It was terrible when Greg left me for another girl," she told us. "I could hardly sleep and I could hardly eat.

"I had no appetite for anything. If you'd put my favourite dinner down in front of

★ Does your stomach simply go "Yeuk" at the thought of eating in the first place?

Stop?

me I would have pushed it away in disgust."

Gradually, Pam's feelings about Greg got less intense until she actually started to forget about him. She started going out and getting interested in other boys, and of course, her appetite came back.

So if *you're* off your food you can be sure there's something worrying you — maybe just minor worries, an argument with Mum, a bust-up with a friend, being up-tight about exams — all these things are likely to spoil your appetite. But, usually, as soon as the cause of stress is removed, you can go back to your three square meals again!

Are You Starving Yourself To Death?

JUST as over-eating can become an emotional habit, so can the Skinny-Liz habit of neglecting yourself by not eating enough. Like 16-year-old Wendy, who'd love to put on weight but can't help her fussy, finicky eating habits . . .

"My mum's always nagging on at me because I don't eat enough," Wendy told us. "I'd love to eat more and put on weight, but the more Mum nags the more I go off my food."

Wendy is the nervous type who reacts to stress by rejecting food. As a personality, she's inclined to put herself down and have a poor opinion of herself. It's also significant that her mum's nagging only puts Wendy off her appetite more. **Food is a symbol of love,** and Wendy is rejecting her mum's love when she rejects the food her mother puts in front of her. It's a way of rebelling.

So if *you've* got into the habit of eating mouse-sized meals, your food problem can be cured by building up more self-confidence and a better opinion of yourself. Be nice and kind to yourself, indulge yourself with new clothes, perfumed baths, funny films, outings, treats, *anything* that'll make you feel better.

You'll have more energy, you'll look healthier and soon eating will become a pleasure rather than a pain. And most important of all, you'll start liking *yourself* a lot better too!

* * * *

So you see, the way you treat your body is a reflection of the way you feel about yourself.

But if you at least *know* why you overeat or undereat, it's much easier to change your attitude to food.

Once you've sorted out your nosh problems, you can afford the occasional luxury of a doughnut binge or a greedy feast without feeling guilty, and you can also afford the occasional bout of keeping going on nothing but a crumb or a crust because you're so busy and hectic and life's so exciting you can't sit still for long enough to eat a meal.

And if you want *more* food for thought, always remember that your eating problems are in your mind, *not* in your stomach!

HOW SWEET ARE YOU?

Had a good sniff recently? No, we don't mean a good cry . . . we mean have you noticed any nice smells around? Delicious perfumes, sweet-smelling flowers, your favourite foods. There are super smells all around you . . . so start now and sniff out some of the nicest ones!

TOWN smells aren't always pleasant, there are just too many cars and dustbins around. The nicest smells come from baker's shops where they bake their own bread and cakes (don't go in!), perfume counters in department stores and coffee shops where you'll smell the wonderful whiff of freshly-ground coffee beans.

Country air is good for your sense of smell except when you pass a pig-farm or a dung-heap! Better to head for the woods with the tangy whiff of pine needles, the smell of woodsmoke from a cottage, the hedgerows in summer with all the flowers and newly-mown hay (fine, unless you get hay-fever!).

Now that we've reminded you of some of the delicious smells around, you'll start noticing others. How does your boyfriend strike you these days?

Does he smell irresistible and manly? Or does he just smell rather peculiar most of the time?

If he's not very sniffable you could try a campaign to change all that by buying him some aftershave or talc powder you'll both like. A little patchouli oil can smell good on boys . . . you'll find it at Indian shops.

Another good wheeze is to get him to try a super-smelling shampoo . . . Earthborn Apricot, Apple and Avocado shampoos smell great on boys!

You'll have to make sure *you* smell good, too, of course, which means finding a cologne or perfume to suit you. If you've no idea where to start, then why not choose one to suit your personality? Check with our list and see what's right for *you*!

SWEET DREAMER?

If you're the shy, quiet and dreamy type, try floral perfumes on a single note . . . Boots Original Formula Lavender or Rose, for instance, or Mary Quant country-sweet oils in Honeysuckle or Country Garden.

SPORTY TYPE?

Are you a sporty outdoor girl? Fond of horses or a keen football fan? Try Revlon's Charlie which is sweet but tangy, or go for Smitty or anything lemony and fresh.

MYSTERY GIRL?

If you long for faraway places, want to travel and see the world, try special oils such as patchouli, ylang-ylang or vetivert. Go for Stowaway or a French perfume spray, too.

A RAVER?

Are you the life and soul of the party? The girl who's always ready to dance the night away? Try Mary Quant's Havoc or any of the Musk perfumes. Try Rive Gauche by Yves St Laurent, too . . . it's very sophisticated. Look for sprays on offer!

GIVE your bedroom a romantic Eastern atmosphere by burning joss-sticks. You can buy them in lovely perfumes such as Mimosa, Ylang-Ylang and Frankincense! If you want something a little less heavy, try scented candles — poppy-scented perhaps?

For the sweetest dreams, try a herbal pillow as a very special treat. These are available in different sizes, from a normal pillow size down to a tiny size which will cost around £2.00 from craft shops. Kitty Little has a range of herbal pillows available all over the country. Re-fills are usually available when the pillow seems to lose its freshness.

Surround yourself with delicious smells and give your nose a *real* treat!

When Steve went away, Julie promised she'd love him for ever. Then she met Martin . . .

I Really Thought I Loved Him...

STEVE'S letter arrived on Saturday morning, just as I was leaving the house to meet Martin.

I've been away a long time, Julie. It's been hard for both of us. I just can't believe what you say – I can't believe it's over.

He was coming home. He had leave due and he was coming to see me, to try to sort things out.

We'd been in love, Steve and I. Really in love. Or it had seemed that way . . .

Joining the army had always been part of his plan. We knew it would be hard being apart, but we'd have letters, phone calls.

And the times we did spend together would be extra special because they were so precious . . .

Only, it didn't work out that way . . .

Sitting in, night after night, had driven me right up the wall.

When I couldn't stand it any longer, I phoned up my best friend, Jacqui, and we arranged to go out to a disco.

I chatted up a boy with dark hair. He danced like a dream and we spent the whole evening together.

I liked having him chat me up. I liked letting him take me home.

I liked the way he kissed me . . .

I felt a pang of conscience when I got ready for bed that night, though, and I couldn't write my usual letter to Steve.

What was the use of a letter? I was lonely. I missed having someone around, someone to hold me, to kiss me.

I didn't mean to go to the disco again. But I couldn't help it. Suddenly I was having fun again.

I thought it could go on like that forever — playing games, having fun. A different boy every week.

Nothing serious, nothing that could harm me and Steve.

Martin changed all that. When he asked me out I didn't even think about Steve once.

Martin was different from the others. I knew there was no way I was going to be able to forget him . . .

IN the end, I had to write to Steve, telling him it was over. I posted the letter right away, glad it was done, glad he would soon know where he stood with me.

And now — now when I was on my way to meet Martin — I had to read Steve's reply. Oh, if only he would stop being so stubborn and just accept things!

Martin sensed there was something wrong as soon as he saw me.

"Hey, what's up, Julie? You look like you're on your way to somebody's funeral!"

I tried to grin, but my mouth trembled a bit and Martin's arms tightened around me.

"Come on — we'll go for a coffee and you can tell me about it."

We found a little corner table in a cafe and sat down. I looked at Martin, just not knowing where to start.

In the end, I just pulled Steve's letter out of my handbag and gave it to Martin.

I watched him as he read it. He folded it up and put it down on the table

"I didn't know," he said.

I stared at the letter, unable to say anything.

"He's got a nerve," Martin said, after a while. "Don't see him, Julie."

"I feel — I have to, Martin. I owe it to him, I suppose. And maybe then it'll be straightened out and I'll feel better . . ." My voice cracked. "I — I'm sorry I didn't tell you before . . ."

He leaned over and kissed me.

"It doesn't matter," he said.

I REALLY dreaded having to see Steve again. He'd said he'd come to the house and I walked round all that morning, not able to sit down even, because I was so tensed up.

And it turned out to be worse than I thought . . .

He came to the door and he looked really nervous. We just couldn't seem to talk to each other at all.

"Julie, let's get out of here," Steve said. "It's no use trying to talk here."

I nodded. "All right."

We turned into the park, and Steve shoved his hands into his pockets.

"Julie, you know how I feel about the army, but if it comes between us, it's just not worth it. It's not worth anything."

I turned to him, dismayed.

"It's what you've always wanted, Steve! You don't mean that!"

"I mean it. You come first with me."

"Don't talk rubbish," I said and pulled away from him. I walked on a bit, and there were tears in my eyes because I knew he wasn't talking rubbish, that he

meant every word he said.

He came up behind me, and I started to cry. His arms went round me.

"Forget about me, Steve," I whispered.

He tilted my face up towards him and began to kiss me. Slowly my arms went round him till I was kissing him back.

Then he held me away from him.

"Don't throw it all away, Julie, it's too important. OK, so things have gone wrong between us, but we can put them right again.

"Because get one thing straight, Julie, I'm not going to lose you . . ."

HE kissed me again and smiled at me. I buried my face in his chest, crying with relief because I knew now Steve had been right to trust our love. I'd made such a mess of things. Convinced myself it was Martin I wanted. But he'd just been there when I needed somebody.

"There's just one thing I've got to know," Steve said. "Do you love me, Julie?"

"Yes, I do love you, Steve . . ."

He held me very tight, and then he said, "Let's hang on to that, then."

I knew, of course, I'd have to try to explain everything to Martin. It'd be difficult — he loves me and he believes I love him. After all, I told him I did, didn't I?

How could I have made such a mistake? It's Steve I really love — only I was almost too late in finding out.

I just hope Martin will understand . . .

A Reader's True Experience

TAKE A GOOD LOOK!

If you always want to look your best, two different looks are all you need – one natural for any time at all and one dressed-up look for special occasions. Follow our step-by-step guide to these two perfect make-up looks designed specially for Jackie by make-up artist Mary Vango. The looks are easy to follow – and they'll give you lots of helpful tips on skin and make-up!

The NATURAL LOOK

The natural look means clear, healthy skin, shining eyes and just a little make-up to define eyes, cheeks and lips. Skin care is really important and a regular cleanse, tone and moisturising routine is what you need to keep your skin clean, soft and healthy.

Remove eye make-up with an eye make-up remover lotion. Soak a pad of cotton wool in the lotion and hold it over your eye — never rub the delicate skin around your eyes.

Use a lotion cleanser or cleansing milk to clean make-up from the rest of your face, then wash gently with a very mild soap and water to remove dirt and grime.

Tone with a gentle toner for your skin type, then moisturise with a light moisturiser for your skin type. Even greasy skins need a little moisture!

Make-up should be really light and fresh for the natural look. It should be used to help make the best of your features — not to cover up blemishes! A greasy skin should be treated with great care and kept really clean — use medicated products for cleansing and treat existing spots with a treatment cream.

A great number of spots which never seem to go away could mean that you have acne. The best idea is to visit your doctor as there are several treatments available for acne now in different forms from special lotions to courses of tablets.

Whatever your skin type, your skin and hair can be improved if you eat a balanced diet, take regular exercise, get lots of fresh air and lots of sleep. Be kind to yourself and cut out sugar and processed foods which are so full of additives that their natural goodness has disappeared completely.

Now, follow these simple steps to perfect make-up and a perfect natural look!

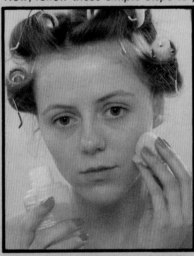

1. Make-up artist Mary Vango cleansed, toned and moisturised model Arabella's skin. The moisturiser makes a smooth surface for the base colour.

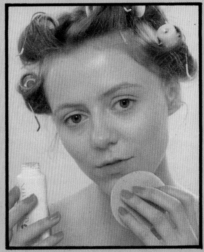

2. Base colour is a cream in ivory-beige shade, applied all over face and neck with a dampened cosmetic sponge for a really smooth finish.

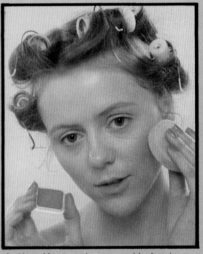

3. Next Mary used a cream blusher in a dusky pink, applied with a sponge from cheek-bones to temples. The edges are blended so there aren't any hard lines.

4. On eyes Mary used a golden brown for lids and a frosted ginger shade for brow bones. Powder colours, applied with a brush, last longer than cream colours.

5. Black mascara next, with two coats for a perfect finish. Allow the first coat to dry before you apply the second – the last thing you want is thick, clogged lashes.

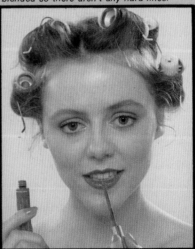

6. Lip colour is the final step and Mary used a russett automatic lip colour to give colour and shine.

7. The finished look – with hair styled on rollers for a bouncy, natural look!

CREDITS: Make-up from Boots 17, Max Factor and Lancôme. Blouse from a range at Laura Ashley.

The DRESSED·UP LOOK

The dressed-up look also calls for clear skin, of course, and more make-up. Using more make-up takes time and needs practice to get it right. The trick is to build up the layers gradually, especially on eyes.

The colours you choose are important, but sometimes it's difficult to know which ones will suit you. There are some special rules to follow, though. Here's some to help you.

Choose a foundation colour according to your own skin tones. Test it on your *face* if you can, and if you *can't* see the colour, it's the one for you. A base colour is used to even up skin tones and cover tiny blemishes — *not* to add unnatural colour, while blusher should be chosen to tone with skin and to go with lip colours. Lips and nails should tone with the clothes you're wearing and should go with your skin tones, too. For instance if you have quite sallow skin and dark hair a blue/red lip colour will look terrible! Colours should look good on

your skin and should make it look warm and glowing.

Eye colours are perhaps the most difficult to choose because there aren't any proper rules. There may be one shade that makes your eyes look *really* amazing — a shade that perhaps tones with the little flecks in your eyes. A green shade may bring out the flecks in hazel eyes, for instance, and a lilac may be just the thing for grey/blue eyes.

Mascara depends very much on your hair colour as well as your skin tones and eye colour. Dark hair usually means black mascara, brown, auburn or ginger hair means browny/black or brown mascara, light brown to blonde means brown or russet mascara, or perhaps navy.

Once you've chosen your colours, practise until you're really good at putting them on. And now, here's how Mary created Arabella's dressed-up look, step by step!

1. After cleansing, toning and moisturising the first step is the base colour. Mary used an ivory liquid foundation applied with a dampened cosmetic sponge all over face and neck.

2. Translucent powder went over the foundation before the powder blusher. Blusher is a light tawny colour carefully blended from just below cheek bones in a V shape out towards temples.

3. Eyes are all important and Mary used a light brown on the inside of each lid, applied with a brush. Next came a soft green applied to the outer lids and just under the lower lashes.

4. Arabella has quite deep lids, so Mary used a soft brown to shade along the socket-line, following the line of the brow bone.

5. For a special effect Mary used a soft green pencil along the lower rims of each eye. She then added two coats of black mascara.

6. Lips come last and Mary carefully outlined the lips with a lip pencil, then filled in with a deep red-rose lip colour applied with a lip-brush for a perfect finish.

7. The finished look with hair rolled back on each side from a centre parting. The side sections are secured with combs and topped with yellow flowers.

CREDITS: Make-up from Evette, Lancôme and the Babe range by Fabergé. Blouse from a range at Top Shop.

WANTED

ROD STEWART

LOCATION — Of Northern British origin, also known as The Tartan Terror, this species migrates between the United States and the U.K. mainly returning to let his thousands of followers catch a glimpse of his leopard-skinned, tightly-clad body and hear his incredibly sexy, husky voice. He's usually accompanied by a blonde — having fun.

THE CAPTURE — Adopt Scottish nationality. Bleach your hair — although if you're not also a willowy 5ft. 11in. this won't work too well. Say you're a distant relative of Kenny Dalglish — this may well work. Never *at any time* mention Argentina or Britt Ekland.

JOHN TRAVOLTA

LOCATION — Easily the most popular of the Travolta species. Can be found in America on film sets, or at private airports — this one loves flying. He may though, only be interested if you're an older, mature female. But you can always try to change his mind!

THE CAPTURE — You'll need to be nimble on your feet. Win "The Disco Dancer Of The Year" contest and be introduced, or pretend you're over 30 and just love young, dishy males with gorgeous blue eyes. Tell him you know all about how to pilot a Cessna 100 or whatever. As long as you don't actually have to *do* it, he'll be impressed, all right!

LEIF GARRETT

LOCATION — Usually found in discos or on TV and film sets. At one time he spent a lot of time in skateboard parks — now he gets around in fast sports cars. A youthful member of the species — noted for his good looks and his dancing ability.

THE CAPTURE — Go to New York and learn the New York Hustle. Or fly to California and live on the beach outside his home. Practise with hair-dryer in front of mirror to get that "windswept" look that goes so well in an open sports car. Thumb a lift in any sports car emerging from this wanted male's house.

BOB GELDOF

LOCATION — This species is Irish, full of fun, and a bit of a rogue — so watch out! He's an incredibly nice rogue, though, and his roving eye will pick you out in recording studios, TV studios and generally every party that's going.

THE CAPTURE — Tear up a John Travolta poster in his presence. He'll love you for it! Make no mention of any similarity between himself and Mick Jagger. He'll hate you for it!

PRINCE ANDREW

LOCATION — Any old palace or castle. His country seat! On the High Seas . . . this creature's pretty hard to track down! Often seen with his mother or brothers. Tweed jackets and a behind-the-back-with-his-hands stance is often adopted.

THE CAPTURE — Throw on all your diamonds and make sure that you're in the vicinity if there are any film premiers to attend or bridges to be opened — or even the odd ship being launched. Read up on polo and rugger. Being filthy rich and royal would be a real asset here.

MEN!

John Travolta, Rod Stewart, Bob Geldof — what have they all got in common? Apart from the fact that they're all magnificent specimens of masculinity, they're all among the world's most wanted men! Wanted by us, of course! So if *you* want to know how to go about locating — and capturing! — some of the world's most wanted men, read on . . . If you can actually manage to catch any of them, we bet you'll find it a rewarding experience!

MARK HAMILL

LOCATION — Often to be found with his head in the clouds and stars in his eyes, this one! One of the characteristics of this gorgeous creature is its fascinating blue eyes — hypnotic if you get too close. He's a little old fashioned really and has an incredible desire to rescue princesses . . .

THE CAPTURE — Either take up spaceship maintenance or hang around looking like a princess who needs rescuing. If you're also incredibly brave and not at all afraid of space creatures or being followed around by a film crew all the time, this will be a real asset.

PARKER STEVENSON

LOCATION — This one's a keep-fit freak and often found to be doing all sorts of energetic things to keep itself in shape (and what a shape!). You'll tend to find him around in secluded areas of Beverly Hills involved in an ancient rite called jogging! His eating habits are quite definite as well — lots of healthy wholemeal bread and yoghurt and salads and yoghurts and salads and . . . Anyway.

THE CAPTURE — The first thing to do is attract him to you by wearing a track suit and bobbing up and down, shouting "Who's for a quick one round the park, then?" Once you've caught his attention you could then make sure he's firmly yours for ever by presenting him with a huge tuna fish salad (we have it on good authority that that's his favourite).

RICHARD HATCH

LOCATION — On a battlestar called Galactica — you mean there isn't a battlestar stop near your house? He's generally to be found with some sort of beautiful creature wrapped around him, fighting off monsters and looking stunningly attractive — clever chaps these Hatches . . . And if he's not doing that he's likely to be swimming, playing tennis, jogging or admiring cats — they *love* cats.

THE CAPTURE — Hire a panto cat outfit and fling yourself off the roof at him the next time he's jogging past. Admit that you don't know a *thing* about anything even remotely energetic but you're *awfully* willing to learn. Oh, and if you happen to be a beautiful star maiden who's looking for help and a bit of romance, it might stand you in good stead for capturing the heart of this particular battlestar trooper.

THE FONZ

LOCATION — Fairly limited species this — in fact, it's nearly extinct. One last outpost where it's still hanging around is a hamburger joint called "Arnold's." It generally dresses in black leather and denim and can move at high speed, especially when it's on a motorbike. One of the quirks of this chap is his desire to stick both thumbs in the air and utter a kind of strangled yell.

THE CAPTURE — Read up on twin overhead cams and sprockets and always carry a selection of spanners around. Enjoy running your hands through greasy hair (your own if you've forgotten to wash them after fixing the bike!) and learn to survive totally on Coke and hamburgers. It also helps not to be too jealous as this male tends to attract hundreds of members of the opposite sex wherever it goes.

CAN YOU MAKE FRIENDS?

Do you want people to love you instantly? Do you want to be surrounded by warmth and friendship wherever you go? Do you want to feel relaxed, at ease, charming and sympathetic the moment you're introduced to someone?

If you've answered "yes" to all three questions then you're just the same as everyone else who belongs to the human race! You want to be liked and appreciated by other people and make a good impression on them.

The first impression you make on someone, though, is very important, because that is the one that tends to stick in their minds until they get to know you better. And, of course, their first opinion of you will determine whether or not they *want* to get to know you better!

For this reason, meeting new people can be fraught with worry and difficulty. The great temptation is to put on an act to convince people what a super person you are, and to hide your real personality by presenting an image which is very misleading.

It's odd how many people think they can make a good impression by putting on an act. The truth is that an insincere or defensive act is hardly ever impressive and is most likely to turn people *off* instead of *on*.

Just take a look at some of the most common mistakes people make when they're trying to impress someone and, if you recognise yourself — be warned! Remember — the simple fact is, the most impressive person to be is — yourself!

Are You A GUSHER?

Gushing takes the form of treating the other person like a god. A warm-hearted person with a genuine sympathy for others, who's naturally outgoing and really likes people, can be so desperate to be liked that she'll launch off into a stream of senseless gush, totally embarrassing the other person, and just making a complete fool of herself.

She currys favour with phrases like: "Oh, what a beautiful dress — you make me feel so dowdy — can you make apple flan, that's so wonderful, I really admire people who can do that . . ."

But in her heart of hearts, she doesn't, you see, and the person she's telling is even less convinced.

People see through overdone charm, and have no respect for you for over-praising them. In the process, too, the gusher is also putting herself down, and so presenting a completely false picture.

This is unfortunate, because the gusher does mean well, and she genuinely wants people's friendship. She has a lot to offer, but it's her lack of self-confidence that has got her into the habit of thinking that people will only like her if she falls at their feet and worships them.

So if you find yourself gushing, cool it! Get rid of the gush — people will appreciate you much more, and your warm and friendly nature will be revealed.

This way, too, you can still compliment people, and they'll know you *really* mean it, and like you even more!

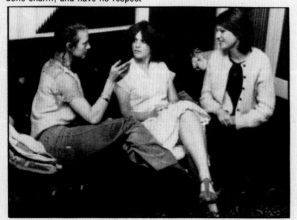

Are You TOO TIMID?

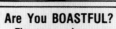

Are you an individual with strong views and opinions of your own, who just hates small-talk? Then make sure you're not falling into the trap of coming across as a very ordinary person, responding weakly to witty remarks, when in fact you could be sparking off a stimulating discussion.

Show your real personality for what it is — unusual and fascinating. You're interesting and original, a great conversationalist on a deep level, so get involved in the kind of conversations that *you* like — if people aren't keen to comply, they'll just make a polite excuse, and walk away.

Besides, you'll be surprised how many other people get tired of silly chatter and would long to share a good conversation with someone like you!

Are You BOASTFUL?

The person who comes across as boastful tends to be very insecure and feels that they're so ordinary they could never make a good impression on anyone.

In reality, if they would only see it, they're kind, good company, and fun to be with. But to make up for that bad opinion, they boast, and their poor victim is given a blow by blow account of love conquests, amazing accomplishments, privileged childhoods — all totally false.

The person being spoken to is also aware that the boaster isn't interested in them as a person, so there's no real basis for a relationship at all.

But if you boast, you're being' your own worst enemy. If you could present your real self, you'd realise that you're not any more ordinary than anyone else. And you're hiding your good qualities, too — cheerful temperament, sense of humour, vitality and enthusiasm.

You'd realise, too, that your real personality is far more impressive than your big boasting act!

Your Special Jackie POP-A-CROSS!

CLUES ACROSS

1. Pretty fair band (7).
4. Ma Bakers' kids (5, 1).
7. You can't play noughts and crosses without it! (1).
8. --creatures Great and Small? (3).
9. Idol band (10).
13. Speedy group (5).
16. ? and behold he's a record producer with 17 (4).
17. A Christian name that sounds like steal (4).
18. A Christian Reg Dwight? (5).
20. A record label that sounds painful! (3).
21. She limited herself to Nutbush City initially (1, 1).
22. Reverse veteran horror film actor (1, 1).
24. These two letters make up Abba's name (2).
25. Starsky and Hutch's base (1, 1).
26. Queen once had a day at them (5).
30. Band's name needing assistance (1, 1, 1).
31. Well, Elvis C. likes them . . . (11).
35. Joins many lead singers to their groups?! (3).
36. Fonzie's nephew? (4).
37. Dury, and others, answer to this? (3).
38. Michael's speedy film manoeuvres? (3).
40. You're a hit if you're in this top? (3).
41. A blond, fun-loving football fanatic? (3).
43. Marie's big brother (1, 1).
45. American band that sound like The Motors (4).
46. What you did with Noakes? (2).
47. Zuko's pal? (5).
48. Three lovely ladies just above freezing point (1,1).
49. He rode to fame on the motorway? (1, 1).
51. You'll be ecstatic about this band! (1, 1, 1).
52. Laboratory measure that added to 40 across makes a band? (1, 1).
53. Tough TV brothers? (5).
55. Child-like lookalikes? (5).
57. Phil kept his whiskey here! (3).
58. Fan club members are "wild" about *this* group (5).
59. Supergroup's kid brother? (4).

CLUES DOWN

2. What joins Dave Travis together?! (3).
3. This band sounds hungry! (5).
4. We're not saying Ian's band are stupid, but . . .! (10).
5. --,honestly,John Alderton appeared in it! (2).
6. Old "Rubberlips" first name! (4).
9. You'd slip a disc(o) if you stepped in it! (6).
10. A common greeting and band name? (1, 1, 1).
11. "Happy Days" Ritchie's real name (3).
12. Potsie's initials off the set (1, 1).
13. This Ray's always "darting" around! (4).
14. Actors do this! (3).
15. Village People stay here (1, 1, 1, 1).
19. Richard's "stand and deliver" role (6).
22. Superman's *first* lady (1, 1).
23. A precious stone and a Wings hit (3).
24. Dirk and Richard operate on one of these? (10).
27. A star is Shaun? (7).
28. Barbra Streisand was born one? (4).
29. Geldolf, Dylan, and Monkhouse have it in common? (3).
32. The real Mike Upchat (1, 1).
33. Sha -- na! (2).
34. How Baccara would say "Yes, I'm a lady" (2).
37. Take the first letters of The Saint's real names . . . (1, 1).
39. Currently one of the most electrifying bands around?! (2, 2).
40. See 49 across . . . again!
41. Ferry's band rocks on (4).
42. Hit the deck and add on A for a record company (5).
43. This band shouldn't be thrown at bullseyes!! (5).
44. Blame it -- the Boogie (2).
48. What Officer Dibble calls Boss Cat. (1, 1).
50. Initially The Sundance Kid (1, 1).
53. If you get this one you're laughing! (3).
54. Low-voiced singer once with Darts (3).
56. . . . and the Sunshine Band (1, 1).
57. Initially he wrote Annie's Song.

Solutions on page 36

My sister, Vicky, was a couple of years older than me. But sometimes I really hated her—as far as Mum and Dad were concerned, she couldn't do anything wrong . . .

I'M GLAD I WAS THE ONE WHO TOLD MUM AND DAD THE TRUTH. IT WAS GREAT OF VICKY TO PROTECT ME, BUT I REALLY REALLY DESERVE TO BE PUNISHED FOR WHAT I DID TO HER . . .

THERE SHE GOES AGAIN! IT REALLY MAKES ME SICK THE WAY SHE CARRIES ON! SHE'S ONLY HELPING MUM SO THAT SHE CAN GET ROUND HER FOR THAT NEW DRESS SHE WANTS.

I HAD TO GET EVEN...

Fiona had had enough of being treated as the baby of the family—so she set out to get her revenge . . .

Whereas Mum was always picking on me . . .

HOW MANY TIMES HAVE I TOLD YOU NOT TO DO THAT, FIONA? YOU'LL RUIN THE CAKE. WHY DON'T YOU MAKE YOURSELF USEFUL, LIKE VICKY!

VICKY . . . IT'S ALWAYS VICKY! YOU'D THINK THEY DIDN'T WANT ME AT ALL THE WAY THEY GO ON . . .

I KNOW SHE'S MY SISTER, BUT SOMETIMES I HATE HER! I MEAN, WHY CAN'T MUM AND DAD TREAT ME LIKE A PERSON, TOO? THEY STILL THINK OF ME AS A LITTLE KID, RUNNING AROUND IN ANKLE SOCKS . . .

DEAR LITTLE VICKY WOULDN'T LET BUTTER MELT IN HER MOUTH! BUT THEY'RE ALWAYS TELLING ME HOW IMPOSSIBLE I AM . . .

I had to share a room with her, too—worse luck!

WHAT'S UP? YOU DON'T LOOK VERY HAPPY, FIONA!

THERE'S NOTHING TO LOOK HAPPY ABOUT! NOBODY ROUND HERE CARES ABOUT ME—I MIGHT AS WELL BE DEAD FOR ALL YOU LOT CARE!

29

HOW TO MAKE HIM WARM TO YOU IN WINTER!

Just because the warm days are over and winter's well and truly here, it doesn't mean you have to hibernate. This is, in fact, one of the best times of the year to meet boys! So stop sitting in front of the fire wishing for summer to come round again — instead, put on your fur-lined underwear, step outside, and grab a guy! Here's how!

IF IT'S SNOWING

WHAT TO WEAR:

Wellies and jeans, a big warm sweater, a scarf and a woolly hat with a bobble on it. Fluffy ear muffs are rather *sweet* so wear a pair if you've got any. If not, you can get the same effect by strapping two of your long-haired guinea-pigs to the sides of your head.

WHAT TO DO:

Enlist the help of a small brother or sister. No brothers or sisters? Then bribe a neighbourhood kid to accompany you.

Choose a nice snowy area and start building a snowman, keeping your eyes peeled for passing dishy males. When you spot one, attract his attention by catching him just below the ear with a well-aimed snowball, then blame it on your small companion.

Explain that small companion is rather fed up as you're not very good at making snowmen.

In no time he'll have forgotten whatever it was he was planning to do, and will be happily piling up snow — while you babble happily into his uninjured ear about how kind he is!

If it's snowing hard, you don't need a small child with you. All you need is a bewildered look.

Approach any likely guy and tell him you've been wandering around in the snow for an hour and you're completely lost and exhausted. Let him lead you home/to a nearby coffee bar/to the disco and *insist* he stays with you until you've recovered.

If the worst comes to the worst and the other two approaches fail, borrow or steal a sledge and rocket down the side of a hill at any passing boy and flatten him. If you're profuse enough with your apologies and you haven't actually broken any bones, he'll at least agree to give you sledge-driving lessons. If nothing else.

IF IT'S COLD AND ICY

WHAT TO WEAR:

A big fluffy fake fur coat and hat. These will make you look soft and cuddly and remind him of a childhood teddy bear he once loved dearly . . .

WHAT TO DO:

Make a really slippery slide at the end of the road and wait. It may be a little while before a suitably dishy guy comes along but you can pass the time until then by helping up the milkmen, postmen, little old ladies and various other people who will have accidentally tested your slide.

When the right boy does turn up, you'll be expert enough to save him before he does himself a permanent injury. He'll be grateful, of course, and what with the added advantage of reminding him of his much-loved childhood teddy bear, you should have a friend for life.

If it's really slippery underfoot, a simpler and more effective way to attract his attention would be to cling to a lamppost in the centre of town, looking helpless just as he comes along.

"It's so slippery," you gasp when he pauses to ask why you're holding the lamppost up, "I'm afraid to move." He'll either pass on with a comment like, "Don't worry, the weatherman says there's a thaw on the way," in which case he's not worth bothering with, or he'll offer to hold you up and help you to

wherever you want to go, in which case he *is* worth bothering with!

IF IT'S SLEETING AND HAILING

WHAT TO WEAR:

Wellies, an ankle-length plastic waterproof coat and a waterproof hat with a big brim. Carry an umbrella.

WHAT TO DO:

Stand around, keeping a beady eye open for a suitable boy. The suitable boy will have a drowned-rat appearance. He will have come out unprepared for the weather and

will be wet through and in the first stages of double pneumonia.

Kindly offer to let him share your umbrella. He'll be touched by your kindness and remember you with gratitude when he's got over his pneumonia. If he gets over his pneumonia.

If it's windy as well as wet, let your umbrella turn inside out and wrestle with it in a hopeless kind of way. The passing boy won't be able to resist proving his superior strength and he'll stop and give you a hand.

By the time you've triumphed over the umbrella, especially if it's blowing a gale, you'll be practically old friends.

Or wander into the disco, dripping water, and shake your coat over the nearest good-looking male. Then look horrified, go red and apologetic.

He'll forgive you — probably — then you can discuss the appalling weather and you can tell him how brave he is to have come out at all. The next thing you'll know is that he'll be buying you Cokes and dancing with you. Boys are easily flattered.

IF IT'S SNOWING AND HAILING AND SLEETING AND FREEZING

WHAT TO WEAR:

Your warmest, fleecy nightie and two dressing-gowns.

WHAT TO DO:

Make a list of all the boys you used to know and still fancy. Then phone them up one at a time and ask them how they're getting on.

With luck, one of them will remember you well enough to want to relight the old flame and you can arrange to meet up as soon as the weather breaks!

So, you see, winter isn't such a bad time after all, is it? By taking advantage of the weather instead of just dreaming about summer, you'll be one step ahead of all the girls who spend their time dreaming about summer instead of taking advantage of the winter weather! By the time they come out of hibernation and start looking around, they're going to find that all the best guys are already hooked. And serve 'em right!

The way to his heart!

"Come round to my place, and we'll have something to eat" — sounds good, doesn't it? But there are distinct disadvantages to making too much of this kind of invitation!

For a start, you don't want to spend hours slaving over a hot oven and find that when everything's ready, you just can't face eating it yourself! Neither do you want to find that, once you'd paid the earth for your elaborate meal, you'll have to starve until pay-day comes round again!

So it's important to choose food that's easy on the budget, fun to cook AND delicious to eat — and that's not as difficult as it sounds, if you try one of our special recipes . . .

THE REAL THING!

MAYBE you're really looking for the works -- sitting down, with knives, forks and soft candlelight, no less! Well, here's a winner — but don't mess things up by trying to go too far and serving anything before the main course or after it, which will only add to the work. This is quite a substantial meal, so if you want a three-course job, all you really need is grapefruit or melon to begin, and cheese and biscuits to end, neither of which take any cooking.

Ingredients:
1 large potato per person
Chicken joint per person
2 oz. butter
lemon juice
1 tablespoonful flour
½ pint milk and water mixed
2 oz. grated cheese
1 large onion, sliced
mushrooms, sliced
salad or peas

First, scrub a large potato each, rub the skin with a little cooking oil, then wrap loosely in aluminium foil and put at the top of a hot oven (400° or gas mark 6).

Next, fry the chicken joints in a pan with 2 oz. butter and a good squeeze of lemon juice. Shake the pan and stir the joints about, turning them until they colour lightly on all sides. Lift the meat out, and put in individual ovenproof dishes. Leave on one side. Add 1 tablespoonful flour to the juices in the pan, and stir until well mixed in. Slowly add the half pint of mixed water and milk, stirring all the

time, until you've got a smooth sauce. Turn the heat even lower, and add the grated cheese. Add a dash of salt and pepper. The mixture, when again smooth, should be like thick custard, not solid and not runny. Add more water if necessary, or cook for a little longer if it needs to be thicker. Scatter the peeled and sliced onion and the sliced mushrooms in the bottom of the dishes, around the meat. The amounts aren't important — use as much as you like. Pour the cheese sauce over, so it covers the meat and the excess runs into the bottom of the dishes. Cover with metal foil.

★ ★ ★ ★ ★ ★ ★ ★ ★ ★ ★ ★ ★ ★ ★ ★

When the potatoes have been cooking for about half an hour, put the covered dishes into the oven under them, and continue cooking for a further hour at the same temperature.

When everything seems ready, put the meat at the top of the oven, and the potatoes below. Remove the foil over the meat dishes, to let the cheese sauce brown. Now's the time to prepare a green salad, or cook some frozen peas, whichever you prefer. When this is done, the meal will be ready to serve!

Before going to the table, you should unwrap the potatoes, make slits in the top and insert a small piece of butter OR a small piece of cream cheese. If you want to be really impressive sprinkle a teaspoonful of chopped green chives or half a teaspoonful of finely chopped raw onion on top of the potatoes. Delicious!

FLIP IT AND FILL IT!

You can't beat pancakes for a meal that's fun to make and good to eat. If you think ahead and get all the separate ingredients prepared in advance, nothing could be easier.

It can be romantic to have a pancake supper for two by candlelight, or you can cater for as many as you like, and have stacks of pancakes and a choice of fillings for a party. You can make all the fillings 24 hours ahead — even the batter.

The basic batter is easy. Just put 4 tablespoonfuls flour into a bowl with a pinch of salt, mix one egg with about half a pint of milk-and-water, and start adding the liquid slowly whisking it up with a fork or an egg beater, rotary whisk or electric beater as you go. You should finish up with a thin, creamy

liquid. If you're preparing the batter in advance cover it and put it into a cold place. This makes enough large pancakes to feed two or three people.

Fillings can be sweet or savoury, hot or cold. The hot fillings can be made in advance, and reheated gently.

FILLINGS

Chocolate and nut: Mix 1 tablespoonful cornflour and 2 tablespoonfuls drinking chocolate to a paste with a little cold milk. Heat half a pint of milk, and pour it slowly on to the paste, then pour the hot mixture back into the pan and re-boil, stirring all the time, for one minute. It should be quite thick, but smooth. Pour a dollop inside the cooked pancakes, roll up, and sprinkle nuts on top. Add whipped cream if you're feeling really gluttonous.

Cheese and egg scramble: Beat up an egg with a little milk and a pat of butter, and cook over gentle heat, stirring, until it's just turning into scrambled egg but not completely set, and then remove from heat. Chop up a couple of little cheese triangles, stir into the egg mixture, add salt and pepper and use to fill the pancakes.

Cherry and ice-cream: Have some vanilla ice-cream to hand, and as the pancakes are prepared, put a spoonful of the ice-cream on the centre of each, and pour a little cherry pie filling (from a can) on top — then roll up the pancake quickly and eat right away.

On the night, have everything set out easily to hand. Heat a thick frying pan until hot, drop in a small piece of butter or a little cooking oil, and when this smokes LIGHTLY, add just enough batter to cover the pan.

If the batter was made the day before, beat it up well before using.

When the first side is set, flip it over or turn with a spatula, and cook the other side.

You can either cook the pancakes one at a time, and get your boyfriend to fill them, or stack them up as you cook them and, once the batter's finished, let everyone help themselves to the fillings, which can be dished up into large bowls for serving. That way you can be sure you'll get to taste your creations, rather than standing in front of the oven all evening!

SOLUTIONS TO SPECIAL JACKIE POP-A-CROSS!

ACROSS – 1 Blondie, 4 Boney M., 7 X, 8 All, 9 Generation, 13 Racey, 16 Lowe, 17 Nick, 18 Elton, 20 RAK, 21 T.T. (Tina Turner), 22 L.C. (Christopher Lee), 24 A.B., 25 L.A. (Los Angeles), 26 Races, 30 E.L.P., 31 Attractions, 35 And, 36 Baio, 37 Ian, 38 Wiz, 40 Ten, 41 Rod, 43 D.O. (Donny Osmond), 45 Cars, 46 Go, 47 Sandy, 48 T.D. (Three Degrees), 49 T.R. (Tom Robinson), 51 X.T.C., 52 C.C., 53 Hardy, 55 Atack, 57 Jar, 58 Child, 59 Andy.

DOWN – 2 Lee, 3 Eater, 4 Blockheads, 5 No, 6 Mick, 9 Grease, 10 E.L.O., 11 Ron, 12 A. W. (Anson Williams), 13 Rita, 14 Act, 15 Y.M.C.A., 19 Turpin, 22 L. L. (Lois Lane), 23 Jet, 24 Battlestar, 27 Cassidy, 28 Star, 29 Bob, 32 R.N. (Robin Nedwell), 33 NA, 34 SI, 37 I.O. (Ian Ogilvy), 39 AC DC, 40. T.R. (Tom Robinson), 41 Roxy, 42 Decca, 43 Darts, 44 On, 48. T.C., 50 R.R. (Robert Redford), 53 HA, 54 Den, 56 K.C. 57 J.D. (John Denver).

How's Your Dream Life?

Dreams tell you a lot about what's going on in your mind and are dead give-aways to all your secret hopes and fears! Some dreams are so obvious they don't need any interpretation — say, for example, you dream that you've fallen in love with a gorgeous boy you know . . . well, it's obvious that in real life, you probably fancy him a lot! This is called a Wish Fulfilment dream, for obvious reasons, and you don't need anybody to interpret that for you!

Other dreams aren't so easy to see through, though. Read on and see if any of your dreams are here — and find out what they might be telling you about your life and your love life!

FLYING

SOME people dream that they can fly, zooming and swooping about in the sky!

THE MEANING of this Science-Fiction fantasy come true is that you're a pretty lucky girl. You're free and independent in spirit, and feeling adventurous. Nothing will hold you back. You'll enjoy yourself in life without feelings of guilt or duty to spoil it.

The flying in your dreams represents this lovely, free-flowing energy that you have — so be grateful, and enjoy it!

CLIMBING

YOU could be going up steps, or climbing a mountain, or just going up and up a winding path.

You might dream that you're carrying a heavy bundle with you, and it's definitely hard going — a bit of a struggle. You won't be afraid of **falling** in this dream, so much as afraid that you'll never get to the top . . .

THE MEANING of this dream revolves around **getting to the top**. You're an ambitious soul, and you've set your sights on something big — success in exams, getting a really good job, or maybe attracting a really super boy who's really way out of your class! Whatever it is, you're stubborn and you're not going to be put off! You're obviously finding it a bit of a struggle, though!

FALLING

DREAMING that you're falling or tripping up is very common. For instance, you might dream that you're walking on the edge of a cliff when suddenly your foot goes over the edge.

Or you might be walking about in a building which has rotten floors — gaping and paper thin. You're sure you're going to plunge through and, suddenly, it gives way under you — and you do . . .

Or you might find yourself dreaming about crossing a deep chasm, and the only way to get across is by a rope-bridge. You can see right through it. It's swaying about dangerously, and you can see it's all thin and fraying . . . Help!!

THE MEANING of dreams like these is that you're feeling very insecure about something. It could be that you've got some big challenge ahead – such as exams, organising something, or sorting out an emotional tangle with your best friend or boyfriend – and you're really scared because you've got no confidence in your own ability to sort it out. You're terrified of failure. You're **sure** you're going to let yourself down, and so you dream about **falling** . . .

The dream is just bringing the problem to your attention, so try to face up to it as best you can, and solve it!

BEING CHASED

THIS is really more of a nightmare than a dream. Maybe you're all alone in some creepy place — like a deserted street, or a dark, ploughed field, and all you know is that somebody's after you!

You're not too sure who they are, or why they're after you, but you're absolutely desperate to escape. As you try to run away, though, your legs get heavier and heavier, your knees go weak, and you feel as if you're sinking into the ground. Meanwhile, your dreaded pursuer is getting closer and closer.

THE MEANING of this dream can be quite complicated. It might be that you're trying to ignore something which you feel is threatening you in real life.

Or it could be that what's threatening you is actually inside yourself – feelings of some sort that are just too much for you. Maybe you want something too much, and you're afraid to face up to it.

Whatever it is, it's really troubling you – so much so that you feel, in your dreams, that it's actually **chasing** you. Think deeply about your life and your problems. You may be able to identify who or what your mystery pursuer is, and then you can start to work on it!

Most of these dreams are rather anxious ones because they're usually the hardest to understand — it's easy to see the meaning in a nice dream! Let's hope most of your dreams are sweet dreams, though, but if they're not — try to work out what it is they're trying to tell you!

STAR SPOT

How well do *you* know your favourite stars? Try our quiz and find out! You could be in for a few surprises!

Superhunk

This handsome hunk is really a mixture of the eyes, nose and mouth of *three* goodlookers — who are they?

WHO'S MASK-ERADING NOW?

Who are these masked marauders? And which one's the *real* Dick Turpin?

EYE-CATCHING BLONDES!

Whose eyes are these? Clue: They're all blondes!

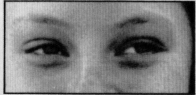

Answers

SUPERHUNK!
EYES — Lewis Collins
NOSE — John Travolta
MOUTH — Billy Idol

EYE-CATCHING BLONDES!
1. Debbie Harry
2. Farrah Fawcett-Majors
3. Anna from Abba
4. Jodie Foster
5. Rod Stewart

WHO'S MASK-ERADING NOW?
1. Richard O'Sullivan
2. Nicholas Ball
3. Leif Garrett
4. Bob Geldof

38

Penny For The Guy!

What we all wouldn't do to have lots and lots of lovely money . . . or a guy with lots of money to share it with!

But money's supposed to be the root of all evil, and it's true it can do strange things to people — it can certainly bring out the very worst in them! Money also tells us a lot about *boys*, according to their attitude to it . . .

So, depending on how important money is to the boy in *your* life, here's how to make him fall *wildly* in love with you, also how he's likely to treat you once you've captured him, *and* how best to get rid of him — if you need to!

MEAN MIKE

He's the boy who just won't spend money. While other boys have masses of pens and Biros, Mike just has one grubby old pencil, and while other boys are flashing their calculators around, Mike's adding up his sums on his grubby little fingers.

HOW TO DAZZLE HIM

So far, Mike sounds pretty repulsive. But what if he's gorgeous, has a dazzling smile and is great company? You'd want to dazzle him, right?

Well, it's going to cost you, because you'll have to keep reaching down into that purse of yours. Every boy has his price — and once Mike realises what a Generous Girl you are, he's yours!

HOW HE'LL TREAT YOU

A mean person basically can't give — financially or emotionally.

And that means that you mustn't expect too much of Mike. Oh, he can load you with compliments (they cost nothing), but when it comes down to the real nitty-gritty of your relationship, he'll avoid getting serious — and he'll change the subject if anybody mentions love.

HIS ADVANTAGES

Mean Mike won't ever get into trouble with the police, scream at you in a public place, or slip on a banana skin. He's far too cautious to look a fool . . .

HIS DISADVANTAGES

What fun is a guy who won't ever scream at you or slip on a banana skin?

HOW TO DITCH HIM

When you're finally sick of having to pay all the bills and disgusted by his birthday present to his mum (a tiny hankie) just stop paying. And he'll stop playing!

MONEYMAKING MARK

Mark could well end up as a millionaire. He's got that moneymaking bug, you see. He's full of bright ideas, but they're always leading in the same direction — money.

HOW TO DAZZLE HIM

First of all, try to give him the idea that you're rich — or at least, that you've got a millionaire Great-Uncle Fred who lives in Miami.

And throw out the odd remark about "Aunt Emily's Emeralds" and "Cousin Monty's Mercedes." That'll intrigue Mark.

HOW HE'LL TREAT YOU

Mark will see you as a girl of many talents. If you don't exactly look like the back of a bus, he'll be sure you could be a fashion model.

If you occasionally sew a Snoopy badge on to your T-shirt, he'll be sure you could be a great designer. If you can stagger through a couple of reggae tracks at the disco without actually falling on your bum, he'll assure you you should be in Legs & Co. All this worship will be quite nice . . .

HIS ADVANTAGES

He'll make you feel pretty, clever and talented. A real investment . . .

HIS DISADVANTAGES

Millionaires (and boys who are going that way) are usually single-minded – and incredibly boring.

HOW TO DITCH HIM

Tell him you dream about living on potato soup in a primitive village in the Shetlands, and knitting jerseys for a living. And that'll be the last you'll see of him!

SPENDTHRIFT STEVE

Money runs through Steve's fingers like water. He just can't resist temptation — anything with a price tag on it he must have.

HOW TO DAZZLE HIM

The quickest way to get yourself noticed would be to have yourself gift-wrapped with a price tag saying, "Special Offer £4.99." But that might make you feel a bit . . . well, cheap.

Instead, cultivate a bit of variety. That's what Steve really likes. Dress up as a punk one day, then at the weekend, put on your prettiest, daintiest dress. Steve knows a bargain when he sees one — two girls for the price of one!

HOW HE'LL TREAT YOU

Life with Steve will be a lot of fun. He always acts on impulse — there's never a dull moment with him.

One minute you'll be planning to go to the movies on Saturday . . . next thing you know, he's dragging you off to a party he's just heard about.

HIS ADVANTAGES

If you like your life to be a whirl of frenzied activity, Steve's the boy for you. He's always

hurtling off after the latest thing that's caught his eye.

HIS DISADVANTAGES

The latest thing that's caught his eye might be blonde and beautiful . . . yes, he's a bit of a flirt, and among the many new things he can't resist are new girls.

HOW TO DITCH HIM

No problem here. Wear the same old dress every time you see him, chew gum and look vacant. Then he'll ditch you!

GENEROUS GRAHAM

Graham likes spending money, too — but not on himself, like Steve! Oh, no. Graham's generous — and that means he feels he must give people things (whether they want them or not!).

Admire Graham's tie at a party, and he'll whip it off and give it to you. (For goodness' sake, don't admire his trousers!) Say you love the soundtrack of "Superman" and it'll appear on your doorstep, wrapped in pink tissue paper. Say you like pink tissue paper and a huge, gossamer-light parcel will arrive on your doorstep . . .

HOW TO DAZZLE HIM

Graham likes giving because it makes him feel important, powerful and appreciated.

So whatever you do, keep accepting his gifts. Don't get embarrassed and send them back. As you unwrap a pair of hideous purple leg-warmers, cry, "Oh, Graham, you shouldn't have! You're wonderful!"

HOW HE'LL TREAT YOU

Graham likes to dominate. In a way, his constant buying and giving is a way of imposing himself on you.

HIS ADVANTAGES

Are obvious. He likes to give. He'll give you lots and lots of love, but he'll want you all to himself.

HIS DISADVANTAGES

Graham's basically trying to buy you, to make you all his. And just let anyone else try and buy you things! Graham'll punch him in the wallet!

HOW TO DITCH HIM

Send all his gifts back to him gift-wrapped, with a copy of the Beatles' old song, "Can't Buy Me Love." He'll get the message.

A Jackie Quiz

1. You're invited to your friend's bonfire party. Would you plan to wear —

c. a new jumper you've just bought — you want to show it off,
a. a pair of old jeans, leg-warmers, an extra jumper and a duffle coat,
b. your usual autumn outdoor gear — you don't really give it much thought,
d. something really wild — dress up as an old tramp or a Guy Fawkes?

2. When you arrive at the bus stop, you discover you've missed the bus. Do you —

d. burst into tears and kick the bus stop,
b. set off to walk, telling yourself you'll soon be there and it's good exercise,
c. try thumbing a lift, though you're a bit nervous and don't really want to,
a. phone up your friend and ask if her parents could come and fetch you — after all, you're their guest?

3. When you arrive at the bonfire party, the first thing you notice is —

c. the dangerous-looking, badly-organised bonfire,
d. the way everybody seems to be standing about shivering and looking miserable,
b. the fantastic smell of baking potatoes, hot soup, and frying onions,
a. a group of people you've always wanted to get to know — and now's your chance?

4. The party seems to be getting off to a pretty soggy start — it's drizzling and cold. Do you —

b. begin to wonder if you'd be better off at

home watching TV,
a. decide it's up to you, and run around slipping hot spuds down people's backs to get them going,
c. lose interest in the party, and nip off towards the house — maybe there's a stereo unit and some LPs in there,
d. sink into a really bad mood, glare at everybody, and swear when a firework singes your eyebrows?

5. Suddenly, a dark handsome boy comes up and says, "Do you want a hot-dog?" You hate hot-dogs but you really like him. Do you —

d. say, "Ugh! No thanks!" but offer to hand them round,
b. shake your head but give him a lovely smile, and ask him what else there is,
c. ask, "Do they bite?", giggle, and run off,
a. refuse, but decide he's the only decent-looking guy around, and ask your friend who he is?

6. An almighty Russian Thunderer goes off right behind you. Do you —

c. scream with terror and fling yourself into the arms of the nearest dishy-looking boy,
a. feel a bit startled, and decide it's time to follow the hot-dog boy into the house,
b. tell the people who are running the party

that you think it's getting a bit dangerous,
d. feel like exploding yourself?

7. A lot of rockets are soaring into the sky, and the hot-dog boy is standing quite near you. Do you —

b. ask your friend to introduce you,
c. grab him by the arm and then say, "Oh, — sorry — I thought you were my brother,"
a. go up and ask him a few questions about

FIRE?

Do you light up people's lives wherever you go, or do black moods often engulf you and put a damper on everyone's enjoyment?

In short, are you a sparkler, or more like a damp squib?

Try answering our special fireworks quiz to find out the secrets of your personality, and how you get on with boys . . .

rockets, hot-dogs, anything you think he'll know about,

d. creep up beside him and ask him what he's doing next weekend, 'cos you've heard there's this great disco happening?

8. The hot-dog boy (who's called Tony) seems to be pretty popular. A girl comes up, gives him a sparkler and tries to wriggle in between you and him. Do you —

c. decide you're wasting your time and flit off to try your luck elsewhere,

d. give her a few smouldering looks and if she doesn't get the message, spill hot soup down her anorak,

b. give up trying to chat him up and start a conversation with your friend instead,

a. stay around and eavesdrop, to try to figure out just how well she knows him and what chance you've got?

9. Suddenly, the bonfire flares up, and the Guy (the real Guy, not Tony!) goes up in a sheet of flame. His hat explodes and his hair shrivels up. Do you —

b. think how sad it is, really — and feel a bit sorry for the poor old Guy,

d. feel quite excited — the more lifelike the Guy is, the more thrilling it is,

a. have a good laugh — he looks really funny with his hat over one eye,

c. feel quite upset — the way he twisted up and writhed about was really horribly life-like?

10. Finally, towards the end of the party, you really get talking to the dishy Tony, and find you have a lot in common. But he still hasn't asked when he can see you again. Do you —

d. gaze deeply into his eyes and whisper, "This has been a fantastic evening, don't you think?"

b. decide that this is one time you can't hope for more, and say goodbye gracefully,

c. get nervous and flirt with him like mad, hoping he'll ask you out,

a. mention casually that you'll be having a party soon, and ask him for his address so you can invite him?

11. The last sparkler's sparked, the bonfire's dying down, and you stare at the scene before you go. You'll never forget —

b. what a great time you had — despite the awful weather. Food, fireworks, fellas — it was perfect,

c. how terrified you were when the banger exploded just behind you,

d. how sexy the hot-dog boy was — and how furious you were when that other girl tried to pinch him,

a. it was the night you met Tony — and you've got *plans* for him — even if he doesn't know it!?

12. You get home much later than you'd promised, and Mum yells at you. Do you —

a. just relax and let her shout — she'll soon get over it,

b. feel guilty, apologise, and try to think of ways of making it up to her,

c. get really rattled, and have a row with her,

d. say nothing, but sulk about it all the next day?

13. As you drift off to sleep, you dream about —

d. the row with Mum — you're still seething,

c. the beautiful shapes of the shining, shimmering fireworks,

b. flickering fires and someone's arms around you,

a. meeting Tony again, and how you're going to sweep him off his feet?

If your answers were mostly a:

You're a rocket! You don't just trust to chance when it comes to the future — you always plan ahead, and because of this, you're very much in control of your life. When unexpected things happen it can throw you, but you soon bounce back and re-adjust to new situations.

You're pretty ambitious, too, and when you've set your heart on something, you won't be budged — whether it's an exam result, a career, or a boy you've set your sights on. And when it comes to boys, you attract them because of your energy and your common-sense.

You share ups and downs like anybody else, but you're usually confident and optimistic, and you can take disappointments well.

If your answers were mostly b:

You're a sparkler! In other words, lively, charming and attractive, but not terribly ambitious. You enjoy the domestic side of life and you're very fond of people — especially the very old and the very young. You have a protective instinct towards them.

If things don't go your way, you can be quite obstinate — but basically you're cool and calm, and capable of taking an easy-going view of things. In fact, you're very rarely bad-tempered, and you hate rows. So you're a pretty positive character through and through — popular with boys and girls alike, and often relied upon to help other people sort out their lives and problems!

If your answers were mostly c:

You're a Jumping Jack! Totally unpredictable, you shoot from one mood to another. You're a fairly nervous character, and you react strongly to whatever happens. You're very lively, though, and enjoy people's company — and they enjoy yours! But they sometimes feel a bit uncertain with you.

You're quite a flirt where boys are concerned — sometimes you can do and say quite mad things you don't really mean. When you're in the mood, you can attract boys with your sheer vitality — other girls probably envy you for your quick wits.

Although you tend to be nervous, you've got quite an adventurous attitude to life. You can be quite daring and that often gets you into trouble. But you're always likely to do something that'll give you a laugh — however crazy! With you, life is never dull!

If your answers were mostly d:

You're a squib! Squibs smoulder quietly for a while and then ... POW! They explode. And that's the way you react to things. You're a girl of extremes — either up in the air or down in the dumps.

You're capable of really turning on the charm when boys are around ... but although boys are instantly attracted to you, they often find you hard to get on with because you're so unpredictable and moody. So you probably find you have no trouble in attracting boys, but have quite a lot of trouble keeping them!

You can be quite aggressive when you want to be — and you're not afraid of having a blazing row once in a while if necessary. People probably think twice before inviting you along to their parties, in case you have a bad day and pick a fight with somebody!

However, when you're in a good mood, you can be really great. You've got a creative, imaginative attitude to life and you really know how to enjoy yourself. In fact, you can create fun like no-one else. Sometimes you find it hard to concentrate on things and get bored easily. Basically, you're a bit lacking in self-discipline, and can let people — and yourself — down. The problem for other people is trying to keep pace with your moods!

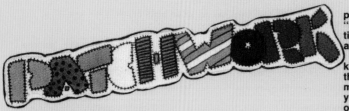

Have you ever felt you'd like to give someone a little present just to say, "Thank you" or "You're nice" or even, "I'm sorry"? The trouble is, it always seems to be just those times when you're stony broke and next pay day seems like a million years away!

So why not make your own presents? It's true that a hand-knitted egg cosy or a home-made bookmark aren't exactly the stuff dreams are made of, but there are things you can make that are original and attractive — and what's more, you don't have to be an artistic genius to make them! So read on and have a go — you might surprise yourself!

HANG IT!

A PENDANT is dead easy to make, and doesn't look any different from a bought one, as long as you don't finish it off with an ugly, lumpy knot! There's a neat trick to avoid this, which is easily done.

First, though, assemble your bits and pieces! The actual pendant motif could be an unusual button (keep an eye on market stalls, junk shops and jumble sales for those), a large bead, an initial traced from a capital letter in a newspaper or magazine, and cut in leather or suede, a small bell, or an interesting shape twisted in wire, or cut out of plastic or card and covered with self-adhesive plastic or glued-on fabric.

If you aren't good at thinking up shapes, look at things like the patterns on a blouse or wallpaper. Pick out a simple shape and keep it roughly oblong, oval or triangular, in other words, something which is longer than its own width, then it'll hang nicely.

Next you need to choose what the motif is to hang on. Use odd lengths of narrow chain, from an old belt or broken pendant, or narrow thongs cut from leather. Or you could use narrow ribbon, gold or silver-covered string, wool or embroidery silk in a suitable colour, plaited or twisted to the right thickness for the pendant. This is important — if your pendant motif is small, the chain must be light-weight, and if the pendant is heavy, the chain must be thick.

Now to make the pendant look professional! Thread the cord or chain through the motif, and make a tight, small knot that lies flat (a reef knot, as illustrated, is best). Snip off the loose ends, fairly close to the knot, and dab a little glue on the knot itself.

If the pendant is a bead, or something similar, force the knot into the bead, using a knitting needle or a skewer, and then the glue will hold it there, unseen. If the pendant motif is a flat object, like an initial, cut a small circle of paper, fabric or self-adhesive plastic, (glue it unless already self-adhesive), pull the knot into position and press the circle over it, hiding the knot completely. And that's all!

If you're making a pendant from a large bead, or several beads, and want to have your string or chain with the bead suspended from it, rather than running through it, here's how. Take the chain or string through the large bead, and then make a knot, and thread the chain back through the bead, so that the knot wedges just inside the bead.

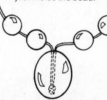

If your chosen chain is too large to go through the bead, tie a thread round a small bead and pull it through the large bead, so that the small bead jams at the bottom of the large one. Tie the thread to the chain and pull it through the large bead again, pulling the chain slightly into the hole at the top of the large bead. Knot firmly, and cut off the end.

IT'S A MUG'S GAME

TRY handpainting mugs. Buy some plain ones, and make your own decorations. You can buy suitable paints in craft shops, and you can also get transfers suitable for use on china and glass.

If you don't want to buy special paints, you can use nail varnish, though it tends to wash off after a time. Still, it's easy enough to do again!

BITS AND PIECES

KEEP your eyes open for really nice pictures on old Christmas and birthday cards, from magazines, calendars, and so on. Cut them out carefully, and ink in the cut edge with a red, purple or black felt-tip pen. Cut a small square of foam rubber or card, about 1 cm thick, and glue to the centre back.

Cut out a piece of cardboard a good bit larger than the picture, and cover it with hessian, lining silk, self-adhesive plastic in a plain colour, or with glued-on wallpaper in a plain design, and then glue the small square of foam rubber or card exactly in the centre.

Add a loop for hanging, and you've completed the picture!

GET SHIRTY!

BUY some plain T-shirts and decorate them, the next time you're racking your brains for a special gift for a friend who's got everything (we can all do with just one more T-shirt!).

You can use paint-on fabric dyes, from Dylon stockists (full instructions come with the dye).

You can also buy a special transfer pencil from good haberdashery counters. Draw your design on greaseproof paper — it's very easy to trace the design with the pencil — from anything you like. Now pin the greaseproof paper in position on a T-shirt, or pillowcase, or anything else you want to decorate. Iron over — and the design is transferred!

You can embroider over the design or sew on small beads in lines or blocks, or colour with fabric to make it more lasting.

Another good gift idea is a Krazy Karpet. You can often buy very small squares of carpet cheaply – from carpet shops' sample books, or on sale in carpet shops as off-cuts and on market stalls.

Cut the pieces into fun shapes, to make unusual bed-side rugs. How about a pair of giant feet – one on each side of the bed? Or a mouse, with a string tail?

COVERED IN BEADS!

USE lots of tiny beads to brighten up plain clothes or bags. You simply sew the beads into a pretty pattern on a pocket, cushion, skirt or a velvet bag.

It's easy, once you know how to sew on the beads so they don't shift about afterwards. Use a back stitch — bring your threaded needle up through the material, place the bead on top of the material, to the LEFT of the needlepoint, take the needle through it and down through the material. Take a long stitch to the RIGHT, on the underside, place the next bead to the left of the needlepoint and so on.

There's also a quick way to sew on beads if you want to work in straight lines. Thread them all on to a thread that fits the holes in the beads fairly tightly, and arrange this thread on the surface, as you want it.

Now thread the needle with a much finer matching cotton, bring the needle up from underneath the material, and just catch down the thick thread between the beads with a small stitch every four or five beads. Make sure the thread is fastened off underneath the material.

You can also glue beads on things like glass, china, leather, plastic, etc., for a decorative effect — use a glue suitable for the material. Pretty up an old plain plate either by sticking on beads in your own design, or use the design on the plate already, and fill in areas with tiny coloured glass or metallic beads.

A Time For Love!

What was it like to be a girl in the past? Was it really as romantic and glamorous as it seems? Or was it a very uneasy time, threatened by illness, wars and cruelty? We've had a look back through time to see just how different life would have been if you'd been growing up then. So read on — and find out if *you* could have survived in the past!

Roman

IF you were a Roman girl, you'd wear cool, comfortable dresses, enjoy heated rooms and hot baths and probably be a lot cleaner than any girls for the next 1900 years!

You'd certainly be courted. Ovid, the Roman poet, wrote a book called "The Art of Love" telling all would-be lovers how to set about it! One of his recommendations was that you should write messages to your lover on your maid's back in milk. Then he would rub her back with coal which would make the words visible. You'd have had to watch out, though, that your maid wasn't prettier than you!

Medieval

THIS was the age of courtly love. While the husbands and fathers were away at the Crusades, the women made full use of this chance to enjoy themselves. With your hair hanging in plaits or ringlets to your waist, and dressed in a close-fitting dress with fur-trimmed cuffs, you'd enchant every young man within miles.

This was the age of real Romantic love. Your lover would write poems to you, and sing sad songs beneath your window. It was almost your duty to be cruel to him — for a while, at least!

Part of the reason for all this intense passion may have been that life was very uncertain. The plague was everywhere, and once it got into your town, you wouldn't last more than a day or two. So perhaps it was a case of making the most of things while you could . . .

Puritans

OLIVER CROMWELL soon changed all this. If you'd been a Puritan girl your hair would have been pulled back out of sight under a modest cap, you'd wear a thick black dress up to your chin and as for make-up, well, any girl daring even to think of it, was sure to go *straight to the fires of hell*! (In fact, doing just about anything seemed to guarantee you a place there, in Cromwell's time!)

Any kind of contact with boys was a sin. Punishments for "wicked behaviour" included head shaving, being ducked, and being put in the pillory or stocks for people to pelt you with rotten eggs. Merely talking to a boy

was enough to get you into serious trouble. Better to sit at home reading the Bible, and let your parents arrange a marriage for you with some religious man who was probably forty years your senior, and who wouldn't have any ideas of fun even if it had been allowed, anyway!

Regency Times

IN the early nineteenth century, life was delicious. You could have your hair cropped, curled or wear it long. Your dresses were of featherlight muslin — so fine that they could be passed through a ring.

Courtship was open and daring. The Waltz — the new dance which was all the rage — enabled you to drift around the ballroom in a close embrace. The wildest place in Britain was Brighton, where the Prince Regent led a life of wine, women and song. It probably wasn't a good idea to pursue the Prince, though; he was vastly overweight, and *very* sweaty.

Victorian

AS usual in history, people soon reacted against a period of wild fun. If you'd been alive in Victorian times, you'd have been corseted more tightly than ever — women often fainted from tight-corseting and sometimes even had deformed ribs!

You'd have to stay at home all day — surrounded by potted plants and furniture that had skirts on to hide the legs! You'd only be allowed out with a chaperone: usually a crotchety middle-aged spinster with eyes like an eagle.

Marriages were usually arranged by families, and even if you happened to *like* your fiancé, your behaviour with him even when you were engaged would have to be absolutely perfect. "Courtship in public is selfish, vulgar, indelicate and offensive" — or so they believed. So your idea of fun was likely to be a quick giggle with your sisters over your embroidery. A pretty limited life!

Well, that's the way it was. Do you wish you'd been there? Or does it make you realise just how lucky you are to live in our pulsating, punky, plastic, dare we say, perfect age?

A Happy New

January

BE AN ICE MAIDEN

It's the month of frosts and glittering snows . . . So why not be an Ice Maiden, someone who's pale and interesting, with a not-quite-real, fantasy atmosphere about her? With just a *touch* of frost, of course!

LOOKS: Hair. If you've got long hair, wear it pulled over to one side. If your hair's short, give it a blonde rinse (the sort that lasts for 3 to 4 shampoos). For evenings, sprinkle a little glitter dust over it.

Clothes. Stick to ice-cool colours — blues and whites. If you've got any satin clothes, or glittery tops, wear them. Silvery accessories look really good with this look.

THE WAY YOU ACT. Try to be a bit more mysterious than usual. Talk less, and listen more. Watch people and study their reactions. Don't get too carried away by your emotions. Read a lot more than usual, and try to find out as much as you can about subjects you're interested in. That way, you'll not only look interesting, you'll sound interesting too! Make a point of listening to all-sorts of music as well — not just the sort you know you like. Don't let people upset you and *don't* get angry — remember, you're staying SUPER COOL!

March

BE A MAD MARCH HARE

March is the traditional month for going mad — and why not, once in a while? Live it up, really have yourself a ball and be outrageous!

LOOKS: Hair. If you're brave enough, have something really wild done — a wild gipsy perm, or a really short cut. If you've always hankered after a pink streak, now's the time! But if you don't fancy that, go for hats — knitted hats, tweed hats, Mum's old hats from the Sixties, bowlers, berets. Try a different one every time you go out.

Clothes. Well, it's your mad month, so anything goes! Try out male gear — ex-Army combat jackets, boiler suits, basketball boots. Or go off wildly in the other direction and try out fishnet tights, stilettos and satin skirts. Root around Army & Navy Stores, and market stalls for medals, badges, interesting beads and belts, and make your own accessories!

THE WAY YOU ACT. For once, don't worry what people think, just do what *you* want to do! (Unless it's downright dangerous, of course!) So go for a run in the park, play on the kids' swings, have a bonfire, write a fan letter to Prince Andrew, hold a jumble sale — and liven up the neighbourhood in any way you like!

February

BE A VALENTINE

Try for an early thaw by becoming every boy's ideal Valentine for this special month of love — sweet, gentle, and tender-hearted. Be a bit of a romantic, and terribly feminine . . .

LOOKS: Hair. Something soft and feminine will do the trick. If your hair's naturally curly, great. If you've been wondering about a light perm, go ahead! And if your hair's dead straight and staying that way, soften it up by wearing a flower attached with a hairslide just behind the ear, or even a pretty clasp.

Clothes. Wear something pretty and flowery — maybe a Laura Ashley dress or blouse. Choose warm, delicate colours — pink, rust, brown, warm greys.

THE WAY YOU ACT. After the January freeze-up, let your emotions thaw! Watch sad movies and have a good weep. And laugh till you cry if you really feel like it. Get a hyacinth in a bowl and put it by your bed, so every night as you doze off to sleep, the sweet smell of spring will creep over you. Tell your family how much you love them. And if you're too shy to tell them — *show them*, by running errands for them . . .

You!

— A NEW YEAR'S CALENDAR OF COOL NEW LOOKS — JUST FOR YOU!

It's fun trying out new ways of looking and acting. So why don't *you* ring the changes throughout the coming year, and have a New Look and a New Style for every month of the year? Here's how!

May

BE QUEEN OF THE MAY

Traditionally, the May Queen is crowned with flowers and led in triumph through the streets. She's definitely the First Lady for a day, and you can certainly take a few tips from her!

LOOKS: Hair. May stunners should make the most of their hair. Try rolling it on big rollers if it's long, and see what a headful of tousled curls does for you. If it's short, try the effect of a daisy chain round it, or a twisted silk scarf, or thongs and beads.

Clothes. Got any really *nice* dresses? If not, now's the time to look out for a few. The second-hand market stalls usually have some. Romantic ones are nice for summer, and always look good.

THE WAY YOU ACT. Forget your usual shy self and be really outgoing. And that means smiling at people as often as you can. They'll smile back, and it feels great to spread a little happiness. And ask that boy you fancy to come out with you. He may be dying to get to know you better but be too shy to ask. Give a party. Tell people what *your* ideas are, for a change. Make them sit up and take notice!

April

BE A COUNTRY GIRL

With spring beginning to — er — spring in every hedgerow, why don't you turn yourself into a true nature-lover, and be a real country girl?

LOOKS: Hair. It should be casual, natural, and gleaming with health, of course. Treat it to lots of lovely herbal shampoos, such as Wella's, or Boots *Original Formula* range. And try the super range of shampoos by Leryss.

Clothes. You'll go for lovely, practical, warm country clothes. Casual, brown and green jumpers and tops, tartan shirts worn with waistcoats, and good, warm boots — the sort you can walk in for miles, which won't let the mud in. (Hush Puppies are best, and Kickers look really smart.) Stick to natural fabrics: things like wool, cotton, corduroy.

THE WAY YOU ACT. Really look at the natural world all around you for once — the trees, the rivers, the grass, and all the newly-growing plants. Get out into the country if you can, and watch the fields being sown and the birds building their nests. And then look up into the sky and find time to wonder at what's behind it all . . .

June

BE ON FIRE FOR FLAMING JUNE

Flaming June it's supposed to be — but so often it's soggy and disappointing instead. So why not become flaming June yourself — a fiery girl who'll send everyone's temperature soaring, even if Wimbledon's rained off!

LOOKS: Hair. If you've never tried henna, now's the time to try it out! If you're a blonde, though, don't go for the red henna unless you want to end up with bright orange hair, 'cos that's how it'll turn out! But Henna Hair Health Ltd. make a Golden Henna now, specially for blondes, which gives shine and condition.

Clothes. Cut a dash. Choose strong, bright, dramatic colours. Go for something really sharp, a white suit, maybe. Or if it's really hot, a billowing red er white chiffon dress.

THE WAY YOU ACT. Now's your chance to really come on strong, to get ahead, to be always on the move. Make a point of exploring new places, going out as much as possible, planning a foreign holiday, maybe. And try to get to know a lot of new people, by going to lots of summer events, fairs, jumble sales, cricket matches, sports events . . . there's lots going on!

A Happy New

July

BE A BIKE GIRL

July's the month of the open road, the start of the holiday, and get-up-and-go. So get your own looks together around the idea of the road, and bikes!

LOOKS: Hair. You don't want to do anything too elaborate with your hair. Shove it away under a cap or scarf. Short hair is really best for this look. If yours is long, make bunches or tie it back.

Clothes. Shorts are a must, for this look! Look out for vests, plain white T-shirts, towelling tops and sandals, too.

THE WAY YOU ACT. Put aside your ultra-feminine feelings and go in for a bit of adventure. Try out things you've never done before. Also, get fit by jogging or weight-training. Working out at the gym can be fun — think of all those glistening musclemen!

August

BE A BEACH BELLE

Even if you're not going anywhere near the sea, now's the time you should be cultivating that sun-kissed Californian beach-girl look . . .

LOOKS: Hair. If yours could possibly be called fair, try and bleach it in the sun. If the sun won't come out, go to the hairdresser and get a few streaks put in. It'll make you look really good. If you're dark, make your hair gleam with lots of conditioner and the occasional application of henna.

Clothes. When you can't actually wear your bikini, go for really cool, casual looks. Look for off-the-shoulder T-shirts in pale, sun-bleached pastel colours, shorts, sandals and skirts which show off your bronzed, beautiful legs!

THE WAY YOU ACT. You're a Beach Belle now, and your job is to relax to the very depths of your being. If you haven't tried yoga, make a start on it now! As you lie back and soak up the sun, too, let your mind swim idly around all sorts of subjects . . .

September

BE A SUNBURNED GIPSY

The month of fairs, and the end of summer. Say goodbye to the sun in style and be a gipsy — even if you're not travelling anywhere!

LOOKS: Hair. If you're blonde, cover it up with headscarves! If you're dark — great! Dark curls clustering around the face are really flattering.

Clothes. Colours should be bright, and patterned. Shawls go well with this look, so do headscarves and big, chunky earrings. Try boots if the weather's cold — if not, it must be bare legs and flat sandals!

THE WAY YOU ACT. The gipsy life is very simple, and close to Nature. Try and live simply. Really learn to appreciate the basic pleasures of life — being warm, the smell of cooking, good company . . . And have a look at that other gipsy thing — the supernatural . . .

You!

November

BE A SPARKLER

This is the month of Guy Fawkes and Bonfire parties. So make sure you're a real fire-cracker — bringing dazzle and sparkle everywhere you go.

LOOKS: Hair. Make sure it's in tip-top condition and try out lots of new looks — hairslides, hair ribbons, little hats. If it's long enough, try lots and lots of fine plaits. Or get some little beads and thread them into your hair (specially nice if your hair's crinkly).

Clothes. Go for a cuddly-but-dazzling look. Lacy jumpers, gloves, jeans worn inside boots. Ankle boots go well with this look.

THE WAY YOU ACT. You're a fire-cracker, right? So you've got to be very *sparky!* Keep smiling. Laugh at people's jokes — even if they're a bit weak — and whatever anybody suggests, react *positively.* Keep your energy level high with lots of exercise. Spring a few surprises on your friends and family — pleasant surprises, that is!

October

BE A FORTIES FLIRT

By October, the best of summer's gone and we're all back at work. A time for looking back, a mysterious month of shadows. Take your own look back, too . . .

LOOKS: Hair. Basically, try out hairstyles from the past. If your hair's very long, try putting it up. Or try a Fifties pony-tail. If your hair's short, get that Twenties look with a really close, boyish crop. If it's mid-length, try some of those Thirties and Forties looks — with little rolls and quiffs.

Clothes. Go round all the second-hand clothes stalls, jumble sales, and Oxfam shops. They really are a gold mine! You can find wonderful clothes at very cheap prices there. Beautiful crepe dresses for 60p or £1 . . . amazing hats with birds and feathers on . . . old fur coats for £8 . . . Go along and see what you can find!

THE WAY YOU ACT. This month's all about the past, so why not read a historical novel and be a bit more aware of history all around you? And think about your own history. Ask Mum and Dad to tell you what life was like when they were young. And go browsing through the photograph albums!

December

BE A CHRISTMAS CRACKER

This is a magical time of year, with parties, presents, and a very special atmosphere. It's time to try out a new, sparkly, crackly look . . .

LOOKS: Hair. If your hair's long enough to put up, try it, and show off the shape of your neck and ears. Maybe even put some silver or gold sparkle in it for special parties (but first make sure it's a spray for *hair!*).

Clothes. Try to find something really out of this world. An old silk dressing-gown, maybe, or a satin dress or an old lacy blouse. Any of these, worn with silvery sandals, would be stunning

THE WAY YOU ACT. If you want to be a Christmas Cracker, you'll have to sparkle! So try to liven things up wherever you are! Sing in the bath, be nice to everyone, organise parties and carol singing and generally be sweetness and light to everyone. And don't worry too much about all this niceness — when it's time for a Christmas party you can get up to a little naughtiness — just to liven things up!

Everybody talks about it, everybody sings about it and most of us think about it . . .
What is it? Love, of course! But what exactly *is* this thing called love? There are lots of experiences
that feel a bit like love, and lots of different *kinds* of love, so it's all pretty confusing and
not at all straightforward . . .
Here, we talk to some girls who've all had different experiences
of love. Hopefully, their stories will help you decide
what it is *you're* feeling — and what
it'll be like once you do
fall in love!

This Thing Called Love...

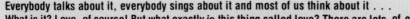

UNREQUITED LOVE

. . . IS when you care very deeply for someone who doesn't care at all about you. It's a very painful experience. Carole, who's 16 now, knows all about the hurt of unrequited love . . .

"I was about thirteen when I met Mark. He was in the Sixth Form at school — a lot older than me and he seemed very grown-up. He wasn't at all like the boys in my class, who were pretty awful. I got to know him through being in one of our school plays.

"I always made sure I was sitting in a group around him, so I could be near him. I remember the time I realised I was falling for him — it was during one of the rehearsals. Mark had arrived late — and suddenly, I went weak at the knees when I saw him. He never ever noticed me, of course, but I couldn't take my eyes off him . . .

"We got to know each other quite well during the play, and he said some nice things to me. Then there were the Christmas holidays.

> **'HE NEVER NOTICED ME — BUT I COULDN'T TAKE MY EYES OFF HIM . . .**

"When I went back to school, I had to face the fact that I'd hardly ever see him — the play was finished and his Sixth Form had their own block and everything.

"He always smiled and said hello, and that kept my hopes alive. But then he started going out with a girl in the Sixth Form. It felt like the end of the world. I was so miserable.

"I've got over him now, of course, but I don't think I'll ever forget him, or ever feel as deeply about anything or anyone as I did for Mark . . ."

Carole's experience is very normal. It's natural when you're 12 or 13 to fall for much older boys — simply because boys your own age are still so much more immature than you are.

If you find yourself feeling this way about a boy, content yourself with harmless day-dreaming about him, but just don't kid yourself that anything will ever come of it — though it might, of course, but it's unlikely to happen for a while, until you're much older, anyway . . .

PHYSICAL LOVE

WHEN you're young, it's pretty hard to make sense of all the different feelings you have about boys. Di, who's 14 and recently finished with her boyfriend, Ricky, explains the physical kind of love she experienced . . .

"Right from the start, it was the way Ricky looked that attracted me. He was gorgeous.

"When he came up at a disco and asked me to dance, I felt great! And when he asked me out, I felt on top of the world. I was so happy. I used to love just looking at him, his

eyes especially.

"After a while, though, I began to notice something. Whenever we were together, I'd listen to what he'd be saying without actually listening, if you know what I mean. I didn't concentrate on what he was saying, I was just looking at him.

> **'I USED TO LOVE JUST LOOKING AT HIM . . .'**

"Once I'd realised that, it made it pretty hard to carry on. I still fancied him like mad, the way he moved and looked, but it just isn't enough, is it? In the end I chucked him, I still fancied *him* — but not his mind, if you see what I mean!"

Just fancying someone — being fascinated by their looks and wanting to touch them — is great in itself.

But there's got to be a lot more to a relationship for it really to take off. For a start, there's got to be a lot of interests to share, and a real ability to communicate and stay interested in each other — absolutely vital if you're going to build a relationship that really lasts.

PLATONIC LOVE

. . . IS when you love a boy the way you love a brother. It's what you feel for a guy you're fond of, but whom you don't really fancy. Some girls find they feel this way about their boyfriends — especially towards the end of a relationship — but it's more usual to feel this way about guys who are just friends. Listen to Janice who's 16 . . .

"I was 14 when I got to know Terry. We were both pretty serious people and we used to spend hours and hours sitting talking about anything and everything under the sun.

"I did love him, but in a very straightforward kind of way, like a brother, only without all the irritation you sometimes feel for your brother. Once I'd realised that Terry fancied me though, I began to get really nervous.

"One day, the inevitable happened — he started to tell me how he'd really fallen for me and how he'd like us to start going out properly. I didn't know what to say, so I kind of went along with him.

"The trouble was, it never felt right. I did love him in a way, but not the way he wanted. I wanted to talk to him and be

> **'I DID LOVE HIM IN A WAY — BUT NOT THE WAY HE WANTED'**

with him but that was all. And when I was pretending it was more than that, it all seemed horrible — the really nice, affectionate way I felt about him kind of sank under a feeling that it was all wrong.

"So I told him. It was awkward for a while but we managed to get back to our old relationship. In the end, too, it was better than ever, simply because we'd got the physical thing out of the way."

Janice and Terry were lucky that their relationship was strong enough to withstand that sort of strain.

But then, Platonic love really is strong. It's sexual feelings that usually cause trouble in a relationship.

You can discuss things without feeling the strain you might with a boy you were physically involved with. You can ask his advice about how boys feel and about their problems, and tell him about girls, without feeling embarrassed. In fact, it's a lovely feeling! So if you've got any boy friends (as opposed to boyfriends!), look after them!

IS IT THE REAL THING?

WELL, maybe there isn't such a thing as "THE REAL THING." There are lots of different ways of feeling real love, and a lot of people go around really worried because they think they haven't felt "it." What Penny felt, though, is obviously the "Real Thing," despite the times she had a lot of doubt and anxiety . . .

"I met Martin when we were both on a course at a big house in the country. It was a really romantic place to meet: trees, a lake . . . fantastic! I noticed Martin straightaway and he noticed me, too. By the first coffee break we were chatting away to each other.

'I WAS SCARED IT WOULDN'T LAST'

"We seemed to like so many of the same things, it was . . . well, weird! I seemed to know exactly what he was thinking.

"When the course finished, we had to part. But we only live ten miles away from each other, so we still meet a lot. I was scared stiff that it wouldn't last, but it has. We see each other at weekends — and from time to time in the week, if there's a chance. It's eighteen months now since we met.

"When I'm going to see him I feel really excited. When he looks into my eyes I feel myself sort of melting inside. And I sometimes feel agonies of jealousy if I think he might be falling for another girl. He hasn't yet, thank goodness!"

Penny and Martin are obviously in love — they've got a lot of common interests, a similar outlook on things and an almost telepathic ability to read each other's thoughts! The fact that Penny still feels excited when she's going to see him shows their love is still fresh, though it's perfectly possible to enjoy a gentler kind of being truly in love, where you don't feel your heart turning somersaults as soon as you see him! That exciting stage is usually only at the beginning of a relationship, anyhow.

It must be clear from all these girls' experiences that there's a huge range of feelings possible in your relationships with boys. The great thing is to be able to recognise what you're feeling and not mistake it for something else.

The sort of love that's going to last must include physical attraction, similar interests, and the ability to talk honestly together. But if what you're sharing with a boy doesn't quite come up to those high standards, don't worry – enjoy it anyway!

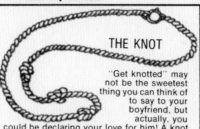
Are You Charming Enough?

Are you a little bit short of luck at the moment? Maybe you need some help with your love life? — or a bit of protection from the "Dark Forces"? Well, here's how to charm your way to success!

From the very beginning of civilisation — even before people got round to wearing clothes! — people have been wearing lucky charms.

Nowadays, though, we tend to take lucky charms for granted without realising their true significance and their strong astrological connections.

Unlike lucky stones, charms can be very ordinary, commonplace objects, and the same shapes and symbols appear again and again throughout history as bringers of luck, with magical properties.

So read these rules which govern all lucky charms — and you'll discover they can't just be treated any old how!

★ No charm which has been obtained unjustly can be a bringer of good fortune.
★ No charm will bring good fortune to one who is unworthy of it.
★ No charm must be allowed to touch the ground. If it falls accidentally its luck will be lost, for a time at least.
★ Charms are more powerful when worn on the left side of the body, rather than the right.

Got that? Good. Now all you have to do is to find out what objects are most likely to be lucky for **you** — it all depends on your astrology sign, and what area of your life you need some help with!

THE KNOT

"Get knotted" may not be the sweetest thing you can think of to say to your boyfriend, but actually, you could be declaring your love for him! A knot stands for the joining of things, and is particularly useful for a girl who wants to draw a certain boy to her. Everyone has heard of the "true lover's knot" and a particularly effective charm is to get hold of a tie he has worn and tie three knots in it, while saying: "Three times a true-lover's knot I tie secure, Firm be the knot, firm may his love endure." Usually, the knot should be made of silver and it particularly favours those born under *Gemini* and *Pisces*.

THE PADLOCK

It might seem strange as a lucky charm, because to some people it suggests locking up, or loss of liberty. But, in fact, when it comes to love and romance a padlock is very lucky. Especially when used to fasten a bracelet or bangle, it is a securer of affection, the lock that holds romance safe and also brings long life and happiness. It's especially fortunate for *Taurean* girls.

THE FOUR-LEAVED CLOVER

This charm is of Irish origin and is still commonly held throughout Ireland to have luck-bringing powers. Each leaf has a separate meaning.

The first leaf on the left of the stalk helps to bring fame; the second moving clockwise assists in the obtaining of wealth (i.e., it helps you get rich!), the third to the right brings a faithful boyfriend and the fourth, on the right of the stalk, brings good health.

This charm is particularly associated with the signs *Cancer* and *Pisces*.

THE HEART

The heart as a mascot stems from Ancient Egypt where they believed that people's hearts were weighed before they were accepted into heaven! Now, of course, it's a symbol of true love and affection, and is especially fortunate for *Leo* and *Libra* people.

THE FROG

You may think these are pretty ugly-looking creatures, but right back through the ages they turn up in myths and fairytales, magic spells and brews — remember the one that turned out to be a prince? Frogs are small but powerful! Small frogs in gold or gilt metal are amulets against illness, or may be worn to speed recovery from disease or injury. And to kill or hurt a frog in any way is supposed to bring illness and ill-fortune.

THE KEY

In ancient Greece and Rome the single key was the most important of all mascots as it was the oldest mascot known to them, and was a symbol of life and knowledge.

A key is particularly suitable as a lucky mascot for *Virgo*, *Scorpio* or *Aquarius* people and should be gold, silver or stainless steel.

And one last tip: gipsies say that if you hang a door key upside down near your bed you will be safe from all forms of evil, including Mare, the evil spirit of the night — the bringer of "nightmares"!

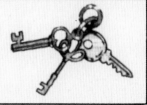

Catch Him If You Can!

Most boys are sportsmen at heart — tennis players, footballers, boxers, cricketers, bikers, skateboarders, fishermen — and most of them play the love game the way they play their favourite sport, to win!

Find out the rules he follows to win your heart, and you'll find out all about the kind of boy he is — and the kind of game *you* should play to win *him*!

THE FAST BOWLER

Tell him by his fixed and glaring eyes, the way he scowls to try and terrify the opposition (you — or any other half-decent girl who's within 3 feet of him), and the restless way he prowls around while he's waiting to pounce on you!

How he'll treat you

His aim is to bowl a maiden over. He'll shower you with compliments, send you flowers, buy you lots of lovely pressies — in short, bowl you right off your feet. If you show signs of resistance, he'll just keep on trying and trying . . .

His interests

A physical type, he's attracted to a nice pair of legs — that's why he seems obsessed with legs before wickets!

If you like him

Make it easy for him to ask you out. It's worth the effort, as he's quite a catch himself.

If you don't like him

Tie his bootlaces together, so he'll slip and pull a tendon.

THE CLEVER BOXER

Tell him by his dead classy, ever-so-clever bobbing and weaving style. He's a real knockout, but what he enjoys is all the slippery-footed dancing about that leads up to it.

How he'll treat you

He'll dance round you, all lively, and soften you up with lots of clever little jokes and cunning moves. Then, when you're getting a bit weak at the knees, and a bit groggy from all his charm . . . WHAM! You'll see stars, 'cos he'll have moved in for the kill.

His interests

What he relies on is his speed and fitness, so all his spare time is spent getting into shape — sharpening up his chatting-up and exercising his girl-hypnotising footwork.

If you like him

Box clever and don't pull your punches and you could be *his* champion!

If you don't like him

Tell him you're going to float like a butterfly — right out of his reach!

FISHERMAN

Tell him by his calm, peaceful, very patient look as he sits hunched up, waiting for the Big One (you) he knows sooner or later he's going to land . . .

How he'll treat you

The fisherman's cunning approach is to cast handfuls of bait to get you interested. Cinema tickets, invitations to discos, cups of coffee, spearmint chews. If this "ground bait" works, you'll be nicely lined up for something really tempting — a double album, or a trip to London to see a live Elton John concert. Then, you're hooked!

His interests

He's a guy who can relax and take his time. He's not going to rush after you when he can tempt you right up into his backwater just by playing his cards right.

If you like him

Swim right up to him with a saucy flick of your fins and let him land you.

If you don't like him

Be the one that got away!

THE LONG-DISTANCE RUNNER

Tell him by his slow but steady trot, his lean and hungry look, and the way he hangs back and bides his time while lots of other fellas are buzzing around you. He's saving himself for the last straight.

How he'll treat you

His technique is to stay with you, gently pottering along in the background for weeks and weeks, as flashier boyfriends come and go. In the end, he's usually rewarded for his stamina.

His interests

Since his effort depends upon stamina, what he really needs is lots of sweetness — from you — to keep him going. A smile here, a compliment there, and a friendly pat on the head now and then ought to be enough to fuel his fires and keep him interested for months . . .

If you like him

Ask him: "Is this the last lap?" — and then jump on to it!

If you don't like him

Tell him he's for the High Jump.

HAVE YOU GOT BAD TABLE MANNERS?

Whether you're a chomper, a guzzler or a nibbler, the way you eat your food is a dead give-away to your personality. Read on and taste the difference . . .

SWEET SHARON

How She Eats — She's always sucking sweets, chewing gum, and slinking into the corner shop to stock up her rations. She doesn't eat very much at meals (not surprising, really. Could you, with a hundredweight of gob-stoppers rattling round inside?), but between meals, her jaws are never still!

Her Character — It's obvious she likes to indulge herself and this extends to other things, too. She'll put off even the tiniest of chores, as she's so lazy. If you're relying on her to do something for you, forget it — *she* certainly will! She's very affectionate, though, and makes you feel needed.

Her Attitude To Boys — This girl is boy mad and spends most of her time dreaming about some guy or other! She can be very faithful and stick to one guy for months on end, but, there again, she can also fall madly in love three times a week, if the mood takes her! Boys like her, because she's sweet and attractive, but they soon tire of her because she can be clinging and possessive.

Her Disadvantages — She won't do a thing for herself and relies on her friends and family. Sometimes she puts on an act of being a helpless fluffy little creature who's totally incapable. The truth is she hasn't really grown up and still yearns for Mummy to come and sort things out for her!

GUZZLING GERTIE

How She Eats — She positively wolfs down her food. Great mouthfuls of pies and tarts, huge forkloads of roast beef — all disappear without trace! It's not that she's *greedy*. She doesn't

eat *more* than other people, just *faster*. (Twenty times faster!) By the time most of us are halfway through our soup, she's licking her pudding spoon.

Her Character — She's really ambitious and doesn't waste time on such unimportant things as eating — not when there's the rest of life to get on with! She wants to go far and do great things. She's got bags of energy, and she's the sort who could walk 20 miles, swim 40 lengths, and run 10,000 metres in the same afternoon! Nobody ever finds her hard to talk to — she's very outgoing.

Her Attitude To Boys — She doesn't wait for boys to chat her up. If she fancies one, she'll dive straight in and ask if he wants to join her rock-climbing club, squash team or drama society. When she hasn't got a boyfriend (which isn't very often), she doesn't bother to think about them. There's plenty of other things to do and say!

Her Disadvantages — Guzzlers suffer from indigestion. And she gets it in lots of ways! Often she rushes into things without enough thought, and then finds herself in circumstances beyond her control. She's not very tactful and tramples on people's feelings quite often.

FANATICAL FRAN

How She Eats — Her attitude to food is *all* that's important. She has theories about it. Maybe she's a vegetarian, or a wholefood fanatic, or even a macrobiotic freak? Or it could be she's into one particular kind of cooking — Chinese, French or Greek.

Her Character — Her head just buzzes with ideas. What's more, she's very strong willed and can follow an idea right through, against all sorts of difficulties. You might call her a bit of an intellectual, and in fact, she's certain to be interested in all sorts of things — books, plays, politics and science.

Her Attitude To Boys — She sets her standards pretty high. She finds boys easy to talk to and get on with, but she can be fooled by a guy who's just ordinary. She sees things in him that aren't there and when she realises she's wrong, she blames herself for her foolishness. In fact, she feels quite a lot of guilt generally — about things in the wider world, like whaling and conservation, as well as in her own life.

Her Disadvantages — She can be a little out of touch with reality. Sometimes she can be intolerant and difficult to persuade about things, too. But in general she's a really great girl — a good mate and an inspiring girlfriend!

NIBBLING NORAH

How She Eats — She goes around the house like a mouse nibbling an apple here, a bit of chocolate there, "tidying up" a piece of cheese that's been left on the kitchen table . . . she's never still. Or at least, her teeth never are!

Her Character — The most important thing about this girl is she's rather nervous and insecure. Really she's convinced she's fat and ugly (or thin and ugly, for despite all her nibbling, she *can* be thin because she worries such a lot). Or maybe she's always arguing with her parents, or doesn't get on with

her mates at school. Whatever the reason, she's lacking a little in confidence.

Her Attitude To Boys — She'd love to get to know some, and maybe even go out on a date, but at the moment that's unlikely, unless a guy's very determined to take her out. Unfortunately, she's so nervous and shy, she hardly ever opens her mouth when boys are about, except to pop a crisp or nut in it, of course! She's so tense she finds it very hard to talk to people, especially boys.

Her Disadvantages — Well, they're obvious! She's a bag of nerves, and however nice, gentle, charming, sweet and intelligent she is underneath it all — nobody's going to find out until she's managed to conquer her nerves and stand up to people.

TAKESTIME TINA

How She Eats — She cuts her food up into nice, even-sized chunks, chews each mouthful well, savours it, and enjoys it! She likes to put her knife and fork down from time to time just to talk. Sometimes while she's doing this, her food gets cold. But does she care? Not a bit!

Her Character — She's very secure, very relaxed and has been lucky enough to be brought up in a very happy home, so her reactions to most things are very even tempered. She's good in emergencies and always keeps her head — so if the soup boils over, she's the ideal person to have around.

Her Attitude To Boys — She's well adjusted to boys, too. But her only problem is she finds boys of her own age very immature, as she's particularly mature for her age. She's quite capable of falling head-over-heels in love with a guy, but she'd probably be quite successful at hiding it from her friends, and she'd certainly never do anything silly or make a fool of herself over him!

Her Disadvantages — She can be just the teeniest bit irritating! After all, she seems to find life so *easy*. If only she'd lose her cool now and then, she'd be a lot more popular!

WATCH THIS SPACE!

We've had superheroes and anti-heroes, space villains and good guys, princesses from far-flung planets and weird and wonderful monsters of every size, shape and description — not to mention a fair spattering of luscious space trekkers for us to drool over. Here we've taken a selection of films you've seen, some you'll be watching now, and even a sneaky peek at a few to come! Read on for stars in your eyes and a delicious floaty feeling!

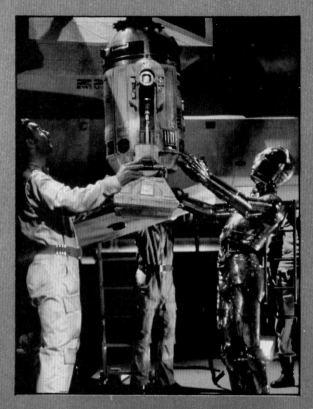

Set in a far-off galaxy, "Star Wars" was the perfect cowboys and Indians adventure — even the costumes were in keeping with the action — black for the baddies and white for the goodies. That all seems so long ago now, especially as the sequel to "Star Wars" has already been filmed. "The Empire Strikes Back" followed on where "Star Wars" left off. Once again starring Mark Hamill, Carrie Fisher and Harrison Ford — not to mention the evil Darth Vadar and the amusing C-3PO and R2-D2, this exciting film has all the action of its predecessor, and lots more!

Space ships are the "in thing" for the film designers. Who can forget that incredible mother ship which appeared in "Close Encounters Of The Third Kind"? CE3K, as it became known, really gave substance to the idea that the Planet Earth was being visited by beings from another world.

A similar visitation occurs in the film "Foes," which is about four people who become the focus of a destructive and tragic series of events, when extra-terrestial aliens attempt to communicate with our planet!

It would be impossible, when talking about space ships, not to give a mention to perhaps the most popular vehicle of them all — the Starship Enterprise. Yes, the full-length film of "Star Trek" is proving as popular as it's TV brain-child, now a staggering ten years old! All your favourites are there: William Shatner, Leonard Nimoy, De-Forrest Kelley and, as an extra bonus, former Miss India — Persis Khambatta, who plays an exotic and incidentally *bald* navigator called Ilia, who comes from the planet Delta.

Disney, too, has not forgotten his fans — "The Spaceman And King Arthur" has the unlikely situation of a spaceman who accidentally travels back in time to the court of King Arthur — and receives a none-too-friendly welcome. Look out for gorgeous Dennis Dugan in the leading role.

"Battlestar Galactica" is almost like a "Star Wars" spin-off, and was originally made for television. Once again the planetary powers are fighting their way into total oblivion. But the special effects, as always in this type of movie, are always worth watching — so is one of its stars — ex-Bond girl, Jane Seymour! Mind you, Richard Hatch and Dirk Benedict are the only two we've managed to see at all!

In "Buck Rogers," Gil Gerard plays an American astronaut whose space probe goes wildly off course and, although colliding with a shower of meteorites, hurtles him back 500 years in time. To help Gil through his troubles is a charming little robot named Twiki — he's played by Felix Silla — aww!

The Women's Libbers haven't been forgotten. "Outer Touch" is billed as a science-fiction comedy and it concerns the adventures of a space ship which has — wait for it — an all-female crew — and about time, too!

Following on from the hugely-successful "Capricorn One," a film about the faking of a United States space mission to the planet Mars, comes Farrah Fawcett-Majors, Kirk Douglas and Harvey Keitel in "Saturn 3." Our heroes and heroine are trapped in a distant space laboratory — sounds like fun!

Even our own James Bond is unable to keep away from sci-fi. His latest adventure "Moonraker" has a marvellous twenty-minute interplanetary battle fought between 007 — Roger Moore — and the evil Hugo Drax, played by Michael Lonsdale.

"Alien" which stars Ian Holm, John Hurt and Veronica Cartwright is a suspense thriller about five men and two women on board a star ship. They realise that, somewhere inside the ship is a horrific alien being — take a hunky boyfriend to hang on to . . . .

So far, we've dealt with nothing but films, zooming to a close on that subject with a last, lingering look at Christopher Reeve, alias "Superman." and on to something that hit our TV screens in 1979 — Mork played by actor Robin Williams, who was the star of "Mork And Mindy." — an odd chap if ever there was one — which is as good a way to end as any!

THE way you react to, and behave with, animals tells you a lot about your personality. You might be the sort of person who'd run a home for strays if you had the space, or you could be the type who can't even sit in the same room as a cat!
Whatever your feelings about small or large furry animals, you'll find out a whole lot more about yourself if you try answering our fun quiz — it's all a question of that old animal magic, in the end !

DO YOU HAVE ANIMAL MAGIC?

1. Which of these pets would you most like to have?
a. A big, healthy, bounding dog.
b. A fluffy kitten.

c. A beautiful, proud Siamese cat.
d. A lizard.

2. Do you think the best thing about having pet is —
c. being able to admire its beauty.
d. being able to observe how other creatures live and behave.
a. being able to run around and have fun with it.
b. being able to cuddle and love it?

3. Would you like a boy who —
c. painted exquisite pictures of multi-coloured birds,
a. had a horse and liked to ride it bareback,
d. kept snakes and made a record of their behaviour,
b. kept pigeons and looked after them meticulously?

4. Which of these would you find most sad?
c. A peacock which had lost all its tail feathers in an accident.
a. A cheetah or other fast-moving animal in a small cage.
b. A dog whose owner had recently died, returning to its old house.
d. An animal from a foreign country suffering because its owners didn't know how to look after it?

5. Do you think zoos are —
d. a good idea, because we can learn about lots of unusual species,
b. a bad thing — those poor animals can't be happy,
a. all right for some species, but for the animals who need lots of space to run about in, they're pretty awful,
c. if they're well planned and set out, they're a great idea because there's so much to see that most of us could never see in the wild.

6. If you could give a present of a pet to a boy you fancied, would you give him —
b. a lovable puppy,

d. some tadpoles,
a. a greyhound,
c. a brilliant Amazonian parrot?

7. If you could go on one of these holidays, which would you choose?
a. Pony-trekking.
b. Working at a kennels.
c. Bird-watching in the mountains.
d. A trip to the jungle to search for rare species.

8. What do think about wearing real fur coats?
b. It's awful because it means suffering for the poor animals.
d. It's a bad thing because certain species could become extinct.
c. You don't really approve, but you'd find it hard to resist if someone offered you one.
a. Men have always worn animal skins, so don't let's be over-sentimental.

9. What's your attitude to "creepy crawlies"?
b. You hate them — if there's one anywhere near you, you have a screaming fit!
c. You're not hysterical about them, but they're not exactly nice to look at.
d. You're interested in them, and wish you had a microscope so you could examine them more closely.
a. You're not frightened of them, but they're boring because they don't do anything.

10. What would you think about watching a Chimpanzee's tea-party?
a. It's a crack-up!
c. There's something grotesque and rather nasty about it.
d. You'd rather see a film of them in their native habitat.
b. It's quite funny, and makes you think you'd like one for a pet.

11. What's your attitude to the controlling of rabbits?
a. If they have to be controlled, ferreting is the best way, because it's natural.
d. They do have to be controlled, and we should do it the most humane, scientific way.
b. Why do they have to be controlled? They're such sweet, cuddly things.
c. It's a shame rabbits have to be killed off, because it's such an ugly business.

12. Your attitude to hunting is —
b. it's absolutely awful, cruel, and you can't bear to think about it,
c. there is some cruelty, but a hunt can look very fine in a winter landscape,
a. whether or not it's cruel, it's a marvellous sport,
d. there are better ways of controlling foxes?

13. If you could come back to Earth as an animal, which would you like to be?
c. A bird of paradise.

d. A rare species of lizard.
a. A dolphin.
b. A fat dozy farm cat.

Now add up your score, mostly a, b, c, or d, and turn to the conclusions.

CONCLUSIONS

★★★

If your answers were mostly a:
You're an energetic, action-packed girl. You're not over-sentimental — you take a realistic view of life and don't get led astray by your feelings. You appreciate natural things, and it's real nature that you like: not a watered-down pretty version. You accept that there's cruelty in life but because you're so clear-sighted you're likely to be able to deal with your own problems without being overwhelmed.
Boys like you for your energetic approach to life, and the fact that you probably appreciate sport. (We bet you're a football fan!) You've got none of the irritating feminine attitudes so boys won't tease you. They're likely to accept you as an equal. Another thing they like about you is your sense of humour.
Girls, however, may find you a bit too cool. They may find you hard and unfeeling but they'd be wrong. You're a lively, fresh, down-to-earth girl!

If your answers were mostly b:
You're a home-loving character. Very emotional and full of feelings. Your reactions to things are very direct and full blooded. You feel very protective towards children and animals. However, your emotions often blind you to facts and make it very hard to look at things objectively. In arguments, you get het-up very easily and the strength of your feelings makes you easily upset.
Boys like you for your gentle, loving approach to life. They probably tease you, because your reactions to things are so predictably soft hearted and illogical. You sum up everything that they think of as feminine. Your gentleness and affection make you very appealing to all males — Dad and Grandad as well as boyfriends!
Other girls like you very much. You're totally at home in girls' company. You share their interests and reactions, and are sympathetic to their problems. You're the loving, muddle-headed girl everybody loves!

If your answers were mostly c:
The most important thing to you is beauty. You love it in animals, in nature, in the landscape, and in your life. Your reaction to nearly everything is determined by the beauty of it — or otherwise. You don't react to things with violent emotion, but with a sense of whether it looks good or not. You're not sentimental about nature, and you know what you like. But you won't get involved in hot-headed arguments. It's much too undignified!
Boys admire your style. You know how to dress and emphasise your good features, but some boys may find you rather frightening — you're just a bit too stylish for them. So make a point of hanging around in scruffy old jeans once in a while — to prove you're human!
Girls like you. Some of them may envy your looks and style, others may imitate you, others may ask for your advice. You're certainly a trend-setter in your group!

If your answers were mostly d:
You're quite an unusual sort of girl. You have a great curiosity about the world and you're probably very interested in the natural sciences — biology or zoology. You're highly intelligent, and very logical and careful in your approach to life. Nature is a ceaseless source of interest to you, but you don't react emotionally to it — you'd rather find out about it. The more unusual a subject, the more it captures your imagination.
Boys may be a bit intimidated by you, but they'll certainly respect you and wouldn't dream of talking down to you or regarding you as less than equal — in fact, most boys probably think of you as downright superior! The really intelligent boys will be interested in you, but they may be a bit shy of approaching you.
Other girls admire you and find you interesting. They'll feel in awe of your highbrow ways, but they'll probably be proud to know you.

★★★

ARE YOU A DATING DISASTER?

OK, so the boy you've been keen on for weeks (months? years??) has finally noticed you and asked you out. You think your troubles are over, that from here on in it's going to be moonlight and soft music and romance all the way. You *think*. But *is* it? Your troubles could be just beginning . . . and here's why!

LOOKING on the bright side, your first date could turn out to be absolutely perfect, of course. On the other hand it could turn into a *disaster!* The reason why a lot of dates go wrong is because the girl has used the three simple words, "I don't mind." He asks her out — she happily agrees — he asks her where she'd like to go — she says, "I don't mind," and instantly leaves herself wide open to any loony idea he may think up!

A lot depends on the type he is, though. And, as you obviously don't know him all that well yet, you don't know what type he is — yet. Don't worry. You soon will . . .

Here's all you need to know about dating disasters — and how to avoid them!

If he suggests A NICE EVENING AT THE ZOO

Fine, you'll think. He's an animal lover. As you're probably quite fond of elephants or duckbilled platypuses yourself, you won't mind in the least.

You'll happily follow him around until you suddenly find yourself in the reptile house with him cooing at the cobras and pythons and slithery vipers, and telling you how *crazy* he is about snakes. He's probably even got a pet boa constrictor at home he's just dying for you to meet.

Or you'll find yourself in the very authentic Brazilian Jungle House, complete with dark undergrowth and creepers and even an authentic black widow spider crawling down your neck . . .

WHAT TO DO

Head for the elephant house. If the boy's really interested in

you, he'll have guessed by now that you don't share his love of snakes or spiders, so obviously he'll come after you. If not, well, elephants don't mind being stared at for an hour or two, and thankfully the only dates they're interested in are the ones in cakes!

If he suggests A MEAL

This could mean prawn cocktails, mouth-watering tender steaks and strawberries in delicious ice-cream in a discreet, candlelit restaurant.

So you put on a slinky dress and make yourself up to look really cool and sophisticated. Then you find yourself in Greasy Joe's All Night Chippery eating sausages and chips. Or even standing around in the rain eating fish and chips out of a soggy newspaper.

WHAT TO DO

There's not much you *can* do, unfortunately. This boy is suffering from a fairly common complaint known as poverty. He may recover on pay day but don't count on it. If you like him, grin and bear it. At least he's not into collecting snakes or spiders. (You hope!)

If he suggests you GO TO THE PICTURES

Don't get carried away with the idea that you'll be going to see Superman II, Grease II or Star Wars XXI. You could be disappointed because some boys have funny tastes in films.

You're more likely to find yourself in a downtown flea-pit watching "Dracula Meets Frankenstein's Mummy."

Of course, he may be quite willing to let you choose the film. If he is, it means he's not in the least interested in it. His plan is to get you in the back row and eat you! Actually, he's not really intending to eat you at all — that's just the impression you'll get. You'll also get the impression he's got three pairs of hands.

WHAT TO DO

Watch the film. It's very off-putting for a boy to make amorous

advances at a girl who's so interested in what's going on on the screen that she doesn't even notice him. It's also a bit unfair. You could say you can't see too well from the back row and insist on moving nearer the screen. This should slow him down. Eating sweets also slows down kissing activity. On the other hand, if the film is so boring, why put him off? If you like him, kissing and cuddling is a pretty nice way to spend the time!

If he suggests A NICE LONG WALK

Whether this is a good idea or not depends a lot on the time of year — and the weather. A nice long walk with an east wind blowing and hail pelting down, isn't going to be much fun.

A pleasant evening in spring or summer, on the other hand, could be very enjoyable. But why did he suggest a walk? You might find you're stuck with a fitness freak whose idea of a walk is a ten-mile trek over the hills. Or maybe he's got the same disease as the boy who suggests a meal which turns out to be fish and chips — poverty. Well, at least a walk is free! Or he could simply be the sort of guy who loves the great outdoors and birds and flowers and things.

WHAT TO DO

It all depends on what he does. If he turns out to be a fitness freak and sets off at a trot, go along with him for a while and then pretend you've twisted your ankle. Having to carry you home *ought* to slow him down a bit. If he's the outdoor enthusiast — enjoy the walk. You might learn something about flowers and birds. And if he's only

suggested a walk because he's short of cash, go along with it. You don't want to embarrass him, do you?

If he suggests THE DISCO

This is more like it. Now you're getting somewhere. This guy either likes to dance or he knows you do.

It doesn't really matter which, unless he turns out to be the World's Worst Show-Off and only wants you to admire his style.

WHAT TO DO

Enjoy yourself, that's what! If he does turn out to be the World's Worst Show-Off, it doesn't matter too much. While he's busy showing off, you can be looking around at the talent. Maybe you'll be luckier next time??

The thing about first dates is that they don't have to lead to second or third dates. If the boy doesn't turn out to be quite what you were hoping for — make an excuse when he asks you out again. It's not so difficult to do and you won't hurt his feelings too much if you're kind about it.

Not that you'll need to make an excuse, will you? You will be the girl who gets the right guy first time, won't you? **Won't you?**

Something In The Way He Looks

Does he love you? Does he hate you? Do you bore him, drive him wild, or simply send him to sleep? You can find out all these things and more with the help of our extra special feature on body language! Here's everything you need to know about all those mysterious facial expressions of the boy in your life — and what they *really* mean!

1. THE DAZZLER

A dazzling smile, dancing eyes, not a trace of shyness or second thoughts about anything . . . If this is the way he looks when he meets you, well, you've got absolutely nothing to worry about! He's well and truly hooked. There's nothing false about the smile, so count your blessings — and smile back, of course!

2. THE DOUBTER

Oh, dear, what have you done? Let him down in some way, that's what! Could be he thinks you're lying; could be that you're saying or doing something he disapproves of. The under-the-eyebrows look shows that he's signalling to you to come clean, and his pursed lips show he's none too pleased!

3. LITTLE BOY BLUE

Downcast eyes are a sure sign of depression — and that he can't face looking you in the eye. There's a downward-turning, discontented look to his mouth, too, that shows all too clearly how cheesed off he is. If it's about you — put it right! And if it's about something else, force him to tell you.

4. LOVER BOY

He fancies you, all right, and what's more, he's pretty sure you ought to fancy him. His eyes have a thoughtful look — he's giving you the once over. He's looking confident and is obviously very sure of himself. You've certainly made an impression on him, and within 5 minutes he's going to make a pass, so . . . watch out!

5. THE SNEERER

This guy's feeling pretty superior. See the sneering half-smile playing around his lips and nose? And those sarcastically-raised eyebrows? He may be feeling hurt, angry, or just malicious, but whatever it is, somebody's going to get a mouthful of sneer any minute! If it's you, make a quick exit. You've got nothing to lose but a few insults!

6. THE GIGGLER

This guy's feeling absolutely fine — the way he's thrown his head back, showing all his teeth and opening his mouth means he's totally relaxed. Bright, sparkling eyes show he's feeling really good — and the whole impression is one of terrific happiness. Could you be the cause of this insane joy? If so, you're laughing, if you see what we mean!

7. THE THINKER

Touching his nose is always a sign of doubt. Basically he's pretty interested in something (or someone). You can tell that by the way his eyes are looking sideways into space. He has his doubts, though he's not too put off. He's likely to make a grab for whatever it is (Doughnut? Job? Girl?) pretty soon!

8. THE DOZER

Eyes closing, face slumping . . . either he's practising meditation, or yoga, or he's so bored with you, he's dropping off! So sharpen up your small talk quick, before he nods off completely! It could just be lack of sleep. Was he up all night writing love poems to you?!

9. SHY GUY

He likes you, he really does. But do *you* like *him*? He's not at all sure how you feel about him. He's smiling, but it's not a *proper* smile. His eyes are alert, open for any tell-tale signs that you don't really like him. Put the poor guy out of his misery — give him a great big hug, or tell him to go!

You just won't be able to resist the chance to own this pair — and they're so simple to make, too! We must warn you, though, that making Madge and Beryl is the easiest bit — it's once you've got them that you've got to look out! Make sure you've got a heavy-weight boxer on hand to separate them if any squabbles start, and for goodness' sake, don't you be the one to fall out with *them* — we hear they tear up all their enemies' weekly Jackies — a fate worse than death, as you're surely aware! Seriously, though, Madge and Beryl are an asset to any household, so get out your pins and start knitting!

BERYL BEAR

NEEDLES — A pair of 3¾ mm (No. 9) knitting needles.
WOOL — Sirdar Superwash Wool 4 ply, 2 (25 g) balls in Honey Beige (060) and 1 ball in White (051). Also a small amount of black 4 ply wool.
PLUS — A scrap of black felt, glue and kapok.
ABBREVIATIONS — K — knit, sts — stitches, beg — beginning, inc — increase by knitting into front and back of stitch, tog — together. Knitted in garter-stitch (knit every row) throughout. When counting rows, remember that 1 ridge equals 2 rows.

LEGS AND BODY

FRONT
*With beige wool cast on 15 sts and K 4 rows.
Next row — Inc in first st, K6, inc in next 2 sts, K to last st, inc in last st (19 sts).
K 6 rows.
Next row — K2 tog, K6, K2 tog twice, K to last 2 sts, K2 tog (15 sts).
K 1 row.
Next row — K2 tog, K to last 2 sts, K2 tog (13 sts).
K until work measures 32 rows from cast-on edge.*
Break wool and push these sts to end of needle. On to same needle cast on 15 sts and repeat from * to *
**Work across both sets of sts and K 2 rows.
Next row — K11, K2 tog twice, K to end (24 sts).
K until work measures 56 rows from cast-on edge.
Cast off 7 sts at beg of next 2 rows.
Cast off remaining 10 sts.

BACK
With beige wool cast on 13 sts and K 32 rows. Break wool and push these sts to end of needle. On to same needle cast on 13 sts and K 32 rows. Repeat as for front from ** to end.

ARMS (2 alike)
With beige wool cast on 18 sts and K 1 row.
Next row — Inc in first st, K7, inc in next 2 sts, K7, inc in last st (22 sts).
K 6 rows.
Next row — K2 tog, K7, K2 tog twice, K7, K2 tog (18 sts).
K 1 row.
Next row — K2 tog, K to last 2 sts, K2 tog (16 sts).
K 18 rows, cast off.

HEAD (2 pieces alike)
With beige wool cast on 15 sts and K 2 rows.
Next row — Inc in first st, K to end.
Next row — K to last st, inc in last st.
Inc 1 st at beg of next 2 rows.
Repeat last 4 rows once more, then first 2 rows once more (25 sts).
K 8 rows.
Next row — K2 tog, K to end.
Next row — K to last 2 sts, K2 tog.
Repeat last 2 rows twice more.
Next row — K2 tog, K to end.
Next row — K to last 2 sts, K2 tog.
Next row — K to last 2 sts, K2 tog.
Next row — K2 tog, K to end.
Repeat last 4 rows once more, then first row once more.
Cast off.

BRA
With white wool cast on 48 sts and K 6 rows. Cast off.

MADGE and BERYL

KNICKERS (2 pieces alike)
With white wool cast on 24 sts and K 2 rows.
K2 tog. at beg and end of every row until 4 sts remain on the needle.
Cast off.

TURBAN
With white wool cast on 50 sts and K 2 rows.
K2 tog at beg of every row until 2 sts remain on the needle.
Cast off.

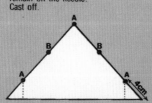

TO MAKE UP
Join body pieces together, leaving neck and feet open. Gather up feet openings and stuff neck with kapok. Join head pieces, leaving cast-on edge (neck edge) open. Stuff firmly and join head to body. Fold each arm piece in half lengthways and sew seams, leaving cast-off ends open. Stuff firmly and sew

to body. Join knicker pieces by catching at each point with a couple of stitches. Join bra along short sides and gather seam. Make turban by following diagram, putting points A together and sewing seams AB. Gather along dotted lines. Embroider features on face and make leopordskin by making three beige satin stitches and surrounding with a single black chain stitch. Sew turban to head. Cut 4 small black felt ovals and glue to hands and feet.

MADGE DUCKWORTH

NEEDLES — A pair each of 3¾ mm (No. 9) and 3¼ mm (No. 10) knitting needles.
WOOL — Sirdar Superwash Wool 4 ply, one (25 g) ball each of Festive Scarlet (085), Royal (023), and Camel (041); Sirdar Fontein Crepe, one ball of Horse Chestnut (055); a small amount of emerald green 4 ply wool.
PLUS — A scrap of white felt, red and black felt-tipped pens, glue and kapok.
ABBREVIATIONS — K — knit, P — purl, sts — stitches, beg — beginning, tog — together, inc —

increase by knitting into front and back of stitch.

LEGS AND BODY (2 alike)
With 3¼ mm needles and blue wool cast on 9 sts and continue in stocking-stitch.
*Work 19 rows.
Next row — Inc 1 st at each end.
Repeat last 20 rows once more.
Work 10 rows (13 sts, 50 rows)*
Break wool and push these sts to end of needle. On to same needle cast on 9 sts and work from * to *
Work across both sets of sts and work 2 rows.
Next row — K2 tog, K9, (K2 tog) twice, K9, K2 tog. (22 sts).
Work 9 rows.
Change to red wool and work 14 rows.
Next row — Inc 1 st at each end.
Work 2 rows.
Cast off 4 sts at beg of next 2 rows; then 3 sts at beg of next 2 rows.
Cast off remaining sts.

HEAD (2 pieces alike)
With 3¼ mm needles and beige wool cast on 10 sts and proceed in stocking-stitch.
Work 2 rows.
Next row — Inc in first st, K3, inc in next 2 sts, K3, inc in last st (14 sts).

Next row — Purl.
Inc 1 st at beg of every row until there are 22 sts on the needle.
Work 8 rows straight.
K2 tog at beg of every row until 12 sts remain.
Cast off.

NECK
With 3¼ mm needles and beige wool cast on 18 sts and work 6 rows stocking-stitch.
Cast off.

ARMS (2 alike)
With 3¼ mm needles and beige wool cast on 18 sts and proceed in stocking-stitch.
Work 2 rows.
Next row — Inc in first st, K7, inc in next 2 sts, K7, inc in last st (22 sts).
Work 5 rows.
Next row — K2 tog, K7, (K2 tog) twice, K7, K2 tog (18 sts).
Next row — Purl.
Next row — K2 tog, K to last 2 sts, K2 tog (16 sts).
Work 19 rows.
Change to red wool and knit 6 rows. Cast off.

FEET (2 alike)
With 3¼ mm needles and emerald wool cast on 32 sts and proceed in stocking-stitch.
Work 2 rows.
Next row — Inc 1 st each end.
Work 5 rows.
1st row — K2 tog, K to last 2 sts, K2 tog
2nd row — P2 tog, P to last 2 sts, P2 tog
Repeat first row once more.
Cast off 6 sts at beg of next 2 rows.
Work 2 rows.
Cast off.

HAIR
With 3¼ mm needles and rust wool cast on 18 sts and proceed in garter-stitch.
K 2 rows.
Inc 1 st at beg of every row until there are 40 sts on the needle.
Working on the first 20 sts only, *knit 2 rows.
K2 tog at beg and end of next and every following row until 10 sts remain.
K2 tog at beg of every row until 2 sts remain.
Cast off.*
Repeat from * to * working on remaining 20 sts.

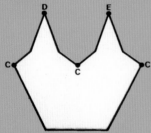

TO MAKE UP
Join body pieces together, leaving neck and ankles open. Fold feet in half and sew together, leaving tops open. Sew to ankles. Stuff body and sew up neck. Join head pieces, leaving cast-on edge open. Stuff firmly, join neck and sew to head, stuff and sew neck to body. Fold each arm piece in half lengthways and sew seams, leaving cast-off edges open. Stuff firmly and sew to body. Make hair by following diagram, putting points C together and sewing seams CD and CE. Sew to head. From white felt cut 2 ovals and carefully colour edges with a black felt tip. Allow to dry then glue to face and make a few black stitches in centre. Embroider mouth and eyebrows with black wool and make a nose with a few stitches of beige wool. Redden cheeks with a felt tip used very lightly.

Something In The Way You Look!

You may try to hide your feelings, but your eyes will always give you away! Your eyes are the mirrors of your soul, and just by looking deeply into them, other people will be able to find out what you *really* feel.

If you don't believe us, take a look at these pictures, and you'll see what we mean! And the next time that special boy looks into your eyes, remember, you might be giving it all away!

1. She's definitely pretending to be amused by the situation, perhaps because she wants to be polite, and she's certainly unsure. It's a very false laugh — her eyes still reflect bewilderment, and to a certain extent insincerity.

She's probably saying, "What's so funny about this? Well, I'd better laugh along with the rest so they don't think I'm stuck up, or a complete dummy." She's not very sure of the people she's with and wants to make a good impression.

2. In this picture she's showing a mixture of regret and confusion. Imagine your friend in the situation where she's just finished with her boyfriend.

She's probably regretting it slightly, although deep down she knows she's done the best thing. "Should I have done it like that?" she's probably saying, or, "Oh, well, it had to be done sometime — but I'm still not sure..."

She'd really like to think what's done is done, but a feeling of doubt creeps in, which shows all too clearly in her eyes. She could do with reassurance.

3. Someone's feeling pleased with themselves here! She looks as though she's managed to get to know the boy she fancies, and she's going to keep it to herself. "I've done it! He likes me enough to ask me out, but I'm not going to tell anyone about it yet!" she's thinking.

It's a look of triumph — she obviously feels that the boy in question was something of a challenge, and she's proved herself by attracting him!

4. This girl's in love! She's got a slightly dreamy, faraway look in her eyes which tells you she's thinking of him. Recognise the look?

Underneath the calm there's a feeling of excitement, though. She's trying to suppress it, but it still shows. She's probably about to meet him, and can't keep her thoughts off him, but along with the feelings of excitement and strong emotions are feelings of insecurity and worry.

5. She's looking very coy and charming, but there's a touch of nervousness here, too. "Can I get away with it this time?" she's thinking.

She's about to ask a favour which she knows may not be granted. But she knows how to use her charm to persuade — and hopes the whole scene will be over with soon.

6. This is the sort of look you'll see on a friend who's feeling very mischievous. She's spotted someone on the other side of the room and she's in a wicked mood and wants to say, "Why not take a chance on me then, big boy!"

Definitely light-hearted and flirty, this look is teasing and humorous. But deep down she's hoping that the game she's playing will turn into something a lot more serious.

MADGE and BERYL

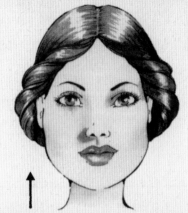

FACE THE FACTS!

When you meet someone for the first time you need all the clues you can to help you get things going. The easiest way to assess someone's character is, quite simply, to look them straight in the face — it's that easy!
Have a look at our Jackie guide to the face shapes below and make sure you're prepared next time you meet someone new . . .

Pear

This is a slightly nervous character who has a tendency to shrink back and let other people take over and run her life. Very often there is an interest in creating things — from pottery to food. She is warm, loving and kind, with a friendly and modest nature.

Oval

The dreamers and the hopelessly romantic all have oval-shaped faces. They tend to be sensitive and highly strung, which means they're easily annoyed. This shape of face shows a character who needs attention and admiration. She tends to be idealistic about romance and is rather in love with love.

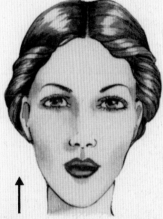

Long

This face reveals a forceful character who likes nothing better than to be physically active. She's always moving around and generally doing everything at the double. Usually with plenty of push and drive, she'll always be in a hurry to get things done and can't wait for tomorrow to come. She'll tend to make very quick decisions where affairs of the heart are concerned.

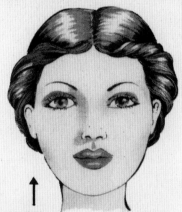

Round

This shape of face belongs to a pleasure-loving and fun-seeking person who thrives on variety and change. She'll be easily pleased but just as easily hurt, because she'll rush into new romantic situations without thinking. She's always full of enthusiasm for new ideas, schemes and plans, whether romantic or otherwise.

Square

This is a bossy type, although dependable and reliable as a friend. However, she always wants to lead rather than follow and enjoys getting her own way. She has strong will-power and so ends up being the dominant person in any organisation. She can't stand being ordered about or made to feel small.

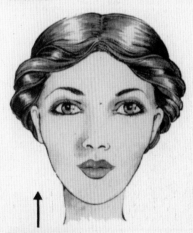

Triangular

Easy going, lovable and just a tiny bit lazy, that's what this shape of face reveals. Her nature is affectionate but she doesn't like making an effort in anything. Being loved and looked after appeals to her and it's very rare for this shape of face to become aggressive or anti-social in any way. Anything for a quiet life, that's this one.

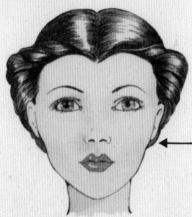

Heart

This face maybe looks really soft but, in fact, there's usually a very hard and determined nature behind it with a strong character. She's usually extremely affectionate and will have a well-developed, possibly off-beat, sense of humour. She'll be good fun to be with and rarely gets annoyed enough to hold a grudge.

Remember that although we've used girls' faces here, the shapes and rules also apply to boys. So, get out there and get looking for your ace-face!

❤

Face Up To Them!

Have you had a good look at your face lately? That noble forehead, that resolute chin . . . have you ever thought that that strong, straight nose shows just what a strong, straight person you are? Well, analysing your face can give a clue as to what kind of person you are — so, we've taken some of our favourite people and given their features the once-over just for *you!*

Mark Hamill

HAIR
Mark has a high, slightly-pointed crown to his head, and this is a sign of a very active mind. His hair is light and fine, indicating a slightly lazy temperament at times.

HEAD
His heart-shaped face and broad forehead indicate his interest in self-expression and the artistic or acting world and there's a love of rhythm and movement in his very widely-spaced eyes.

NOSE
The bridge of his nose is wide and shows that he likes to feel secure in his relationships and he has the will to see a thing through once he's started it.

MOUTH
Mark has a long, thin upper lip creased at the corners, and this shows his off-beat sense of humour and ability to see the funny side of things. He has a thick protruding lower lip, indicating warmth, sensuality and generosity, plus a love of the opposite sex and flirting!

CHIN
His narrow chin is squared off with a flat base, and this demonstrates his hasty temper, which dies down as quickly as it flares up.

Summing up his personality, Mark has a great sense of fun, enjoys being the centre of attention and loves showing off a little.

Martin Shaw

HAIR
Martin has a squarish face and his thick curly hair hanging low over his forehead shows his vitality and energetic nature.

EYES
The eyes are set far apart, and this means that Martin is more of a giver than a taker. The tiny rolls of flesh under his lower lids are a sign of a warm, affectionate and deeply caring nature.

BROWS
His eyebrows show that he's slow to anger and prefers to use reason rather than force to put across his point of view.

NOSE
The tiny ridge across the bridge of his nose reveals curiosity and an enquiring mind, while the flaring-out of the nostrils is a sign of an open and friendly nature.

MOUTH
The wide, generous mouth with its dip in the middle of his top lip is a sign of individuality and shows Martin can be tender, constant and true.

CHIN
The square-shaped chin is a sign of determination and persistence, and the rather plumpish cheeks show a liking for humour and the simple things of life.

EARS
His ears are set low on his head, and this means he is capable of making quick decisions and isn't easily led by other people or their opinions.

Martin's overall personality is a capable, caring and sympathetic nature with a good sense of drama — but one who isn't likely to be carried away.

Lewis Collins

HEAD
Lewis has a pear-shaped face, and this is a sign of a fairly highly-strung person. It shows a lot of artistic talent and a romantic but down to earth streak.

EYES
Lewis has a longish forehead, and this shows his keen intelligence. His eyes are deep set, showing he can sum up people and situations quickly and he isn't easily taken in.

NOSE
His nose is thinner at the ridge, and this means he's extremely active with a love of attention and a need to show off sometimes.

CHIN
The chin comes to a point almost, and this shows that Lewis has a lot of attraction for the opposite sex, but is a bit of an idealist in his choice of partner.

MOUTH
His lips are tightly closed with the lower lip protruding a little, showing he can keep a secret well, and has a warm passionate nature with a need for harmony in his love life.

Lewis' personality is a curious mixture of the mildly aggressive and friendly-guy-next-door-type. But he is a man with a strong sense of responsibility, and this is something he wouldn't shirk, not with that well-formed head on his shoulders.

Dirk Benedict

HEAD
Dirk has a temperament that's a mixture of the dreamer and the action man. His head is shaped well, long and fine, and his hair laying flat against the crown shows that he enjoys physical exercise and has lots of energy and drive.

EYES
His widely-spaced eyes — large and clear — reveal a mind that likes to range over lots of subjects and show that he's quick, alert and fast thinking.

BROWS
The well-formed eyebrows coming to a point towards the nose show his sense of humour and love of life.

CHEEKBONES
His cheekbones are high, and this is a sign of an affectionate, loving and demonstrative nature with a need for close relationships.

MOUTH
Dirk has one predominant feature that stands out above all others and that's his mouth, beautifully shaped and turning up slightly at the corners, showing that he has a romantic soul.
His bottom lip is fuller than the top and has tiny perpendicular lines on it, indicating a passionate and ardent nature!

CHIN
His chin is firm and means that he has lots of willpower, even to the point of being obstinate at times when he wants his own way.

The overall impression of Dirk's head, face and hair is of a nicely-balanced guy with a love of beautiful things and a desire to achieve his ambitions.

Fozzie Bear

What an extrovert this bear is . . . . ! He loves to be in the limelight and enjoys being the centre of attention.

MOUTH
That huge gaping mouth tells us **all** about his personality, and how he loves to talk.

EYES
Watch those eyes set a bit too close together. They show he's great at getting his own way and he doesn't mind taking short-cuts to get it.

NOSE
He's a lovable, noisy, individualistic type who has a large nose for enquiring into other people's affairs, but he does it so cheekily no-one minds.

BROWS
Those high-flying eyebrows show he's always surprised at the way things turn out and he's certainly a character to be reckoned with . . . .

EARS
Those ears, almost large enough to take off, show his love of gossip and you'll always find Fozzie Bear where the action is!

Shaun Cassidy

HEAD
Shaun has a rounded head with a small round face, and this means that he's a romantic and a bit of a daydreamer, but with a practical streak, too.

HAIR
He enjoys an audience, and that thick hair shows his vitality and love of space and movement.

EYES
His eyes are "laughing eyes," very expressive, and show that his feelings are near the surface and he tends to be impulsive and spontaneous.

NOSE
His nose is full and has a very wide bridge, flattened at the sides of his nostrils, showing that he's a trusting, confiding and frank person.

MOUTH
The wide, generous mouth, that crinkles at the corners, demonstrates his amusing, sociable and friendly personality and extravagant, generous, ready response to people.

NECK
His neck is quite long, and this reveals his ready energy and love of action. Those dimples in his cheeks show affection and a loving disposition, tinged with a lack of caution at times in his friendships.

EARS
The ears are forward and low on the side of his head, giving away his love of music, singing and dancing.

CHIN
Shaun doesn't keep many secrets to himself because he enjoys sharing them, and his well-formed chin also shows he has many ambitions for the future.

Nicholas Ball

HAIR
Nicholas has a lot of vitality showing in his face, and one of the things that gives this away is his wiry, very much alive hair. It springs back from his forehead and upwards, showing lots of physical energy and drive.

BROWS
The heavy, thick shaggy eyebrows meeting almost over the bridge of his nose indicate a temperament that's thoughtful, deep and passionate.

EYES
The deep-seated eyes are a sign of persistence and the ability to be practical when necessary. They also reveal an impressionable nature with a genuine curiosity about the world and people around him.

NOSE
The slightly broad top to his nose is a sign of a person who uses the talents given to him to the best of his ability.

MOUTH
The thinner upper lip shows his sensitivity, and yet he has a temper when crossed or under tension, and the fuller lip tells of his generous disposition and sympathy.

HEAD
The overall impression of his face denotes his artistic and creative talents, his imagination, and desire to express his personality through his acting.

Nicholas is emotional, has a slightly sentimental streak, and there's a lot of understanding in his nature, but he's not the type to form superficial attachments. He likes to choose his close friends with care, and he's a difficult person to get really close to.

ARE YOU NICE

THERE are two sides to human nature — the nice, kind, good side and the nasty, mean, bad side. Most of us are a mixture of both good and bad — but what kind of mixture are *you*? Are you a goodie or a baddie? Nice or nasty? Just how do you see yourself and, more important, how do *other* people see you? Well — now's your chance to find out! Just try our fun quiz and find out how nice (or nasty!) you are — and what that means about your relationship with boys!

1. Before an important interview, would you . . .
a. be so nervous you'd feel positively sick,
b. make sure you have a good night's sleep and a good breakfast beforehand so you'll be at your best,
c. keep your fingers crossed and carry your good luck charm with you,
d. say a quick prayer as you go in, and then leave it all in the hands of Fate?

2. If you were visiting an old church while on holiday, what would you be most likely to think?
a. It's got a really weird atmosphere.
b. Just think of all the people who've been here over the years.
c. Gosh! It's freezing cold in here.
d. What beautiful colours those stained-glass windows are.

3. There's a market in the town where your friend lives, and you like going there. Which stall would you find most interesting?
a. The second-hand clothes stall.
b. The antiques stall.
c. The flower and plant stall.

d. The pets and petfoods stall.

4. If you're watching TV with your family, and a sexy statue of a naked woman is shown, would you think . . .
a. what a lovely body! Wish I looked like that!
b. gosh, this is a bit embarrassing,
c. I wonder what Mum and Dad are thinking . . . ,
d. that statue is a really beautiful work of art?

5. While your steady boyfriend is away on holiday, you're asked out by a boy you've fancied for ages. Do you . . .
a. feel it's wrong, but go anyway, unable to resist him,
b. indulge your feelings and have fun without feeling guilty,
c. say no, with a lot of regrets, and still think about him,
d. say no, but go on feeling guilty for being tempted?

6. When you say hello and goodbye to family and friends, do you . . .
a. give them all big hugs and kisses,
b. feel you want to kiss them, but be too shy,
c. give your mum and dad a peck on the cheek, but that's all,
d. not kiss or hug anybody: it feels wrong and you don't want to?

7. How would you most like to spend a summer afternoon?
a. Swimming and sunbathing on a deserted beach.

b. Having a picnic on a riverbank with friends.
c. Lying on your back in a sunny park listening to the sounds all around you.
d. Taking a neighbour's children to the park to give her a break.

8. What do you think of poetry?
a. It's OK sometimes — when it's funny.
b. It's a load of old rubbish.
c. You like reading it; it fills you with ideas and feelings.
d. You even *write* it sometimes! You like expressing your feelings in this way.

9. Music's something you probably enjoy. But what's the thing you like most about it?
a. The great, foot-tapping rhythm of it.
b. The sheer exhilarating noise.
c. The patterns you can hear in it.
d. The words of the songs and the feelings they express.

10. You're at a party where most people seem to be kissing and cuddling. Is your reaction . . .
a. to blush all over,
b. to think it's embarrassing but a bit exciting,
c. to want to join in,
d. to wonder why they're all behaving like that?

OR NASTY?

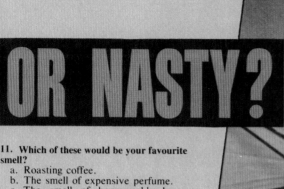

11. Which of these would be your favourite smell?
- a. Roasting coffee.
- b. The smell of expensive perfume.
- c. The smell of honeysuckle by a cottage door.
- d. The cool fresh smell of lemon eau de cologne.

eau de cologne

12. Are you attracted to . . .
- a. mainly good-looking boys,
- b. ugly boys sometimes — if they're interesting,
- c. only interesting boys — and you don't always fancy them, either!
- d. ugly boys quite often, 'cos they're usually nicer?

13. You're at a posh dinner and you want to go to the loo. What do you do?
- a. Quietly ask the nearest person where it is, and feel embarrassed.
- b. Go off and look for it on your own, too shy to ask.
- c. Announce, "I must go to the loo!" in a loud voice.
- d. Wait till you get home, even though you're bursting, rather than ask.

QUIZ CONCLUSIONS

Now count your score and turn to the conclusions.

SCORES

1. a-4, b-3, c-2, d-1.	7. a-4, b-3, c-2, d-1.
2. a-1, b-2, c-4, d-3.	8. a-3, b-4, c-2, d-1.
3. a-3, b-1, c-2, d-4.	9. a-3, b-4, c-1, d-2.
4. a-3, b-2, c-1, d-4.	10. a-3, b-2, c-4, d-1.
5. a-3, b-4, c-2, d-1.	11. a-3, b-4, c-2, d-1.
6. a-4, b-3, c-2, d-1.	12. a-4, b-3, c-1, d-2.
	13. a-3, b-2, c-4, d-1.

If you scored 40-52:

You're much more of a baddie than a goodie! But don't worry — all it means is that you're very basic and down-to-earth. You like to enjoy yourself, and your pleasures are eating, drinking, looking at beautiful things — in short, all the pleasures of the senses, including touching! This makes you very affectionate and warm. You probably come from a very cuddly, happy family — you're a lucky girl and a lovable one, too!

Your feelings are all very immediate, and even violent sometimes. You're quite hot-blooded really! You tend to fall suddenly and passionately in love, but you do find it hard to stay loyal for long. The trouble is, you just can't resist your feelings and get swept along by them. In fact, you haven't really got much self-discipline. You probably find it hard to concentrate on work for long!

You're a very physical person. Looks matter to you, you make the most of your own, and go for good-looking guys. You're also active — you enjoy the sheer sensation of swimming, dancing, and bounding around. In fact, you're a real bundle of fun! If people might whisper behind your back that you're a weeny bit empty-headed, or can't control yourself, what do you care?

If you scored 30-39:

You're mostly bad but with one or two good qualities thrown in! Which means you're a straightforward, pleasure-loving, warm person, but occasionally you are plagued by doubts or guilt or ideas which upset you. However, you're still much more likely to be swamped by your feelings than able to reason them away or rise above them. The result, more often than not, is a feeling of conflict — torn between the desire to do something and the feeling that you mustn't. And you usually go ahead and do it, but feel guilty afterwards!

Boys find you a warm and friendly girl. Easy to get to know, and good fun to be with. As far as being faithful is concerned, you'd be capable of it if the boy was really your type. Try to find a boy who's fond of sports, dancing, and who has a good sense of humour. An intellectual type probably wouldn't suit you so well, and you'd fly off at the first chance — and feel guilty about it!

What you really need to do is work out what pleasures you're going to allow yourself, and enjoy them to the full. And be really firm with yourself about the ones you know you should resist! (Be they jam doughnuts or other people's boyfriends.) If you work hard to develop a bit more self-discipline, you'll be a really well-balanced person!

If you scored 20-29:

You understand yourself and your motives. You know how to enjoy yourself, and in some quite sophisticated ways sometimes. But you'd hardly ever let pleasure get in the way of duty. Which means that you're a very nice girl to know: reliable, loyal, and very considerate of other people's feelings. You think before acting and would be unlikely to commit yourself to a relationship with a boy who didn't suit you. And the sort of boy who wouldn't suit you would be a tearaway, irresponsible and wild, even though he might be really attractive. Boys find you a bit shy but once they discover your warm, balanced personality, they find you pretty irresistible!

You don't chase after boys. In fact, though you like people a lot, you're also happy just being on your own. Peace and quiet, and a chance to feel your own feelings and think your own thoughts, is what you need. Just occasionally your shyness gets the better of you, and it could lead you to miss a lot of what's out there waiting for you. It might be, for example, that there's a boy who fancies you a lot and is just too shy to do anything about it. He needs encouragement, and you might need to encourage him. So try and become a bit more outgoing and confident!

If you scored 13-19:

Where are your wings and halo? 'Cos you're the nearest thing to an angel we've ever heard of! (Unless you cheated?!) This means that you're very highly disciplined, you have incredibly high standards for yourself and other people, and you take a fairly detached, cool and calculating attitude to life. Your sense of duty is strong — so strong, it often interferes with your pleasures. And your pleasures are pretty intellectual — you like reading, art, and learning more about life.

You're the girl who can be totally faithful to her chosen boy. But that boy had better be pretty wonderful, 'cos you've got such high standards for him that he's almost bound to disappoint you. When he does, though, you'll forgive him . . . you're an angel, after all! The thing that's really missing from your life is good, strong, spontaneous feelings. You're never swept off your feet. (Have angels got feet, anyway?) Even when a really attractive, interesting boy comes along, you're very wary of losing your heart too quickly. A little tiny bit of you wants to — and it would do you good to indulge that little tiny spark from time to time. Go on, let yourself go and really enjoy yourself for once in your life! Otherwise, you'll end up just too good to be true!

The one thing there is never any point in doing is slobbing around thinking you're a failure! If you want that boy you fancy to notice you, if you want to be pretty, witty and full of personality, well, you can get halfway there at least by making the very most of things – including yourself! If you want to get the very best out of your life, make a start right now by following our extra-special A – Z which tells you all about how to make the very most of yourself!

A is for ACCIDENTS
Which *will* happen, and they aren't necessarily anyone's fault! So if you're freaking out at the disco, someone trips, and a glass of Coke suddenly pours itself down your new white dress — do *not* scream and collapse into tears! Also, do not immediately punch the offender on the nose! Soak the stain in cold water in the "Ladies," sponge yourself off, pin a smile on your face — and keep on dancing!

B is for BOYS
Without whom, frequently, life wouldn't be worth living! But if you haven't got a boyfriend, don't despair! It could be you just haven't found anyone you fancy enough yet. Boys need to be handled with TLC (tender loving care)! They must *always* be given the impression *they're* the ones doing the chasing! They must *never* be made a fool of in front of their mates! And you've got to remember that most of the time they're just as worried and scared as *you* are!

C is for COSMETICS
In other words, lipsticks, eye-shadows, cleansers, etc. Do not get conned into believing something in terrific packaging costing three times as much as anything else is the best thing out! Quite often own-make brands, like Boots, are *far* better — as well as cheaper! Basic rule to follow with cosmetics is find a make that suits *your* skin, find colours that compliment your own colouring, and stick with them for a bit. Who *needs* 50 different lipsticks, anyway?

D is for DAYDREAMS
Which everybody has, but never get so involved in a daydream you can't be bothered with the reality! Daydreams are great for getting you through boring moments at work or at school or on the bus. They're not so great if you drift off into one when your boy's whispering sweet-nothings in your ear and expecting you to answer him!

E is for EYES
Eyes can send a wealth of different messages from, "I love you" to "Get lost, you creep!" Make the most of yours by using complimenting eyeshadows, lashings of non-run mascara, and lots of fluttering! For tired, dull eyes, first rub a little cold cream round them. Dip some cotton wool in witch-hazel water. Lie down. Close your eyes and put the cotton-wool pads on the eyelids. Relax for ten minutes. If you haven't any witch-hazel, a couple of slices of cucumber will do the same trick!

F is for FASHION
And whether you follow it or not is entirely up to you! Always, though, buy clothes that actually suit *you*, and if they're really fashionable but look hideous — forget them! Keep watching Jackie fashion pages, too, for the brightest and best of what's around.

G is for GROWING-UP
Which is frequently a painful process. Try to remember, though, when Mum gives you a lecture for the 50th time, that *she* had to grow up once, too, and that she wasn't always such a nag! Once, *her* mum nagged *her*! All sorts of things happen when you're growing-up. Your body starts changing . . . you're happy as a lark one minute — in the depths of gloom and doom the next. Relax! You're normal! We've all gone through it!

H is for HAPPINESS
Which means different things to different people, so if you find you're at your most ecstatic catching falling leaves or cutting your toenails — ignore anybody who says you're a twit! Just go on being happy! Happiness brings a sparkle to your eyes, a bounce to your step, and generally makes you *feel* like a million dollars. And if you feel that way — there's a good chance you'll look it, too!

I is for INVITATIONS
And they're great things to get! But a quick word of warning. If, for example, you're invited back to *his* place to meet his folks — do *not* turn up looking like a Punk crossed with a Mod. This will only terrify his mum and worry his dad! So whenever you receive an invitation — try to find out about where you're going. You'll feel a right nanna turning up at a disco that doesn't allow jeans in your newest shrink to fits, won't you? And an even *bigger* nanna appearing on a cross-country ramble in footless tights and stilettos!

J is for JEALOUSY
Unfortunately, it's one of those feelings we all experience at some time or another. You can get pangs when you see your boyfriend grinning at his old girlfriend. You can be furious when your best friend starts going out with the dishiest boy in town and suddenly can't meet you every night. Panic not! Just try not to let it get on top of you, because if you're feeling jealous you can say, and do, things you'll later regret. So take deep breaths, think twice before you open your mouth, and *try* not to turn green. (It's a lousy complexion colour, anyway!)

THE MOST OF YOURSELF

K is for KEEPSAKE

In other words, that wilted daisy he gave you on your first date and that you've kept ever since! Keepsakes are great sentimental souvenirs — but they do have snags! If you keep *every* wilted daisy he ever gave you in your underwear drawer, you may not have room for your tights! And if you happen to stumble across one of these daisies two days after you've split from him, you'll just burst into tears. Face it — keepsakes will bring back memories, and they'll also be classified by your mum in sarky moments as "all that rubbish!" So clear them out occasionally!

L is for LOVE

Never underestimate the strength of it. Never play about with it. If you're *not* in love with a guy — don't tell him you are. And don't, either, ever fall for the old line of, "If you loved me, you would . . ." If *he* loved you, he wouldn't have said *that* in the first place!

M is for MONDAYS

And there is *nothing* good to say about them! They are vile, endless, dreary days, and the only thing you can do with them is get through them without screaming or killing someone! Try, therefore, to make Monday nights special nights, somehow. (Even if you only stay in, have a luxurious smelly bath, then nip early to bed with Jackie and a mug of cocoa-it's *something* to look forward to, isn't it??)

N is for NOTHINGNESS

That awful feeling quite often associated with Mondays! It's a sort of "ugh" where you don't think anything's going to be the same again, and you *know* nobody'll ever understand you — sniff! sniff! Rubbish! That is a very unpositive attitude and you've got to *do* something about it. Nothingness is a frame of mind, so go and spring-clean your wardrobe immediately, or bake a cake, or take the cat for a game of tennis! As long as you stay active — you'll keep the "ughs" at bay.

O is for OPPORTUNITIES

Which should always be grasped firmly with both hands. People who mumble, "I had the opportunity once . . ." are the saddest people around. Don't be like them! If the chance to do something, or go somewhere, or *be* something, crops up — grab it! It doesn't matter how nervous you feel. What *does* matter is that you don't just sit there thinking, "No, I could *never* do that!" That's just soggy! How d'you know anyway — if you don't try!

P is for PEOPLE

Of whom there are all sorts of different types — nice, nasty, and nothing-very-much. If you don't *know* many people — what're you sitting here reading this for? Go forth *immediately* and join a club full of the species! Or find a pen-friend! Or start a "People Need People" Society! The more you know, the more fun you'll have — and the more friends you'll make.

Q is for QUARRELS

Not nice things to have. Somebody's granny once said, "Never let the sun set on a quarrel" — and she had a point! If you walk off in the middle, still yelling at each other, it's that bit more difficult to kiss 'n' make up. So avoid quarrels where humanly possible. If you really can't, have a violently spectacular yelling match and get it all out of your system as fast as possible! Then you can start to calm down — and find out what you're *really* arguing about!

R is for RAIN

Which is very damp, we know, but also does wonders for the complexion! All that soft water trickling down your nose may turn it a delicate shade of purple for an hour or two — but think how soft your skin'll feel! And if you don't believe us — try talking to the plants in the garden. They couldn't survive without the stuff!

S is for SLEEP

Which we all need in order to recharge our batteries. About eight hours a night is average, but some people get by on as little as six — while some need ten! Always have your bedroom window open a bit at night — if you go to sleep in a fugged-up room you'll wake up feeling *ghastly*! Don't have too many heavy bed-clothes — you'll just be un-comfortable. And never have a really heavy meal just at bedtime. Apart from stopping you sleeping, it'll very probably give you indigestion!

T is for TALK

Not the every-day, "How are you? Isn't the weather awful?" kind. More the kind when you're really worried or upset and need help. Finding someone you can talk to, and who'll actually *listen* to you, is worth a great deal, because once you've actually started to put what's on your mind into *words* — the worries and anxieties will seem that bit less.

U is for UGLY

Which you're *not* — even if you *think* you are! You may not have the most spectacular face and figure in the world, but d'you have a nice laugh? Are you good fun? Kind? Sincere? Willing to help people? Kind to dumb animals? Then you're *not* ugly!

V is for VICES

Like stuffing yourself with cream-cakes when you're supposed to be on a diet! Buying *another* pair of jeans when you really need a dress! Playing disco sounds at top volume and giving the budgie a headache! Vices, little ones, anyway, are sort of self-indulgent things that don't really matter unless they directly affect someone else. But try never to let the *little* vices grow into *big* ones — or you could be in a whole heap of trouble!

W is for WEATHER

Or rather it's for feeling under it, the weather, that is — and if you're feeling ill, for heaven's sake tell someone about it! Don't be afraid to speak to Mum or go to your doctor — they are there to help, you know. And don't think it's smart struggling on with a streaming cold — it's not, especially when you infect everyone else . . .

X is for XMAS

Or one of the times of the year when you will *certainly* eat too much, drink too much, and have *far too many* late nights! If you want to make the most of yourself — don't accept the third slice of Xmas pudding (unless you want to make the most of yourself in a very *large* way!); do go on a diet on Boxing Day; don't go to parties *every* night of the week; but *do* have a thoroughly good time!

Y is for YOGA

And Yoga exercises are very good for trimming flabby figures, helping you relax, and generally easing aches and pains. Join a class and try. At least you'll meet a load of new people that way!

Z is for ZIP

Both the variety you find on the front of jeans — and the variety that means you're full of get-up-and-go! If the first variety doesn't meet — you *need* those Yoga classes! And if you've got plenty of the second kind — then you already *are* making the most of yourself!

Your Jackie Guide To... *Kissing!*

First off, it's not such a great idea to kiss a boy you're not all that interested in, even if he is great to look at. If you don't *like* him then you won't like kissing him, it's as simple as that. For any kiss to work, there's got to be some feeling behind it, so try not to kiss just any boy, especially pushy ones who try to Half-Nelson you into doing it, or you'll only end up regretting it and feeling really let down. Remember — your kisses are precious, they ought to be full of honest feeling, definitely not to be wasted on SLOBS!

OK? Now on to the fascinating subject of kissing and how to kiss . . .

YOU'VE probably imagined what it's like to kiss a boy. In your dreams, everything will be just perfect . . . In real life, though, it might not work out like that, so don't be too let down if it isn't all sweetness and light straight off. Here are a few tips to make all your first kisses that little bit special. Of course, there's no one right way to kiss but the following points to remember might help you out when it comes to the crunch, when he wants to kiss you and you think you might panic and run away from him!

Kiss your mum and tell her how much you appreciate her. Kiss your dad and tell him you think he's great. Kiss your boyfriend and *you don't have to tell him a thing* because here, actions speak much louder than words!

There are kisses and kisses though, and no two kisses are alike — a friendly peck on the cheek, for instance, is a million miles from a wild, passionate mouth-to-mouth clinch! So which kind of kiss should you use where and with whom, and, when you get right down to it — how should you kiss a boy in the first place anyway? Read our extra-special blueprint on all you need to know about kissing and you'll find out!

HOW TO KISS

★ *Be prepared for the fact that he probably **will** try to kiss you after he's walked you home, although it could happen any time, any place – at the bus stop, in the disco, in the street . . . It'll help if you remember he's just as nervous as you are, so . . .*
★ *Take a few deep breaths and try to relax.*
★ *Keep your head up, don't stare at the ground.*
★ *Look at him.*
★ *When he moves towards you, don't back away.*
★ *Tilt your head.*
★ *Contact! Your lips meet.*
★ *Move your lips with his, slowly.*
★ *Depending on how things are going, you can stop kissing him now and lay your head on his shoulder. That's all there is to it!*

Once you're with a real, live boy, you ought to find everything goes really smoothly. Just make sure you *like* the boy you're kissing in the first place.

IF YOU DON'T LIKE HIM

If you've only been out with a boy once, and he's taken you home, obviously expecting a late-night snogging session, things can be a bit awkward, especially if you don't want to encourage him. So, once you get to your front door, thank him for a really nice evening, say you'll see him around, then peck him lightly on the cheek, if you like, and go indoors.

Don't allow him to put his arms around you in the first place if you don't want him to, and don't let him kiss you at all if you don't want him to — it'll only make him think you really do like him. So be honest with boys, especially the boys who are nice, not pushy, but whom you don't really fancy.

IF YOU DO LIKE HIM, AND HE LIKES YOU

Here, you'll probably expect your first kiss with him to be out of this world. If it isn't, put it down to nerves and try again. The chances are, though, that your first kiss with a boy you like *will* be wonderful, simply because it's *him* you're kissing!

IF HE WON'T TAKE NO FOR AN ANSWER

If he's too pushy, and he tries to force you to kiss him and you don't really want to, you'll have to tell him to stop. A lot of boys just don't know what's expected of them and so they go completely over the top, especially on first dates. How do you handle a boy like this? You do *not* just stand there and let him do whatever he pleases, that's for sure! You teach him to kiss naturally, the way *you* want to be kissed.

Try to make a joke out of it — say something like, "That may be OK for a female gorilla but I'm a girl." Or simply tell him what he's doing isn't welcome. Ask him to cool it. Or be honest, and tell him you don't *like* it, and will he please stop.

There's absolutely no point whatsoever in pretending to like being kissed in a certain way if you really don't, so for goodness' sake say so. Your boyfriend will probably be glad of it because then he'll stop having to live up to a big he-man image.

KISSING AND LOVEBITES

A lot of girls think lovebites are great and a lot of girls think they're pretty ugly. A lot of boys think that once they give a girl a lovebite that she's his property, while a lot of boys are really turned off by girls with lovebites.

Well, it's up to you really. Most people think kissing is a pretty private and special thing, not something you tell the whole world about. Really, though,

lovebites aren't pretty at all. And do you *really* want your boyfriend to act as if he owned you?

Too obvious lovebites can cause a lot of upsets anyway — your friends think you're a show-off, other boys think of you as being not quite nice, maybe even a bit easy, and as for your parents — it'll hurt them a lot. So is it worth it?

If you don't want lovebites, then tell your boyfriend so.

FRENCH KISSING

French kissing is when you put your tongue into your boyfriend's mouth and he puts his into yours. To a lot of people it's nice and natural. To others it's disgusting. Some people aren't disgusted by it but still don't quite like it.

If *you* don't like it, don't do it, and don't let your boyfriend force you into doing it. He may just be doing it because he thinks that's what you expect or because he thinks it's more grown up, or even a tiny bit daring.

It can be embarrassing to talk openly about your feelings when it comes to the physical side of your relationship with a boy but it's always best to air your views rather than to carry on feeling used and miserable in silence.

So speak up. If there was something he didn't like about you, wouldn't you rather he told you? At least that way, you'd understand each other a whole lot better, and feel even closer than ever.

WHICH KISS SHOULD YOU USE WHERE . . . AND WITH WHOM?

THE FRIENDLY PECK ON THE CHEEK

Use it on a boy you don't want to get serious with. If your evening out together proved a disaster, or even just OK, it's ideal — friendly without being *too* friendly.

THE ROMANTIC KISS

Use it when you're with a boy you really like — one you think you might even get to love!

THE FRENCH KISS

Kiss a boy this way and it ought to mean you've known the boy for some time. French kissing on a first date is a bit pointless and not much fun at all. A lot of boys think you must be pretty experienced if you kiss like this. Well, are you? And can you handle the kind of boy it'll encourage . . . ?

Finally, here are a few do's and dont's to remember. Follow them and you'll keep your kisses really sweet!

Don't *chatter on and on and on because you're nervous at the thought of him kissing you – he'll only think you don't want him to kiss you.*

Do *close your eyes when he kisses you. You don't want any distractions!*

Don't *get into a really heavy session with someone you don't really care about.*

Do *smile or laugh it off if everything does go drastically wrong, if you gulp really loudly, or if your false tooth falls out! Show him you've got a great sense of humour and he'll come back for more . . . and more!*

HOW TO PUT HIM OFF YOU!

If you've fancied a certain boy for a while and you want him to start noticing you, it's up to *you* to take the first step — and here's just how *not* to go about it!

AT THE DISCO

Boys are at discos to eye up the talent basically, and, if there's plenty of other female talent around, you have to be *very* careful about what you do and say. Don't dress up outrageously just to catch his eye. You'll catch his eye, all right, and he'll probably have a good laugh at how stupid you look in your leopardskin leotard and orange wig. Don't make an exhibition of yourself by jumping about like a kangaroo on hot desert sand while grinning insanely at him as you jump above the crowd. He *won't* be impressed!

On the other hand, don't stand there trying to look so cool that ice wouldn't melt in your mouth. It may be OK for Clint Eastwood to chew gum and wear shades — but you'll look out of place in downtown Barnsley. And don't stay with your friends for *every* dance — he'll be frightened to approach you! If you *must* be with your mates, don't keep getting the giggles and pointing at him as if he was some prize ape in a monkey house. If you're desperate for him to notice you, don't pretend to fall over in front of him (that's too obvious), and don't walk up and say, "Don't I know you from somewhere?" (that's even more obvious).

Suppose he actually asks you to dance. Try not to ignore him. You know how it is — you *really* fancy the guy so you look at the floor, other people, the ceiling — anywhere but at *him* while you're dancing! On the other hand, don't grin at him with a fixed smile like a finalist in Miss World, and don't for goodness' sake hang around his neck murmuring, "Oh, this means so much to me."

If he offers you a drink, ask for diluted orange, because most boys don't like expensive girls. Above all, don't try to be something you aren't or you're not going to get very far before he sees that you've tried to fool him. Remember that whatever you do he still won't think you're a patch on Hot Gossip, and if he does come over to ask you to dance, don't run to the loo first to fix your face. He won't be there when you get back!

AT SCHOOL

Either he's a new boy or he's been around for ages and is suddenly, quite gorgeously, different and grown-up. Whatever the reason, you fancy him like mad and you know you've got to do something about it. Try not to let your friends know, or they'll make your life a misery. Despite all their promises not to tell a soul, Anne'll tell Mary, who'll tell her brother, whose best mate's Jim, who lives next door to Brian — and HIS name is Brian, then your secret love's no secret any more.

If you travel on the same bus, and you get on first, don't keep the other half of your seat covered with your bag, only to whip it off and smile charmingly at him

when he gets on. Don't deliberately fall on top of him going down the bus stairs, either. He'll just wish you'd drop dead when you arrive in Ward 7 with your stupid smile and a bunch of grapes.

Don't drop your schoolbooks in front of him. He'll either step over them, or pick them up thinking what a clumsy fool you are and he's never even *likely* to fancy you. It's not a good idea to write *I love Brian* all over your bag, the desk, or the blackboard either, because besides being terribly unsubtle, *he'll* be mortified.

Don't change your whole timetable just so that you can sit next to him in Maths or Physics either — this could ruin your whole future career. Also he'll think you're a banana when you say circumference was one of the knights of the Round Table! Don't do stupid things like joining the same clubs as him if you're hopeless at badminton, shocking at swimming, or you don't know which way up to hold the cricket bat — you don't want him laughing as you crash into the net, drown, or knock yourself, rather than the cricket ball, for six!

AT THE LAUNDERETTE

Launderettes are very boring places, where a lot of deep thinking goes on — simply because there's nothing to do but watch the washing go round or fall asleep! Staring at the washing swirling around is conducive to deep thought, so there he is, thinking about tomorrow's home game, not really seeing anything.

Don't disturb him until he sighs deeply and turns to the newspaper or starts chewing his nails. This means he's done

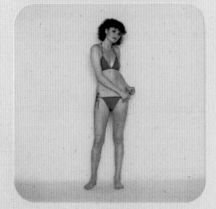

with the thinking — maybe his brain was starting to hurt. So don't start slamming things about, throwing your washing all over, crashing money into the machine, singing "I Got The Washday Blues" and generally being a noisy nuisance.

Don't take along your grottiest undies, mum's tea-towels with half a pot of soup over them and your dog's blanket. He'll think you're a slob and that the dog's blanket is actually *your* blanket.

If, or rather when, you get fed up, don't let him catch you picking at your nose, ears, etc. If you do need change for the machine or the powder dispenser, don't be so obvious as to ask him for it when the woman in charge is in front of you! He'll know straightaway that you're after him.

But don't pretend to be a big know-all about how everything works. If you're lucky, he'll show you how to put the powder in, if you're not, he'll ignore you. Don't for goodness' sake sit next to him and say, "Nice 'ere, innit?" For one thing, you probably don't look the slightest bit like Lorraine Chase . . .!

THE BOY NEXT DOOR

There's something quite sweet about fancying the boy next door — it's sort of, well, homely.somehow, and *nice*. But unless you go about things the right way and have him fancying you, too, just think how awful it'll be for the poor bloke if he can't get away from you because his house is stuck on to yours!

Don't be too obvious. This means *not* brushing your teeth at the bathroom window every morning when he goes out to feed his rabbit, undressing behind the net curtains in your bedroom every night, or hanging over the garden fence looking for your earring every time the poor guy sets foot outside the back door.

Don't do up your bedroom window to look like a Barbara Cartland boudoir, i.e. single red roses, heart mobiles, volumes of love sonnets, or teddy bears with arms outstretched to next door's drying green — he'll just think you're a soft weedie, or a weedy softie. It's a waste of time spending every free minute gardening for your dad hoping that he'll notice you because it'll only make your hands rough, you'll get cold and fed up, and it's very likely that he'll just think you're a mad keen gardener and the two of you have nothing in common.

Playing blaring pop music, screeching along with The Skids, bellowing to The Boomtown Rats and other such raving

things might convince him that you're a raver, but he'll want you to rave off and do it elsewhere. (This could also make you unpopular with his parents.) Also, don't peer into his parents' lounge window on every one of the hundred occasions you just accidentally-on-purpose happen to be walking past every day. The family, including him, will hate you for being a nosey, gawping ninny, and they'll probably complain to your parents.

AT THE LIBRARY

It could be that you have to use the library for a school project, or even for your own amusement. So one day you stroll in, and there's this lovely guy absorbed in a book at one of the tables. So what don't you do? You *don't* make a noise — not even a discreet little cough, or you'll be *most* unpopular.

Dropping the Encyclopaedia Brittanica is a bit risky — and dangerous. He'd notice you all right, but the thing might land on your foot, and if it gets damaged you'll have to fork out (for the book, not your foot!). He'll also think you're a clumsy oaf with no respect for books (presumably he's fairly keen on the things, or he wouldn't be there).

Don't walk up to him and say, "Excuse me, but I think you have the book I want." He's bound to ask politely how long you've been into agricultural engineering or nuclear physics.

If he's obviously studying and taking notes, don't offer to sharpen his pencil, clean his glasses, turn the pages, etc. He's probably feeling quite irritable enough without your kind offers to interrupt him. If you do manage to get a seat opposite him, don't drop things on the floor just so that you can have the thrill of getting near his feet under the table! He'll soon twig to what you're doing, and you might get kicked. Likewise, don't tie his shoelaces together in the hope that he'll see the funny side of it all when he stands up and falls flat on his face. Studious types often aren't too hot on the humour.

Try not to get into a heavy situation you can't cope with. That is to say, pick books with care before you sit opposite him. It's no good getting involved in a literary discussion over the selected works of Tolstoy that you picked off the shelf, when the nearest you've ever been to "War And Peace" is fighting your kid brother for the last piece of chewing gum — and losing.

How Moody Are You?

IF you want to know what sort of mood you're in and what you should and should *not* do about it, try our special quiz and we'll tell you! It's quite simple — first of all, choose your favourite colour of the moment, and just answer the questions that appear in that colour section. Your score will direct you to a certain part of the conclusions, and that'll tell you all about you and your mood of the moment!

If you find it hard to choose one colour, not to worry! You can pick two or three colours (but not more). Then, answer ALL the questions in those sections. Divide your score by two if you used two colours, or divide it by three if you used three colours.

You can do the quiz another day, if you feel in a different mood. Choose a different colour (or colours) and you'll get a different answer, to help you with your mood of that particular moment!

IF YOUR FAVOURITE COLOUR IS RED:

You start with a score of 100 in this section. Deduct the points given.

1. Would you like to have your bedroom decorated in reds?
Would you wear an all-red outfit?
Would you fancy a meal in a café decorated all in red?
  a. Yes to all 3 — deduct 1 point.
  b. Yes to 2 — deduct 2 points.
  c. Yes to 1 or none — deduct 5 points.

2. Do you ever dream of blood?
  a. Yes. Deduct 1 point.
  b. No. Deduct 5 points.

3. Choose a word from the following group: sincere, straightforward, positive, forward, action, definite.
  a. If you chose straightforward or action, deduct 1 point.
  b. If you chose forward, deduct 2 points.

  c. If you chose positive or definite, deduct 3 points.
  d. If you chose sincere, deduct 5 points.

4. Would it put you off a boy if someone said he was aggressive, even if you hadn't met him?
  a. No. Deduct 1 point.
  b. It might put you off, but you'd still meet him and decide for yourself. Deduct 2 points.
  c. Definitely you wouldn't want to meet him. Deduct 5 points.

IF YOUR FAVOURITE COLOUR IS YELLOW:

You start with a score of 80 in this section. Deduct the points given.

1. Do you enjoy eating yellow food (cheese, butter, eggs, etc.)?
Would you wear yellow shoes with a yellow dress?
Would you like a bed with yellow sheets and covers?
  a. Yes to all 3 — deduct 1 point.
  b. Yes to 2 — deduct 2 points.
  c. Yes to 1 or none — deduct 5 points.

2. Do your problems seem less serious when the sun is shining?
  a. Not particularly. Deduct 5 points.
  b. Yes, usually. Deduct 1 point.

3. Choose a word from the following group: cheerful, bright, happy, fortunate, lucky, smile.
  a. If you chose smile, deduct 1 point.
  b. If you chose fortunate or lucky, deduct 2 points.
  c. If you chose any of the others, deduct 5 points.

4. If you spent the evening with your boyfriend and he was moody or unhappy the whole time for no reason, would you feel your romance was on its last legs?
  a. No. Deduct 1 point.
  b. Maybe — it would depend on your own mood. Deduct 2 points.
  c. Yes. Deduct 5 points.

IF YOUR FAVOURITE COLOUR IS GREEN:

You start with a score of 60 in this section. Deduct the points given.

1. Do you make a point of eating a lot of vegetables because you think they're good for you?
Do you think it's unlucky to bring certain green plants indoors — like lilac branches or hawthorn?
Do you like green as a colour but find it impossible to wear?
  a. No to all 3 — deduct 1 point.
  b. No to 2 — deduct 2 points.
  c. No to 1 or none — deduct 5 points.

2. Do you find that a room with pale-green walls has a calming effect on you?
   a. Yes. Deduct 1 point.
   b. No. Deduct 5 points.

3. Choose a word from the following group: belief, choice, attitude, thought, care, decide.
   a. If you chose care, deduct 1 point.
   b. If you chose belief or thought, deduct 2 points.
   c. If you chose decide, deduct 3 points.
   d. If you chose choice or attitude, deduct 5 points.

4. What do you think is the ideal length of time for an engagement?
   a. It varies according to the temperaments of the couple. Deduct 1 point.
   b. 18 months or less. Deduct 2 points.
   c. More than 18 months. Deduct 5 points.

IF YOUR FAVOURITE COLOUR IS BLUE:

You start with a score of 40 in this section. Deduct the points given.

1. Would you like an outfit in shades of blue?
There aren't many natural blue foods — would you fancy eating ordinary food like potatoes or bread if it were coloured blue? Would you like your bedroom to be decorated in shades of blue?
   a. Yes to all 3 — deduct 1 point.
   b. Yes to 2 — deduct 2 points.
   c. Yes to 1 or none — deduct 5 points.

2. Do you believe in the saying, "Pink makes the boys wink, blue makes the boys true"?
   a. Yes. Deduct 5 points.
   b. No. Deduct 1 point.

3. Choose a word from the following group: tension, argument, tiff, bicker, sulk.
   a. If you chose argument, deduct 1 point.
   b. If you chose bicker or tiff, deduct 2 points.
   c. If you chose any other, deduct 5 points.

4. How long do you feel it would take you to get over the break-up of a relationship with a boy you've been seeing regularly for six months, and he did the breaking-up?
   a. You'd never completely get over it. Deduct 5 points.
   b. You'd have forgotten your sorrows in six months. Deduct 1 point.
   c. It would take more than six months to forget. Deduct 2 points.

IF YOUR FAVOURITE COLOUR IS PURPLE:

You start with a score of 20 in this section. Deduct the points given.

1. Do you fancy the idea of yourself in a matching lavender nightie and negligee? When you eat coloured Smarties, do you eat the purple ones first? Do you think pansy-purple eye-shadow looks sexy?
   a. Yes to all 3 — deduct 1 point.
   b. Yes to 2 — deduct 2 points.
   c. Yes to 1 or none — deduct 5 points.

2. Do you dream in colour?
   a. Yes. Deduct 1 point.
   b. Don't usually remember dreams, so can't tell. Deduct 2 points.
   c. No. Deduct 5 points.

3. Choose a word from the following group: star-crossed, misfortune, fate, weird, jinx.
   a. If you chose misfortune or weird, deduct 1 point.
   b. If you chose fate or jinx, deduct 2 points.
   c. If you chose star-crossed, deduct 5 points.

4. Do you feel that somewhere there is a boy who is exactly right for you, and it's just a matter of luck bringing you together?
   a. Yes. Deduct 5 points.
   b. No. Deduct 1 point.
   c. You think there is more than one. Deduct 2 points.

Now count up your score (remember, if you scored for TWO COLOURS, *halve your score*, if you scored for THREE COLOURS, *divide your score by three* and turn to the conclusions.

QUIZ CONCLUSIONS

0-8 points: You're a very emotional person, and you depend a lot on luck. If you tried to be less guided by your heart and relied more on your own brains and talent, you'd be happier and probably make more of a success of your life! You have quite a lot of sex appeal even though you don't think you do, so don't under-rate yourself! Go out and make a splash!

9-19 points: Could jealousy be your big problem today? Remember, if you have a problem it's much better to do something positive about solving it, rather than just brood over it. Whatever you do, don't try to solve it in some underhand or sneaky way — that'll just make things worse!

20-28 points: You're going through rather an unhappy phase. You definitely need a bit of cheering up so this would be a good time to indulge yourself in your favourite treat! Don't be ashamed of feeling a bit weepy, a good cry to get it out of your system will probably work wonders!

29-39 points: A bit ratty or edgy today then, are we? You're probably regretting something you said or did earlier. It's much better to kiss and make up than brood if it's a boyfriend. Try to put things right with a friendly word or two. It could be you are normally more easy going, but you're feeling tense at the moment and need to relax. Try to get more exercise, you'll find it easier to relax mentally and physically afterwards.

40-48 points: You've got everything going for you, but you must act positively to take advantage of opportunities. What you need is some friendly help, just a friend to talk things over with. It could help you a lot to take your mind off any activities that are causing you headaches or heartaches at the moment. Get right away from the usual routine, if only for a few hours, it'll do you the world of good!

49-59 points: You're entering a more serious mood than you've been in and the next 24 hours could be important. Don't be too outspoken — remember, people aren't always as good at keeping secrets as they could be. This isn't a time to make snap judgments about important things like a job, a boyfriend, or a holiday. Take time to think about it!

60-68 points: You're a fairly happy-go-lucky person anyway, and today is a good day for you. Things will run very smoothly so now is the right time to tackle any chores that you've been putting off! It's also a good time to think of a change in your normal routine.

69-79 points: You're a bit too casual at the moment about everything! You have lots of confidence, but are maybe a bit too impulsive for your own good. If you're thinking of spending more than one week's money on one particular purchase, think about it for at least 24 hours.

80-88 points: You're in a very positive mood at the moment, and this would be a good time to be more daring and outgoing than normal. So if you have a favour to ask, a rise to seek, or want to put your foot down, now's the time. But make sure you have all your facts right, first!

89-99 points: Steady — you could be heading for a big row or a challenge of some sort. Take a little more time to make sure that what you're doing is what you really want. Did you feel like this a week ago? Then the action you're considering could be right. If not — if you just woke up today in this dashing, crazy mood — try to put off decisions until tomorrow!

WHAT LINE IS HE HANDING YOU?

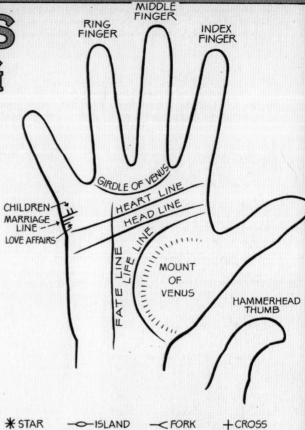

RING FINGER
MIDDLE FINGER
INDEX FINGER

GIRDLE OF VENUS
HEART LINE
HEAD LINE
CHILDREN
MARRIAGE LINE
LOVE AFFAIRS
FATE LINE
LIFE LINE
MOUNT OF VENUS
HAMMERHEAD THUMB

＊STAR —○—ISLAND ‹‹FORK ＋CROSS

Everybody has their destiny in the palm of their hands — literally! All you have to know is how to read it. In this special feature we explain how palmistry works so that you can learn all about the secrets of a boy's true romantic nature. So read on . . . then tenderly take hold of his hand . . . and all his secrets will be revealed!

HOW TO READ HIS HANDS

The lines on his hands show his character and what's likely to happen to him, and *you* if you're with him!

The Heart line, for instance, runs across his palm above the Head line and it reveals the secrets of his romantic feelings.

He's very romantic if his Heart line is a deep strong line that cuts well into his hand. He's a boy who's never bored with love and will always be interesting to be with.

But you'll *never* receive a love letter from a boy whose Heart line runs straight across his palm without a curve. He's definitely too direct and unromantic for such sentimentality. So if it's a romantic boy you're looking for then a boy whose Heart line swoops across his palm is the one for you!

But be on your guard! If his Heart line runs *too* far across his palm, he's a boy who only imagines he's in love. He may be in love with *love* and not with *you!*

Broken marriages break the Heart line, palmists say, but a happy marriage is in store for the boy with a Heart line beginning under his index finger and running strong and unbroken across his palm.

A boy's Heart line will also show his romantic sorrows. Each small line extending down from his Heart line and each break in the Heart line is a disappointment in love.

If you want to know how much a boy's head rules his heart, compare the Head and Heart lines. Whichever line is deeper and longer rules the other. You'll have quite a time swaying the emotions of a boy with a faint Heart line and a strong Head line.

But a boy with a strong Heart line and weak Head line is bound to be over emotional and impractical in love. So, go for a boy with lines of equal strength.

Be cautious with a boy whose Heart line curves sharply upward in a right angle towards his fingers. He tends to act impulsively in love without thinking of the consequences — and you could be the one to suffer.

IS HE SEXY?

Yes he is, if the pad called the Mount of Venus, extending from the base of his thumb into the centre of his palm is fleshy and well developed! His sexiness is also shown by the Girdle of Venus, a semi-circular line running from between the index and middle finger to a space between the ring and little finger.

When this line is strong he's a boy more interested in a girl's physical attributes than her personality! He's probably a male chauvinist, so beware! If broken in several places, he's a boy who makes many physical attachments but no long-lasting emotional ties. He'll be good fun if you don't try to tie him down.

HIS ROMANCES AND MARRIAGE

*A boy who wants to keep his past from a girl should **never** let her look at the small horizontal lines on the side of his hand under his little finger. So try to take a look before he realises what it means! Each weak line is a love affair and the deeper ones represent a marriage. You may even find **yourself** in his hand. If you're romantically involved with him you'll certainly be one of the weaker lines, at least!*

A long engagement is in store for the boy whose Marriage line begins with a fork. But if it ends in a fork this marriage will end in divorce or separation.

HIS FAULTS

The larger the thumb the stronger the ego and ambition. Girls unwilling to do just what a boy wants should avoid boys with large, long thumbs. He'll want to keep you under *his* control. A domineering boy may also have an index finger as long as his ring finger or a thumb which curves backwards like a hammerhead. Such a boy may be overbearing and childish so you'd probably do well to avoid him.

But a boy with a weak, small thumb and short index finger will let himself be nagged by a girl — he may also sweep a girl off her feet with promises he can't keep. So you won't want *him* either!

A short thumb that does not extend to the middle joint of the index finger is a sign of lack of will-power or sense of responsibility. This type of boy may let you down. If his thumb is flexible and bends easily away from his hand, he is generous and easy going and will make a great boyfriend. If his thumb lacks flexibility and does not bend easily away from his hand, he is stubborn and probably mean over money.

So now you know *his* destiny — if only he'll let you take a look at his hands!

We all know what girls are scared of . . . but what are *boys* scared of? We know boys aren't supposed to be scared of anyone or anything, but we went ahead anyway and asked a handful of boys for their honest, considered opinions about the things that frighten them — and we came up with all sorts of fascinating answers, on all sorts of fascinating subjects! Here are our results — we're sure they'll change your attitudes to the boys in *your* life . . .

THINGS THAT SCARE BOYS

NOT BEING NORMAL

Sean, 19: "You wouldn't believe the hang-ups some blokes have about their bodies. I worried like mad because I didn't start shaving till I was nearly 18. What made it even worse was my best mate had a moustache growing when he was 12! I felt like a freak. The first hair on my chest was a landmark for me too — I felt dead butch, like a man at last! It sounds stupid but little things like that can give you incredible hang-ups. It's even worse for small blokes, because they can get these terrible inferiority complexes, especially where girls are concerned — I mean, it's not much fun being 5 feet nothing when the girl you're mad about is a cool 5 ft. 6 in. now, is it? It's much easier for girls than it is for boys, because girls aren't as cruel to each other, and they don't have as much to live up to . . ."

SHOWING THEIR FEELINGS

Danny, 18: "I don't think boys are all *that* different to girls when it comes to feelings — it's just when it comes to showing their feelings that most blokes completely freeze up. I'm pretty squeamish for instance, and my very first girlfriend dropped me because of it! It's funny now, but it wasn't then because I felt a complete failure. Her nose started to bleed really badly one night — so badly that I fainted in front of some of her mates just as we were going into a disco. Now, I suppose, I go over the top — go to the other extreme and act all big and tough and manly. It's not me, really, but I think that's the image most girls go for. Boys have got to hide their feelings more than girls. It's the same with girls though — they hide their feelings and pretend they're what they're not just as much as we do."

MARRIAGE

Joe, 17: "I do want to get married — one day, but not now. One of my best mates who's 18 got married about six months ago — he had to because the girl was pregnant, and even I can see it's just not going to work out between them. I feel really sorry for him because he's made such a mess of his life. He hardly ever goes out with the lads anymore and when he does, his wife — *she's* only just turned 17 — kicks up a fuss. I don't want to end up like that. I'm going to get myself a really good job, play the field and meet lots of girls then settle down when I'm about 30. Why tie yourself to a wife and baby, all that responsibility, when your life's really only just beginning? I think girls are a lot to blame. All they think about is a ring and babies. They can't see in front of their noses."

GOING TOO FAR

Sam, 15: "Sex is everywhere — on films, TV, books, magazines, and most guys do think about it a lot. I know I do. Well, it's hard not to think about it. I hate the way everything's so one-sided though — you know, guys supposed to be after *just one thing*. Well, I'm not. I know a lot of guys are but some girls just ask for it, the way they dress and behave. If they could hear the things some guys say about them behind their backs . . .! Most girls are pushovers — they go all lovey-dovey and will do anything for a guy with the right line of patter — or at least, that's what a lot of my mates say. Most of them talk a lot of hot air though, so you end up not knowing what to believe. A lot of guys are really unsure when you get down to it, though. I mean, where do you draw the line? I think everything should go a lot more slowly than it does. I mean, it's not the end of the world if you don't have sex by the time you're 15. There are too many pressures on young people today. The whole thing is so mixed-up. I don't think magazines like yours help things either." (Well!)

GIRLS

Ian, 15: "At our school there are three kinds of girls — the snobby ones who are dead flash, — flash clothes, make-up, the works, the kind who are caught up in the "who's going out with who and him — I wouldn't look at him twice he's not good enough for me" syndrome; the really nice girls who aren't loud and pushy; and the yobbos — the girls who are all tough and big-mouthed. I'd really like to get to know the nice ones. The other ones I couldn't care less about and I just wouldn't want to talk to them. But it's really hard, and a bit scary too, trying to break the ice. It's still up to the boy to talk to them first, to ask them out and generally do all the running, which isn't easy to do, especially if you haven't even been out with a girl yet. Girls are like things from another planet. I just don't understand them. A guy like me finds it really hard to break the ice — I think most blokes do at first.

Finally (whew!) we think Colin deserves the last word. He's big enough to admit that lots of things scare him . . .

Colin, 16: "What am I scared of? Well, chatting up girls in groups for a start — I hate that. It's the same asking a girl to dance when she's with her mates. One thing I dread is when a mate and I get two girls up to dance and I get the ugly one who won't go away.

"Then there's bed-wetting, at a mate's house. Being made to look a fool by her elder brother in front of her family and knowing that I can't smash him one in the face 'cos that won't do me any good. Taking a new girl to an X film and not being able to get in. Getting beaten up. Being turned down after plucking up the courage to ask a girl out. Will that do?"

Did you know that what you write in your diary gives away an awful lot about what you're *really* like? Everyone's diary is different — as you can see from the pages we've sneaked from the diaries of five very different girls. All *you* have to do is compare their scribblings to yours, decide which is nearest your style — and find out the secrets which are lurking in the pages of your diary. (A double reason for keeping it under lock and key!)

ARE YOU A WRITE GIVE~ AWAY?

WET WENDY'S DIARY

MONDAY Felt sick, but Mum said I had to go to school, worse luck. Felt worse in Biology — no wonder, we were dissecting a horrible THING. Not sure what it was exactly, because didn't dare look at it. But Theresa threw a bit of it at me so I ran out screaming and went to the medical room to lie down.

TUESDAY Still felt very shaky after yesterday. There wasn't any hot water to wash in because the switch was off. And when I cleaned my teeth, my gums bled. I expect I've got that awful disease which makes your teeth fall out.

WEDNESDAY School dentist came so hid in the toilet. At break, John Greenfield came up, got talking and asked me out on Friday. I'm sure he was just taking the mickey so I told him I had to go to my gran's.

THURSDAY Theresa says I should have one of those new haircuts. But my hair's like old rats' tails and nothing would do any good. My hands are mottled today — I wonder if I'm going down with something?

FRIDAY Had a bit of a sore throat today. Theresa says John Greenfield really fancies me — but I don't believe her. How could he fancy me? How could anybody? Looking forward to watching TV all tomorrow.

If Your Diary's Like Wendy's . . .

We all feel like Wendy from time to time — when things go wrong. But nobody's that much of a failure. Everybody's got something going for them. When a boy asks you out, don't assume he's got to be joking. He just might be serious and attracted to you — there's no accounting for tastes!

Try increasing your self-confidence. For a start, endless fretting about your health is silly — it's usually a sign that you've got nothing whatever wrong with you.

If your life consists of watching TV, just get up and go — OUT! Anywhere: for a walk, for a bike-ride. You're far too shy — and when it comes to boys you assume you have nothing to offer, so no wonder you don't get asked out anywhere! Join a few clubs, get your free time organised so you spend it with a drama group, or a photography club, or whatever, and forget about your imaginary problems and worries!

DOROTHY DREAMER

MONDAY A strange and weird day. Dark clouds — all the birds are silent. Why? Came bottom in Geography test. Spent Needlework lesson dreaming about the French assistant M. Plaque. Miss Sullivan read us a ghost story today in English. I was so scared I had to hold on to my desk. M. Plaque still away. I wonder what's wrong.

TUESDAY M. Plaque still away. If only I could be by his bedside and nurse him back to health . . . sponge his brow and brew up his hot lemon drink. I saw a flower in a hedgerow today, picked it and made a wish.

WEDNESDAY It came true! M. Plaque came back! And that rhymes! Maybe I will write a poem about it! He looks very pale but terrifically romantic.

THURSDAY I bit my ruler in half today when M. Plaque walked past the classroom window. Splinters in the gum quite painful, but for him I could bear anything.

FRIDAY M. Plaque trod on me! It was *wonderful!* He said *pardon* in his lovely French voice and looked into my eyes! I shall never wash my foot again! He *touched* me! Came bottom in History and Maths. Got run over tonight outside school, but not seriously. Was looking up at French-room windows at the time.

If Your Diary's Like Dorothy's . . .

Dreaming about things (or to be more exact, boys!) is natural. But being in such a dream about them that you're out of touch with reality is another matter. And what's more, it's a very stupid state to be in. Whilst you're dreaming about Mr Right, a real flesh-and-blood boy might be trying to catch your eye . . . and failing!

It's also pretty dangerous to get yourself into such a romantic frame of mind that you believe in things like premonitions. When you think you're being psychic or feeling that something strange is going to happen, you're probably only just indulging your moods.

As far as boys are concerned, you're too interested in them. It's natural to be interested. But not to think of nothing else. So give yourself a break, and get going with some pastimes that will extend you as a person. Languishing in a romantic dream-world is *not* the answer to life's problems!

VAIN VICKY

MONDAY Woken by golden light streaming in through my curtains. The trees are covered with blossom and I have got a huge spot on my chin. A new boy got on the bus today: tall and dark, with smouldering eyes and a sulky mouth. I turned my face away so he wouldn't see my spot.

TUESDAY Washed my hair in the new **Extract of Dogrose and Cowparsley** shampoo. Smells awful — like a goat with B.O. Today my spot was worse: like a Belisha beacon. Covered it with make-up and buried my face in my scarf.

WEDNESDAY I wish Dad wouldn't wear that awful old suit. He collected me from school today because of the bus strike, and everyone could see his lapels were the wrong shape. I could've *died*.

THURSDAY A fantastic day! I shall remember this day as long as I live! The boy on the bus sat by me! I could feel his shoulder against mine! He's got the most beautiful hands — big, and brown. What's more my spot popped yesterday so I didn't have to hide my face. If only we didn't have to wear school uniform.

FRIDAY He didn't turn up. Good job, too, 'cos there was a girl on the bus who was really fantastic looking. The cow. It's not fair. Beautiful sunset today. Washed my hair in **Extract of Barley and Groundsel.** Smells foul.

If Your Diary's Like Vicky's . . .

If you think you're a bit like Vicky, well, relax a little. It's not the end of the world if you've got a spot or a blemish.

People like Vicky who are interested in beauty are usually aware of all sorts of other beauty in the world — not just their own! This is great. You probably like looking at paintings or sculpture, or just enjoying the wonders of nature. Flowers, sea-shells, feathers — you love them all, you like to collect them.

You're much too aware of your looks when it comes to meeting boys, though. You try to stun them with your beauty, whereas most boys would feel more comfortable just talking casually with a girl to break the ice.

PRACTICAL PAULA

MONDAY Got up early. Was just about to go jogging in the park when Mum asked me to go to the corner shop for some milk 'cos of the milkmen's strike. So I jogged to the shop and back. The result? A milk-shake! (Ho ho!) Mended Steve's bike puncture this evening.

TUESDAY Overslept till 7.30. In an awful rush. Forgot to feed the hamster, didn't have time to clean my shoes or iron my skirt. (Or iron the hamster, ho ho!) Hopeless day. Couldn't do hockey because of the rain.

WEDNESDAY At youth club played Steve at table tennis. Beat him hollow. He seemed fed up. It's his birthday next week. I said I'd make him a cake. That cheered him up. He *must* ask me out soon.

THURSDAY At weight-training tonight, a bloke twisted his ankle. I gave him the old first-aid treatment, and the coach was very impressed. I hope Steve noticed, but I think he was talking to that wet girl Mandy Pillick. She always comes to watch. Never lifts a finger though. (Nor a bar-bell, ho ho!)

FRIDAY I was really enjoying myself tonight making a yoghurt machine out of a few old milk-bottles and a mousetrap, when Sheila had to come round and drag me off to the disco. She said Steve would be there. He was . . . wrapped around Mandy Pillick.

If Your Diary's Like Paula's . . .

If you feel you might be a bit like Paula, well . . . congratulations! You've certainly made the most of your talents and learned a lot of skills that'll help you get on well with people. You'll always be invaluable to any group of people. You're cheery, you crack jokes, you're great in a crisis . . .

If you haven't got a boyfriend, or have trouble keeping them, you're probably putting them off by being too good at everything, too organised. *Ask* him things instead of *telling* him. There's nothing wrong with being a tomboy, but let him know you're a real girl underneath!

SUSAN SWOT

MONDAY Great day. The maths test was everything I'd been hoping for. Had a very good talk with Mark Smith at break, about the maths test. We argued about question 6. He said the answer was $ab_2 = qrt + 2.008 + zrt = 700.000006$ but I disagreed.

TUESDAY Found a terrific old book in the second-hand bookshop: called Ferrier's **Functions of the Brain.** Great stuff. Read it secretly under the desk in the needlework lesson. Pricked myself twice. Blood is interesting. I'd like to do an experiment measuring people's clotting rates.

WEDNESDAY Smashing concert on Radio 3: a new concerto for Harp, Flute and Elastic Band by Erich Twitterguts. I wonder if Mark was listening to it. I thought of him in the slow movement.

THURSDAY Asked Mark if he'd heard the concert, but he said he'd been over at the **Hope and Anchor** in Whistley, watching a band called **The Snots.** Sometimes Mark surprises me. I wonder what his clotting rate is.

FRIDAY Results of maths test! Mark was top but he did get No. 6 wrong! I was second — but I don't mind him being top sometimes. Janice says Mark might take more notice of me if I plucked my eyebrows and maybe my nostrils as well, but I know he's above such things. Read 288 pages of **War and Peace** and fell asleep to the sound of Beetroothoven's Fifth Symphony.

If Your Diary's Like Susan's . . .

If your diary extract is a bit like Susan's, it's obvious that you're highly intelligent, and very academic. Being interested in school work isn't odd — for some people it's only natural. We can't all sit goggling at *Top Of The Pops.*

When it comes to boys, you're a bit frightening to some boys because they find clever girls are a threat to them. But you *needn't* be a threat if you're just relaxed and friendly. Bright boys like bright girls to talk to.

So if you're a bit like Susan, be patient with boys. Talk to them about everyday things as well as the problems of the universe! And don't be ashamed if you want to doll yourself up now and then. Why shouldn't you be clever *and* pretty? It's a winning combination!

SPOT THE GROT

First, check that a Grot *is* what you've got by —
HIS APPEARANCE

His appearance isn't the best guide to a Grot. Some Grots are scruffy, some are smart, some are in-between. But a too scruffy guy who obviously doesn't care what he looks like is likely not to care too much about the girls in his life, either. And that makes him a Grot.

At the other end of the scale, watch out for the *too* neat, *too* smart and *too* well-dressed guy. Ask yourself how he gets that way. All those clean shirts, the perfect creases in his trousers. You can bet he doesn't get as immaculate as that by himself. So he's already got *one* devoted slave pandering to him. Has he got you lined up as Number 2? Then he's a Grot.

THE WAY HE SPENDS HIS MONEY ON YOU

Is he generous? It's important here to separate the poor guy who's low on cash from the genuine meanie Grot. Your genuine poor-as-a-church-mouse guy will happily fork out to buy you an ice-cream. The Grot will fuss about buying you an ice-cream but he'll let you have a lick of his. Even though he could afford 100 ice-creams.

The Grot is likely to carry a purse. Men with purses are careful of the pennies. There's nothing wrong with that, but combine it with the Grot and you've got a first-class Meanie.

THE PLACES HE TAKES YOU

This is tied in with the way he spends his money on you. He's finally got round to agreeing to buy you a meal. You fancy a particular restaurant. He says "Yeah, but there's a cheaper place just round the corner." Maybe he's just being careful with his cash. Or maybe he doesn't think you rate a first-class restaurant. Some guys give girls what they think they deserve. So if you get dragged into a burger bar that's the level you're tagged at in his grotty mind.

THE WAY HE ACTS TOWARDS YOU WHEN YOU'RE IN COMPANY

Is he off-hand, cool? Does he leave you standing on your own while he takes off to chat with his mates? Does he talk to people he knows without bothering to introduce you? He does? Then he's a Grot for sure. He doesn't count you as important, can't even be bothered to show you off. Face the facts, the guy is taking you for granted.

Take a long, cool look at your guy. Does he stand you up, let you down, give you the runaround and leave you stranded? Is he treating you like an old bag? If he is, then the chances are, that what you've got is — a Grot. And what's a Grot? A guy who's not so hot and doesn't care a lot, that's what! So, if you suspect that you're stuck with a Grot, read on! We tell you, first of all, how to check that you have got landed with a genuine Grot and if (poor fool) you find that you have, don't despair — we'll tell you what to do about it!

OK. On the evidence you find you're stuck with a Grot. The next question is — what to do.

First ask yourself if you're genuinely fond of him. Would it hurt badly if you split up? Answer *no* and all you have to do is give him the push. Simple.

Answer *yes* and you've got problems. How are you going to change a guy like that? Because that's what you've got to do, for your own sake and for his. So —

★ Start with his appearance. If he's scruffy and careless about his looks, nag him into smartening up. Or turn up looking mucky and slovenly yourself and see how *he* likes it. If he doesn't, tell him that's just how *you* feel about *him*.

The too-smart guy needs some attention, too. Ask him why he needs to be so immaculate, what's he afraid of. Guys don't like suggestions that they're afraid. It might do the trick. Or if his old mum is behind the scenes slaving away you could try getting at her instead and maybe start a rebellion so he'll have to iron his own shirts in future.

★ How are you going to knock the meanness about money out of him? Not easily, that's for sure. It might pay you to start being aggressive with him. Try lines like — *"What's the matter, you don't think I'm worth spending that much on?"* It might do the trick.

A gentler way is the kindly *"Let me help"* approach. When he's reluctant about parting with his cash, act as if you know he's really very generous and say, *"Haven't you got enough? Look, why not let me make up the difference? You can pay me back later."* This'll put him in a spot.

You can use the same line when he tries to drag you to the cheaper restaurant. *"If you can't afford it,"* you can say, *"let's go Dutch. I'd just love to have a real, romantic meal with you."*

Even *he* will have to admit that there's not a lot of romance in a burger bar. If he has got a heart, this kind of approach should find it and, if you're lucky, he won't even take up your "going Dutch" offer.

★ When you're in company and he's doing his off-hand bit, you've got two lines of action. Stick around and ignore *him* the way *he's* ignoring *you*. He won't like you showing signs of independence. Don't hesitate to break into the group of people he's talking to if you feel like it and introducing yourself. *"You may not have guessed it but I'm his girl-friend."* This'll make him look like an ill-mannered yob to his friends and if he's got any sense he'll save himself future embarrassment by making sure he includes you in the action.

The second line of action is just to walk out and go home. Pretty drastic stuff, but the only way if you can't raise the nerve to do anything else. If the guy is keen on you, he's going to want to know *why* you walked out on him and you can tell him you're fed up with being ignored and treated like you're not important. (A lot of Grots don't realise just how grotty they are until it's pointed out to them.)

If he's not keen on you, then he isn't going to care why you walked out. Then you'd be better off nursing your broken heart. Don't go back to him, no matter how much it hurts not to. If you do, he's going to go on using you as a doormat.

THE important thing is to work up the nerve to be honest with the Grot. And maybe the best time, the time when least embarrassment will be caused, is when you're alone together. A heart to heart talk might do the trick. So long as the guy knows you're keen and you don't want to lose him, he's likely to listen to your list of complaints against him. Like we said, a lot of Grots don't realise how grotty they are.

*But before you start, have a think about **yourself**. While you're listing **your** complaints, is he going to be matching them with complaints about **you**? So don't start on him, unless you're sure you're not also a Grot!*

Do You Know When To Take A Hint?

IF your friends start arriving at your house with clothes pegs on their noses, think twice before shouting, "Oh, is that the latest fashion? I must rush out and buy a clothes peg!" Clothes pegs on noses aren't one bit fashionable. Could it be that your friends are trying to tell you something? Is it possible you may have B.O.? (Hadn't thought of that, had you?)

When hints are being dropped, the sooner you catch on — the better. It can save an awful lot of discomfort, especially in the case of B.O., and save your friends from having to buy gas-masks in a desperate last attempt to let you know what's wrong.

Another example is when you're happy and you want to share your happiness. That's understandable. But if you've just started dating The Most Gorgeous Guy In Town, your friends are going to want to know all about him and you're certainly going to tell them.

But if you keep harping on about it, pretty soon your friends are going to get fed up with hearing about Him (especially if they haven't got boys of their own at the time).

If they start changing the subject every time you mention Him, take the hint. They'll talk about fashion, records, the possibility of life on other planets, and Einstein's Theory of Relativity. Anything except HIM.

If this happens, you should really ease up on talking about Him. Otherwise, in the end, they'll start screaming and tearing out their hair with cries of, "I can't stand any more!"

But what happens when your romance with HIM starts to fade — how is he going to let you know if you're still madly in love with him and haven't noticed him cooling off?

He could come straight out and tell you, but if he doesn't

want to hurt your feelings he won't do it like that.

He'll try to be kind about it. That's when hints will start dropping like rocks.

He may leave a note for you saying, *Sorry, can't keep our date tonight. Have emigrated to North Borneo.* This should give you an inkling that he might be cooling off!

But it's more likely he'll be less obvious than that. He'll start breaking dates with weak excuses you don't really believe.

When love's flown out the window it doesn't come back. Take the hints and retire gracefully before he has to resort to more drastic measures, like putting a barbed-wire fence all round his house so you can't drop

in to ask why he didn't turn up for your last date.

Don't be the Piggy in the Middle, either. Sometimes, when two girls have been close friends for a long time, one of them still expects their regular meetings to continue even though the other one's got a steady boyfriend and would really like to spend some time alone with him.

If *you're* the one who tags along, keep your eyes open for warning signs. Your friend may not mind you turning up and making a threesome from time to time.

But if you find yourself chatting away about the weather and whether the Bee Gees would look any different if they had the

Osmonds' teeth, and your buddy and her guy don't seem to be paying much attention 'cos they're busy cuddling — take the hint.

Even if you ask your friend if she minds if you tag along it doesn't follow that she means no when she says no.

If she doesn't sound as if she means it — that's the hint.

Hints are very indirect. When you've set your mind on buying a particular dress and your friend says: *Are you sure it will suit you? What she really means is, I don't think it will suit you.*

When you've planned a great scheme of some kind and your enthusiasm is met with a remark like, *Well, yes, I suppose it might be a good idea,* you can be pretty sure your scheme will be a dead loss.

A remark like, *Are you sure you know what you're doing?* is very often a hint that the speaker thinks you don't. If you're a non-swimmer and you're about to jump into the deep end of the swimming pool by mistake, it could turn out to be the last hint you'll ever have a chance to ignore.

Most hints are gentle and well meaning. Some can be cruel or unkind. When you find yourself having to drop hints to let a friend know she's being a pain in the neck in some way, try to do it without hurting her feelings.

If your boyfriend is still hanging around when the lovelight has gone out of your eyes, if your best friend has B.O. or is boring you to tears, make your hints as delicate as you can.

And try to avoid such unsubtle hints as clothes pegs on your nose, barbed-wire fences round your house or running around screaming, *I can't stand any more.*

There are better ways. Anyway, barbed wire is pretty expensive stuff.

Clothes For

Clothes can say a lot about you and the sort of person you are to people who don't know you. So it's important to remember that there's a time and place for everything. Who'd go hill walking in stilettos or to a garden party in denim shorts, for example? They're extreme examples, but here are some light-hearted guidelines to knowing *what* to wear, and *when*!·

WHAT TO WEAR WHEN YOU'RE — MEETING HIS PARENTS

You've been going out with him for quite a while, then he suddenly announces, "Would you like to come to tea on Sunday?" And you think: Oh, no . . . ! It's not that you don't *want* to go, but the prospect of meeting his mum and dad is nerve-racking enough without the added problem of what to wear!

The mere fact that he's asked you home means that he likes you a lot and wants to show you off to his parents.

If you care about him in the same way, you'll want to create the right sort of impression with them at first, and let them see what a nice, sensible, attractive, smart and down-to-earth girl you are for their son.

What To Wear

It's a safe bet that you're choosing the right clothes if you go through your wardrobe and pick an outfit that you don't like but your mum has always raved about! The only problem with wearing the little petal-pink suit with the Peter Pan collar that your mum adores is that if you don't feel happy wearing it, it will undermine your confidence and make you feel pretty fed-up, which will show in your face.

So pick clothes you feel happy in. A skirt with a matching blouse or jumper, matching coloured tights (without ladders!), and a leather shoulder bag and matching sensible-looking shoes will appeal to his mum.

Alternatively, if you have one, wear a fairly demure, high-necked dress, which you can pretty up with a nice brooch or a scarf at the neck. Mums seem to like pretty brooches and neck scarves!

If you have long hair, pull it back or wear it up. Mothers in general don't like hair flopping round faces and fringes falling into eyes, tea, soup, etc.

Keep your make-up very simple — just a touch of eyeshadow, mascara and lip gloss. It's very difficult meeting your boy's mother for the first time — if you're too dressed up she may think you're flashy; if you're not dressed up enough she may think you couldn't care less!

The best thing is to play everything down a little to begin with, as far as clothes are concerned. Play up the happy, sweet, kind and friendly side of yourself, and that way it's a safe bet that his mum will stop looking at your clothes and begin to notice the real you.

What Not To Wear

Even if your boy sees you every day of the week in jeans and T-shirts and, more to the point, *loves* to see you in jeans and T-shirts,

the same clothes won't wash with his mum. Jeans, of any size, shape or form, are definitely *out* for that first meeting over the tea table!

In fact, even your brand-new, dead-expensive, straight-legged, £25-a-go, pink satin trousers are out, because mothers seem to prefer a girl to be an old-fashioned girl (with, don't forget, manners to match).

Don't, whatever you do, wear a T-shirt with a slogan like "See me, feel me . . . !" His dad may be impressed, but his better half will be horrified, unless she's a *very* liberated lady.

High, thin-heeled shoes are out, too. Anyway, they might leave holes in his mum's good Cushionfloor when you're drying the dishes.

Avoid anything that's shocking pink, bright yellow, passionate purple or pea-green. Don't wear anything strapless or see-through, or she'll soon see through *you*, and, even though you might be a dedicated punk, for goodness' sake leave the coal-mine eyes, rigor-mortis lips and vampire finger-nails at home.

And finally, even if you have no chest to speak of, wear a bra . . .

WHAT TO WEAR WHEN YOU'RE — ON A FIRST DATE

So he's asked you out. Whether he's seen you around at school, or just around the town, he must fancy you already, and must really like the way you look. But even so, *everyone* gets into a flap about what to wear for a first date, and spends hours beforehand rummaging through wardrobe and drawers, finally ending up wearing what they decided they looked revolting in four hours before!

Whatever you wear, you'll think you look awful — it's all tied up with the whole first date scene — but remember, it's *you* he's

All Reasons !

interested in, and clothes aren't really all that important, though it helps if you feel that you're looking OK.

What To Wear

Unless you've met him at a party or disco, when you've been dressed to kill anyway, nine times out of ten he'll only have seen you in your school uniform or everyday clothes. Obviously, you want to knock him out on that first date, but don't go overboard. Most boys find something really appealing in the girl who's naturally fresh and pretty, so go for pretty clothes, and a hint of flowery perfume!

Wear a self-coloured silky blouse which is nice to touch, and pretty it up with lace round the collar, or a matching piece of ribbon. Choose a pretty skirt in a nice fresh cotton — no butchy tweed or cord.

Boys like dresses, the floatier and softer the better, so if you have a nice peasanty or frilly one, wear it.

Wear your flimsiest shoes or sandals to show off your pretty little feet. If they're big, wear boots, which boys find sexy, as long as they're not wellies, hob-nailed or ankle-length, sheepskin booties.

Borrow one of your mum's lacy hankies, he'll think it's really cute when you cry at the pictures (or you can use it to wipe away his tears when you tell him you don't want to see him again).

If you have long hair, wear it loose, unless you can be sure it'll all tumble down at the crucial moment, in true Hollywood Romance style.

What Not To Wear

If you were decked out at the disco like a Christmas tree when you met him he obviously likes it, so it's OK to dress the same for the first date. But dressing up in garish colours, split skirts, fish-net T-shirts, chain belt and black stockings and suspenders when he's only seen you in school uniform is guaranteed to frighten the life out of him.

The punk look is too aggressive (unless he's a punk himself). Try to avoid trousers, as all male chauvinist pigs like to see the real shape of a girl's legs (one exception here, and that's if your nickname's Tilly Treetrunk or Claire Cricketstump).

On the other hand, if you've got a great figure and look amazing in jeans, slither into them. On the right girl, they're very sexy.

Don't wear rude brooches; he may get entirely the wrong idea about you. Steer clear of military jackets, or anything vaguely masculine, which might frighten him.

Don't wear a woolly jumper or cardigan. There's nothing very soft and sexy about functional old wool.

Stay clear of stockings and suspender belts, on your first date anyway. Again, he might get the wrong idea about you and suddenly become too hot to handle. Don't wear clumpy great elephant shoes which could break his toes when he kisses you goodnight, or tights held together with nail varnish.

Don't wear anything that's not as fresh as it could be — not if you want him to get closer, anyway!

WHAT TO WEAR WHEN YOU'RE — AT THE DISCO

Now the disco's one place you can really let rip with your clothes — if you're not careful! There's absolutely no excuse for being shy and frightened about getting

dressed up for the disco. If you do feel like that, then you'd be well advised to spend your evenings in the public library instead. Discos and disco gear have never had it so good, and unless the gear's right you won't do your boogying any justice at all. You're there to let go, have a good time, and get yourself *noticed!* In all disco-goers there's a bit of the show-off, so throw caution to the wind, terrify the budgie, give your dad a seizure, and dress to kill!

What To Wear

Simply wear whatever you feel really good in, and will make you stand out from the crowd. The brighter the colour, the better — or all in white is great because it shows up well under disco lights. Silks and satins are fantastic — they glimmer in the lights and, if you've a good figure, cling to the right bits of your anatomy when you're dancing!

Choose straight-legged satin pants in any colour of the rainbow, with a skimpy little shimmery top.

The higher your heels, the better, as long as you don't keep falling over, which will ruin the image! If you're happier in a skirt, stick to the same colourful materials.

If you've a waist, nip it in with a wide, glittery or patent belt. Wear lots of jewellery, especially silver or gold to glitter under the lights.

Sprinkle matching glitter on your hair, but whatever you do, wear lashings of lip gloss which really looks good shimmering against white disco teeth!

Above all, don't be frightened to be outrageous, and remember to wear a huge smile — there's nothing worse than a miserable sea of disco faces looking as if they're only there for the beer, and even that's rotten . . .

What Not To Wear

What not to wear, basically, is anything that you wear at work or change into when you get home from school to watch the telly in. Boring everyday clothes will make you

feel boring and everyday. That means plain old jeans, deadly dull skirts and any other boring old clothes that don't turn you, or anyone else, on. Don't wear anything that you'll feel hot and uncomfortable in after half an hour.

That includes anything too tight, which might look good, but leaves you terrified that you'll get soaked with sweat which might show. Or, worst of all, split from top to bottom (literally!).

Don't wear anything blatantly braless and see-through. If you're looking for a nice guy, that's the wrong way to go about it.

In the majority of cases, boys don't really like it, unless they're only after what they can get, and that sort aren't worth knowing. And, likewise, avoid skirts slit up to your bottom, or tops slashed down to your waist.

Again, this kind of gear really will put nice boys off.

Don't wear flat shoes. They look pretty silly at a disco. Don't wear boring, flesh-coloured tights either — not when there's every colour under the sun to choose from.

And don't, *please*, wear your bag on your shoulder, or put it on the floor in front of you when you're dancing. It looks too awful for words.

WHAT TO WEAR WHEN YOU'RE — OUT FOR A MEAL

Going out for dinner does *not* mean the Wimpy Bar or the sitty-down bit of the local chipper. Dinner *does* mean a bit of luxury that doesn't happen very often because boys are usually too hard up.

But suppose your boyfriend's saved up to take you out for dinner to celebrate your anniversary, or birthday.

It's worth making a very special effort to look good for, because it's costing him a pretty penny, more likely than not, and whether it's the local Reo Stakis Steakhouse or a five-star hotel, the whole eating-out

thing in a nice atmosphere is a great experience.

What To Wear

If you're being taken out for a nice evening meal, not a luxury one, that is a Chinese, Indian or Steakhouse-type place, the best thing to go for is simply a pretty dress, provided it's not very tightly fitted because you'll never get past the first few forkfuls of rice or Steakhouse French Fries!

But if this evening meal is in a five-star hotel or expensive, romantic candlelit restaurant with soft music, finger bowls and toothpicks, do him the honour of looking gorgeous! This is the one time to wear a long dress, simple and elegant if possible, to make the best of what's underneath.

Go for halter-necks or tiny shoulder straps to show off your shoulders in the candlelight and wear one very simple silver or gold chain round your neck, with a matching chain round your wrist.

If your dress is simple and self-coloured, pin a rosebud or tiny flower on it — you can even tuck a tiny flower into your hair, which, if it's long, should be swept back or up, or softly waved.

Make sure you take a little evening purse or clutch bag — your everyday takes-every-thing-but-the-kitchen-sink shoulder bag will look too clumsy. Wear lashings of lovely perfume and concentrate on making your eye make-up as pretty as possible to give that big, dewy-eyed look across the table.

Wear a pretty silk or crochet shawl around your shoulders to slip off when you sit down.

What Not To Wear

No-one ever goes out for dinner in trousers — it's just *not* done! Only if you own a really fabulous silk harem suit is it acceptable, and even then some high-class hotels will frown on it. Never wear anything tight, especially if you have a midriff which will begin to expand as the meal progresses. If you're a messy eater don't wear light colours, which, horror of horrors, might show anything you spill.

Don't wear anything that's too way out. Your long shocking pink Lurex tube dress may be OK at the disco, but would look quite out of place at a ritzy restaurant.

Don't wear cheap jewellery — if that's all you have, don't wear anything at all. If you have long hair, don't wear it loose and floppy — it might fall in the soup, and anyway, it looks much more sophisticated when worn off the face.

Don't spoil the whole effect by floating into the restaurant in a plastic mac, tweed knee-length coat or cardi slung over your shoulders.

If you don't have a fur coat, silk or crochet shawl, go without. Don't wear boots under your dress and avoid floaty scarves round your neck. They'll float all right — into the soup.

WHAT TO WEAR WHEN YOU'RE — GOING TO AN INTERVIEW

Everyone, at some stage in their lives, has to face the dreaded interview. Interviews are horrible, no-one likes them, but first impressions are what interviews are all about. No prospective employer is going to be impressed with a girl who obviously hasn't made the slightest effort to look her best; that attitude will reflect on her work as far as the prospective employer is concerned, i.e. lazy, careless and untidy.

No matter whether you're trying to get a job

as a dishwasher or a personal secretary, be as smart as possible, to create an image of efficiency.

What To Wear

The golden rule to remember is that everything must look clean and well cared for. Even if you can't afford a new outfit, make sure it looks neat and tidy. The best thing to wear for an interview is a smart suit, with a well-cut jacket and skirt, but, unfortunately, they don't come cheap, as most interviewers realise these days, so you just have to make do with the next best thing.

Choose a plain blouse and skirt in sober colours, for example, a cream blouse (or jumper) with an unfussy dark or matching skirt. If you feel drab like that, wear a little floral brooch or pin at the neck of the blouse, which must be fastened to a decent height.

Your skirt should be calf length, with dark or flesh-coloured tights, and smart shoes with a matching bag. If you want a touch of luxury, try a silky scarf round your neck.

Polish your shoes like mad, check tights for holes or ladders, and see that your hands and fingernails are spotless.

Wear simple make-up, and if you want to look the cool, efficient secretary type, take a notepad and pen in your bag to jot down notes, because the interviewer will expect you to ask questions.

Make sure you have a clean hankie (blowing your nose is a great diversion when you're stuck for something to say!).

What Not To Wear

Again trousers are out, even in these days of Women's Lib and sexual equality. You have to be sensible about this. *You* may know you look great in trousers, but prospective employers will not be impressed. Even the smooth, camel, stay-press slacks should be given a miss (anyway, who'd *want* to wear them?). Dungarees aren't acceptable, either.

If you're a punk avoid anything even faintly to do with your private punk life — this includes safety-pin-style brooches, tiny silver razor-blade necklaces, even plastic banana badges. You won't get taken on for fear that you'll be more efficient at smashing filing cabinets and hurling tea urns through windows than typing.

Don't wear anything remotely slinky or sexy — you won't get the job if they think you'll spend your time climbing into the filing cabinet with the office messenger boy.

Finally, don't try to make yourself look *amazingly* good, because, if you get the job, it'll take all your pay packets to keep up the image!

WHAT TO WEAR WHEN YOU'RE — AT A FOOTBALL MATCH

It would be interesting to know what percentage of the male population are footie freaks. If you're going out with one of the minority, then you're dead lucky; if you're going out with one of the majority, then hard luck. Unless, of course, you're one of those strange females who actually *enjoys* watching fellas mindlessly chasing a ball round a field! The day will dawn when you'll have to spend the best part of a precious Saturday shivering on the sidelines, but the right gear can make the whole boring experience more bearable.

What To Wear

Well, as football is, basically, a winter sport, you'd look pretty silly in a summer dress — you'd also freeze. Yes, at last, this is where jeans come to the fore. Trousers of any shape or size are a must, but if you want to please the boy who's dragged you along, your jeans, or, even better, tracksuit bottoms, should be in the boyfriend's team colours (this is really so that the other side's fans can single you out and kick you in the bottom when you bend over to retrieve your rattle).

Wear the brightest, biggest, baggiest sweater you can find, with four other jumpers underneath, and thermal underwear under-neath *them*. You may look like a Michelin man, but at least you'll be warm.

Knit yourself a bobble hat, scarf and mitts in the *right* colours, and buy one of those awful rattles — not specifically to cheer the team on, but the physical effort of swinging the thing keeps you warm.

Don't forget your dad's socks under your boots (preferably hob-nailed for defence!). Duffel coats are useful — they're warm, you can twiddle the toggles around when it gets boring, and hide under the hood when you want to fall asleep.

What Not To Wear

Don't wear a dress. That's really stupid, because it's much more draughty than trousers. Don't wear tights, you'll tear them to shreds on the wooden seats and boards, and don't wear heeled shoes. After the game you'll fall flat on your face trying to walk away — the heels will have sunk into the turf.

It's no good trying to do the model look at a football match, play up the sporty theme instead. It's simpler to avoid anything that looks pretty and feminine, because it'll get ruined with the flying mud, rain-drenched pink Andrex, flying pork-pie missiles and the liquid contents of assorted cans.

Don't wear pink lipstick, it might turn blue with the cold. Avoid red fingernails, too, they clash with blue mottled fingers.

And lastly, for very obvious reasons, don't wear the wrong colours . . .

Don't Monkey Around

IF you haven't already heard, this is the Year of the Monkey, as dictated by the Chinese calendar. Certain boys are *really* going to come into their own this year and it's only fair, we feel, that we give you a few tips on what to look for, because there are a lot of MCM's about — Male Chauvinist Monkeys — and you *don't* want to end up monkeying around with the wrong boy, do you?

ALEC APE

STARTING with . . . Alec Ape. He's the life and soul of the party, the centre of attention, and the source of most of that annoying noise when you enter the room.

This is because he lives up to his name and is a mimic. He can "ape" or imitate anybody from famous comedians to yourself, and we all know how annoying bad Elvis Costello imitations have become these days. So Mr Ape's first annoying trait is that he can be a *bore*.

He'll very rarely notice if *you're* feeling bored stiff, because he's so absorbed with his own fabulously aggravating imitations of Mike Yarwood imitating somebody else.

Unless you enjoy being constantly amused, give Alec Ape a *wide* berth.

BRIAN BABOON

BRIAN BABOON is a much more serious proposition. He's the fiercely possessive type. Baboons are notoriously fierce and will guard their ladies and their territory against anybody in the most *vicious* fashion.

At the same time they have a strong sense of humour and propriety. If you're easy-going, like people and enjoy dancing with lots of boys at parties and not being answerable for your whereabouts *24* hours a day, Brian is NOT your sort.

He'll drive you *mad* with his possessiveness; embarrass you in pubs or at parties by socking boys who so much as talk to you; and bore you silly with his regular routines and love of going to the same well-tried places.

If you feel a bit insecure and would like a permanent chap for the Year of the Monkey, then Brian Baboon will love, cherish and care for you, for ever, and ever, and . . .

CHARLIE CHIMPANZEE

CHARLIE CHIMPANZEE, on the other hand, can be *very* lovable indeed. Just think of those endearing tea-drinking chimps on telly, and you know how lovable a chimp *can* be.

Bear in mind though, as your heart begins to melt towards sweet, funny, handsome Charlie, that he can be very, very mischievous. This can take various forms.

He's quite oblivious of the fact that he's been seen two-timing you with that HORRIBLE girl from round the corner, and can't understand what all the fuss is about.

He's also the sort who thinks it's funny to miss the last bus, or get stranded without an umbrella in a rainstorm, or hide round the corner from where he's supposed to meet you and jump out and scare you silly.

If you can stand all this . . . then Charlie's your darling for sure!

GARY GIBBON

NO peace exists for anybody attracted to Gary Gibbon. Gibbons are the smallest, fastest and most agile of the monkey family and are exhausting company. Remember that Goodies song about "Doing The Funky Gibbon" — well it's all that and *worse*.

Gibbons can be found in squash clubs, rugger clubs, swimming pools, gymnasiums and, of *course*, every disco in the land, where they jump about and gyrate all night long, making a very elegant spectacle of themselves with hardly a bead of sweat in sight. Not fair, is it?

They also eat like pigs and stay like sticks. A trip to the cinema with one (a harrowing experience because they don't like sitting still) is accompanied by a mound of yummy chocolate which has you out in spots by Wednesday and leaves not a pimple on old Gary.

And a word of warning — they love heights, so beware of hill-walking, mountain-climbing or tree-climbing suggestions.

GRAHAM GORILLA

GRAHAM GORILLA is a misleading sort of guy. He's the boy you've been watching for a long time and silently hating, thinking he's stuck up, stand-offish, haughty and aggressive.

Then one evening at a party you see him approaching — horror of horrors! And you find he's *totally* different from how you'd imagined.

His fierce manner hides quite a strong vein of shyness and sensitivity, he's got a terrific sense of humour and is very considerate.

He's probably the biggest challenge of 1980 and worth the effort becuase he's full of surprises — most of them nice ones!

ABC OF LIFE,

APPEARANCE

This is one of the most important aspects of making the most of yourself. It's the very first thing people notice about you and the last thing they'll forget!

It's all very well avidly reading the beauty tips in magazines and wishing that you looked like a model, when you've got to be hoisted out of your armchair even to answer the phone! Don't convince yourself that it's expensive to look good — because that's just not true.

Simple, in this case, is best. When you're neat, clean and tidy, you can't help looking good, and even someone in the most fashionable clothes and make-up can sometimes look slovenly!

Take time over your appearance, because if you're feeling good then you'll radiate good looks as well!

BORROWING

It's all very well saying *never* borrow anything, but as long as you're not a consistent borrower, it often saves you buying something that you'd only use once.

But if you borrow something, make sure you return it promptly and in good condition, and if you have damaged it in any way, then tell the owner. It all depends on the situation but it's often best to buy something new if that happens. Just put yourself in their position, try imagining how *you'd* react, and you should be OK.

CRITICISM

It's easy to be critical of friends and boyfriends. Certain things about your nearest-and-dearest are bound to irritate you, but you should only criticise them rarely, and when you do, try to make your criticisms as constructive as possible.

If, for example, you think your friend treats her boyfriend really badly without knowing it, and you know that he's fed up with it, then it's obvious that a discreet word from you might work wonders. Remember, criticism is always most effective when it comes rarely and when it suggests improvements.

DATES

Dating means, simply, going out with a boy, whether once or quite regularly. The most important thing to remember about dates is that they're *not* the most important thing in the world. All they are, in fact, is just two people spending an evening together and finding out a bit more about each other. So *don't* get it out of all proportion, and you'll find that life can be really good fun.

EDUCATION

We all agree that at times, school can be very, very hard, and it can seem as though you'll *never* do anything right or understand *anything*! But another side of school is that it's the place where most of your friends are, where you can have a great laugh and join in all sorts of hobbies.

Schooldays and college days, of course, are just about the most important days of your life — and if you try your very best, then you'll never have anything to regret.

But even outside school, you're learning all the time — about relationships, about your own feelings, your strengths and weaknesses, about the way other people behave. So if you have a bad experience of any sort, just remember it'll have taught you a lot and strengthened you. It's all education for life!

FLIRTING

If you're unattached and so is he, then great! But if you're not — beware!

GOSSIP

It's hard to resist having a good old gossip, especially when there's a bit of spicy news around.

But in fact gossip never does anyone any good, and it can do real harm. So if you really want to make the most of yourself, get a reputation as the girl who *never* gossips!

HELP

Everybody, at sometime in their life, needs a little help, and it's always nice to try your best to help someone. Friends, especially, deserve some of your time when they're worried or in trouble, and even though sometimes you can't do anything, it's often just a friendly ear they need.

There's also such a thing as helping yourself, though. Whenever *you* need help, don't ever feel too proud to ask — because a problem shared isn't always just a problem halved, it can be solved as well!

INVITATIONS

Invitations are always nice to receive, proof that your company is wanted and that people like being with you.

However, don't always leave invitations to others. It's nice to have friends round now and again, and, of course that goes for boys, too. Don't always leave it to *them* to do the inviting, though, try it out for yourself.

JEALOUSY

This is one of the strongest emotions you can feel, and it never does *anything* for you. But it's also one of the most common emotions and hard to keep down. Really, jealousy isn't feeling envious of what someone else has got, it's all about what *you* haven't got — so only *you* can change that. Anyway, after reading this, you'll be well on your way — won't you!

LOVE AND YOU!

Are you really making the most of yourself, as a friend, as a girlfriend, as a daughter — as yourself, in fact? To get the best out of yourself you've got to work at it. If you sit back, and expect your life to flow happily and smoothly all the time, then you're in for quite a shock! Everybody needs to improve themselves a little, and we've got together a whole alphabet of things for you to polish up on. Go on, read it if you dare . . .!

KISSING
Many girls have a fear of kissing. They feel nervous and anxious before they've ever kissed a boy, thinking: I don't know how to do it! He'll think I'm a baby!

There's only one golden rule to kissing: kiss when you want to, and you'll find that you just *know* how to do it — it comes naturally!

LOVE
Love is wonderful, love is everything they say it is — *when* it's real, because it's so easy to fall in love with the idea of love! So just take time and don't try to convince yourself that you're in love with a boy *too* quickly — because you can get very hurt.

There are also many other kinds of love: love for your parents, your friends — love for anyone in fact whom you care for, and if you love people, then you're definitely making the most of yourself!

MONEY
Everybody would like to have money — and lots of it, but when you haven't got any it can really cause problems.

Magazines often tell you to do odd jobs, etc., and if you try it you'll find that the money really does mount up. So use your imagination to get money *and* use your imagination when you haven't got any. Have some fun for free!

NAGGING
Are you a nag? If something about your friend or boyfriend irritates you, and you badly want to change it, the chances are that you mention it quite a lot.

It's always hard to get people to change their ways, and nagging certainly *isn't* the way to do it. So all we can say is, if you have the tendency to nag — button up.

ORGANISATION
There are so many groups, classes and clubs that are just crying out for members, that you've got no excuse for feeling bored. Pop along to your local library and find out all about all of the organisations in your area.

Learn new things, meet new people and thoroughly enjoy yourself into the bargain!

PARENTS
Your parents know you better than anyone else. They've cared for you through the years and have given you all they could, so it's only right that you should do the same for them.

Many girls find that when they become teenagers they don't really get on with their families as well as they used to, but you've got to realise that they *don't* want to hurt you, and they *don't* want to be nasty — they worry because they love you so much.

QUESTIONS
Questions are a vital part of life. With boyfriends especially it's always nice to show an interest in them, and it's a great way of finding out about each other and building up a relationship.

Get into the habit of asking *yourself* questions, too, about your work, feelings and ideas. That way, you're bound to keep an open mind about things.

RISKS
All we can say here is, *don't take them!* Whether it's risks with a boy, your friends or parents, it's always better to think really carefully about the worst possible outcome — and especially with boys. If they want to take risks and you don't — just tell them, and *never* do anything against your will.

SUCCESS
Success for you is what you make it. Your friend's idea of success might be being chosen to represent the school in a quiz, whereas yours might be something completely different. Success has got to be worked for, though, and being successful *proves* you've been making the most of yourself!

TRUTH
The truth sometimes hurts. And a good friend will know the right time for the whole truth, and when it's kinder to say nothing.

For instance, you might know that your friend is being two-timed. If she seems anxious and unsure, and often asks for your opinion, chances are she wants to hear the truth and it would be a relief.

But if she's immensely happy, then you run a great risk if you destroy her happiness by telling her something that will probably wreck it.

US
It's so easy to think of yourself *all* the time, that you can forget about other people's feelings. "Me, me, me" — if that's how you sound when you talk, then you're bound to appear a bit boring. Try to think of others a little bit more, and they're bound to think a little bit more of *you!*

VENOM
Hate is a terrible thing to feel for anyone. And when you're young, it's not an emotion that you should be feeling too frequently! It doesn't make you look big to cause a scene or have public arguments, it's much better to live and let live! So the next time someone does something that really annoys you, then think to yourself: Does that person really mean it the way I've taken it or am I just imagining it? It may not work *all* the time, but you never know!

WORRY
Everybody has worries, and everybody, at one time or another, can see no way out of their problem. When you're young, everybody tells you that you shouldn't worry, that you're too young to worry — but that never helps.

What you *shouldn't* do is bottle up your worries — tell someone! Even better, try not to get yourself into worrying situations!

X-TRA SPECIAL
This is what you are! Everybody on this earth is a totally unique person — and that's quite a thought!

YOURSELF
There's really not a lot we can say except — take care, and always look after yourself well.

ZEST
You should be feeling full of zest after reading this, because now you're going to start to make the most of yourself! Turn over a new leaf and try really hard to be a nice person — it may sound corny, but it'll work!

SOMETHING OLD...

It's always fun to look back on what's been happening on the music scene at this time of the year.

We've taken a light-hearted look at 1981 and selected some famous faces you're sure to recognise. For some of them it's been business as usual as they produce hit after hit, there's also some bright new talent around, some stars who have cheated a little and "borrowed" ideas from other performers, and some who sadly haven't made it at all this year.

See if you agree!

STATUS QUO. Not one golden oldie here, but four! And really they don't look at all that different now than when they exploded onto the charts with a song called "Pictures Of Matchstick Men" in 1968.

So, Status Quo not only have the privilege of being among the top hit-making bands, but also one of the longest running. Francis Rossi and Alan Lancaster have been playing together since 1962, but it wasn't till Rick Parfitt joined the group six years later that things really started to happen for them.

Perhaps this was just a coincidence . . .

CLIFF RICHARD. None of you, or none of us for that matter, are old enough to remember Cliff when he had his first hit in 1958 with a song called "Move It!" It got to number 3 in the charts and stayed around for eleven weeks.

The rest, as they say, is history and not a year goes by without Cliff hitting the headlines.

No-one would deny him the success he's achieved and you can't help but admire the way his music appeals to all age groups.

What we'd like to know is, how he manages to stay so young-looking. Does he know something we don't know?

PAUL McCARTNEY. Most people are well informed about Paul's vastly famous career from the Beatles' first hit "Love Me Do" in 1962 right up to this day with his super group Wings.

Paul seems to have the Midas touch and like Cliff Richard he seems to get even better looking as he gets older!

Apart from being a brilliant singer/songwriter, he's a great solo performer, businessman and, according to his family, a really super dad.

Some people have all the luck!

DIANA ROSS. For a lady who has an almost grown-up family, Diana isn't doing too badly. Apart from a short spell when she didn't reign "supreme," she's been topping the charts consistently since her first hit with the Supremes in 1967 with a song called "Reflections."

When she realised that disco music was making some people very rich, Diana claimed that she could, "Do that stuff with my eyes shut." She did, and proved that there's still a lot to come from this super singer.

SOMETHING NEW...

ORCHESTRAL MANOEUVRES IN THE DARK.
Paul and Andy of OMITD have succeeded in bringing synth music to the fore as an intelligent, lyrical, real form of music.

They've taken care to ensure that it's their music people associate with them and not some clockwork dummy image. So far they've experimented far and beyond other performers working in this field, a move that will guarantee that OMITD will be around for a lot longer than other less creative musicians.

PAULINE MURRAY.
Pauline is a lady who's taking on the music scene on her terms. She's successfully created a niche in the market to suit her music and, though her emergence as a solo performer may not have been as explosive as others, she's quietly and confidently built up a strong following.

Her sense of humour is another asset that should stand her in good stead — not many people are zany enough to play with a band called the Invisible Girls who are all males!

STRAY CATS.
The runaway success of the crazy-quiffed trio has been quite phenomenal. Long before the band had a hit record or even a recording contract there was an incredible buzz amongst talent scouts, the music press and fellow musicians, about their exciting brand of music.

But they held out till someone offered them a contract with enough money behind it and also one that gave them the opportunity to do things the way they wanted.

The three Americans may not be your idea of the perfect guy but their music is definitely a hit. It's given rockabilly music a whole new sound that isn't steeped in the past but new and very exciting.

ADAM ANT.
Adam Ant was just what the doctor ordered last year when he burst on to the pop scene.

Although Adam had been working for a couple of years it wasn't till the original Ants left to join Bow Wow Wow and he formed a new band that he had his first hit with "Dog Eat Dog."

Adam is really a modern-day hero with the looks, talent and image to take the Ants to the top and keep them there. The 80's will surely go down in music history as the years of the Ant!

Now turn to page 90 for Something Borrowed and Something Blue!

SOMETHING BORROWED...

SHAKIN' STEVENS.
Elvis Presley lives on — in the shape of Shakin' Stevens.

How Presley's fans feel about the man, we're not too sure, but Shakin' is certainly cashing in on the King's recipe for success. Not only does the slick-haired singer copy Elvis's clothes, he sounds like him and even has Elvis's gyrations duplicated jerk for jerk.

His dark looks have made him a hit with male and female fans alike, and we suppose that as long as there's a market for the Presley-style sound there will be people like Shakin' popping up in the charts.

TOYAH.
We bet a lot of you had forgotten all about Lene Lovich till Toyah came along. She sounds so like the Lene, who had super hits with "Lucky Number" and "Say When," that's it's uncanny.

Toyah definitely doesn't *look* like Lene, but listen to her vocals and we're sure you'll find more than a passing resemblance to Lene's style of performing. Something else the two ladies have in common is that they've both been the subject of TV documentaries — an honour reserved for the chosen few.

After Lene's was screened however, the lady just didn't seem able to top her initial success. Toyah, take note!

GARY NUMAN.
Listening to some of Gary's music is like hearing David Bowie on an "off" day. But, let's be fair to Gary. At least, unlike some artistes, Gary admits that he's been greatly influenced by Bowie. Though we think it goes a bit deeper than that.

It's a pity,however,that Gary has been unable to take a leaf from David's book on learning to cope with success. Perhaps then he'd still be touring and letting his fans hear his music first hand — after all, there's no substitute for the real thing.

BRYAN FERRY.
Among the things Bryan has "borrowed" from other performers is a repertoire of classic, standard hits to which he's added his magical touch.

Perhaps the most famous tunes that have the Ferry treatment are Bob Dylan's "A Hard Rain's A-Gonna Fall" and "Smoke Gets In Your Eyes" that was first a hit for The Platters in 1959!

But we don't mind what he pinches because he does everything so well we bet he could make the National Anthem into a top ten hit!

SOMETHING BLUE

LES McKEOWN. When Les released his album "All Washed Up," he said he'd chosen the title to prove to his critics that he wasn't! The album however didn't do all that well and Les took to ligging around on the other side of the Atlantic with Britt Ekland. So, what's the star, who was once part of The Bay City Rollers, been up to?

Well, things just haven't worked out for Les without the rest of the band. They're all living it up in America and enjoying some success with the American teen market — they always were a few years behind their British counterparts.

Meanwhile, though, Les certainly looks as though he's well and truly — washed up . . . .

SMOKEY. Though the band still seem to be popular in Germany, things don't seem to be happening for them in Britain.

Smokey have, however, had their fair share of success since their first hit "If You Think You Know How To Love Me" back in 1975.

Perhaps the punk movement was in some way responsible for the band's demise. Certainly it shook up the record industry and gave it a much-needed spring clean, and since then the band seem to have disappeared in a puff of smoke . . . .

THE OSMONDS. The Osmonds have just one thing going for them — their teeth — because they help the incredibly rich performers to keep smiling despite the fact that they're no longer teeny idols.

The Osmonds success seems to have waned since the boys started to get married. Not that we're blaming their wives for the decline, but it now looks as though the family are much too content sitting around at home to go out on the road.

Maybe they're busy working on a second generation group — what a thought!

LEIF GARRETT. Leif is one of those unfortunate people who's been made into a star for no apparent reason. He fits in with the American picture of the good-looking, young blond-haired guy they go wild for. Leif unfortunately doesn't seem to have the talent to go with all the hype.

We're not denying that Leif is a really nice guy — he is — but apart from good looks and nice personality he has nothing. His main ambition is to be taken seriously as a rock singer, but so far all his records have flopped dismally.

The best advice we can give him is to hang on to his skateboard — maybe someone will remember him for that!

EARS TO IT!

You don't have to spend pounds on earrings — with a bit of imagination you only need to spend a few pence — if you make your own!

Pale purple sea shell.

Cocktail parasol with raffia attached.

Christmas tree bauble.

Earrings are very popular just now, with more and more people getting their ears pierced – often two or three times.

The jewellery stands in shops offer an enormous range of sparkly, brightly coloured things to hang from your lobes – many of which seem to be a bit too expensive for what they are, especially if you're prone to losing them!

This year, we've seen a lot of huge, brassy dangling earrings around, which have an ethnic African or Egyptian influence – but anything goes – as long as it's large!

It's very easy and cheap to make your own earrings and the great thing about it is that they'll be unique – you're not likely to see everyone else wearing a pair exactly the same as yours, which is another problem with shop-bought earrings.

Once you start thinking about making your own earrings – the possibilities are endless!

Curtain rings, old necklaces, wooden beads, toys, buttons, are just a few of the things you could use. Even those tiny plastic toys you get inside crackers would make great earrings.

Have a look round the house – there are bound to be hundreds of things you could use!

The earrings shown here were all made from collected objects with the help of a strong glue and the odd coating of enamel paint. They're the handiwork of Deborah Allison, a first year fashion student at Ravensbourne College of Art and Design.

"I started to make earrings because a lot of the ones on the market were too expensive and not individual enough," Deborah told us. "At one time I had as many as fifty different earrings, made from anything I could get my hands on – like marbles, coloured paper clips, and fuses in different colours.

"The good thing about them is that they're just for fun and they don't cost anything, so it doesn't matter if you lose them, as earrings do tend to drop off very easily."

Earring Aids:

If you're interested in making yourself some earrings, the clips can be bought from craft shops, bead shops and street market stalls, or you could send for them. *Creative Bead Craft Ltd., Unit 26, Chiltern Trading Estate, Earl Howe Road, Holmer Green, High Wycombe, Bucks.*, do a small order service, and have a wide selection of beads and earrings clips. Write to them for details, enclosing a stamped addressed envelope.

Remember – don't wear anything too large, heavy or breakable on your ears!

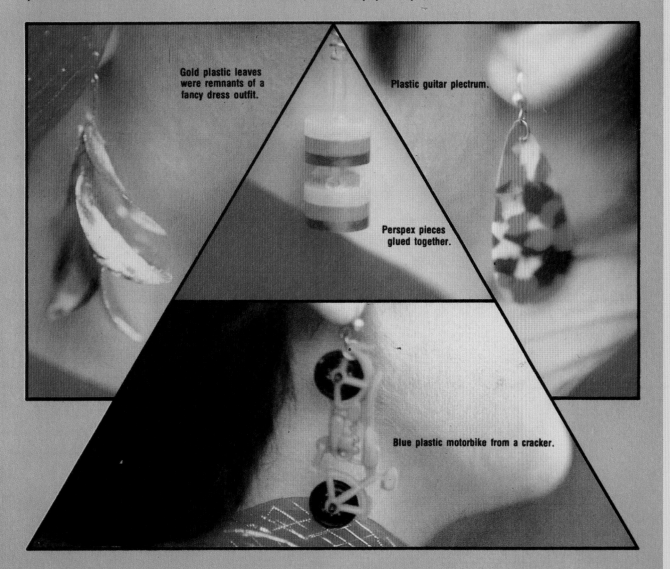

Gold plastic leaves were remnants of a fancy dress outfit.

Plastic guitar plectrum.

Perspex pieces glued together.

Blue plastic motorbike from a cracker.

New Looks

TARTAN TRENDS . . .

Tartan never seems to go out of fashion — it looked good on Bonnie Prince Charlie and looks just as good 1982 style! Mix your tartans and tweeds for a really original look — add knickerbockers, waistcoats and a huge scarf slung over your shoulder — and you'll be all set for your own Highland fashion fling!

. . . or are they? If you get the feeling you've seen the new 1982 fashions before – you probably have – in your history books! This year, the designers have gone as far afield as places like Turkey and Lapland to bring you clothes with an ethnic, peasant flavour – and as far back in time as Bonnie Prince Charlie for the colourful tartans we'll be seeing a lot of. The Pirate styles are still as exciting as they were in Errol Flynn's day – and the romantics can look forward to an even frillier new year!

SWASHBUCKLING STYLE

Pirate styles are still very much part of the picture for 1982 fashion — in true Errol Flynn tradition! Look out for swashbuckling touches like sashes, billowing pants, puffy sleeves, lace-up tunics, thick gold bangles right down to fall-down socks. It all adds up to one of the most adventurous, exciting looks around!

FOLKLORE FASHION
The ethnic influence! Smocks, dirndl skirts, boleros, embroidered blouses, gaucho pants and jacquard socks are all coming back in style! Pile on the layers — not just to keep you warm! Use your imagination and mix different prints together for a really colourful peasant look!

New Looks

ROMANTIC RUFFLES

Take a chance on romance! Go for pretty, softer new styles — ruffled blouses, black velvet bows — with lots of frills and lace. The new romantic styles include knickerbockers, breeches and capes — in old-fashioned fabrics like velvet, satin and taffeta. So take a trip back in time to discover a brand-new way of romantic dressing!

All the things you'll find hardest to understand about your boyfriend, and the things he's most worried about, are all here. If you want to know exactly what makes him tick, just read on!

APPEARANCE

Girls aren't the only ones who are obsessed by their appearance — boys are, too! As they reach adolescence, boys are only too aware of the way they look.

They worry about whether they're muscular or puny, whether they've got anything resembling a beard or not, and whether their voices have broken or not. Even in these days of equality, there's still a lot of pressure on boys to be big and strong and "manly."

So stop and think how sensitive and anxious a boy is likely to be if he's small, or skinny, or a late developer. It might help you understand him a bit better!

BRAGGING

Most boys boast a lot — they can't help it. They boast about their bikes, motor bikes, stereos and girls. Boys together have a bad influence on one another — well, they certainly often feel pressurised by their mates into pretending that they're doing things that they're actually miles away from experiencing.

So beware if you hear a boy boasting about his success with girls. Don't jump to the conclusion that a girl's "easy" just because you overhear a boy saying so (especially if you hear a boy saying so!).

COMMITMENT

Many boys are afraid of having a really deep relationship with a girl. Younger boys want to go out with their mates and they usually only want to see a girl now and then (while still being able to boast that they've got a girlfriend). Older

boys like to play the field. There are some boys who aren't afraid of committing themselves, but they're unusual.

DOUBLE STANDARDS

For hundreds of years the Double Standard has ruled — and ruined —

women's lives. It means that men feel it's all right for them to have lots of girls, but not for girls to have a lot of boyfriends. They also want one special girlfriend or wife — and if *she* goes around with other men, that's unforgivable!

This crazy (and unfair) notion is dying out, but there are still boys around who demand faithfulness from their girlfriends whilst happily two-timing them themselves.

FIGHTING

When boys are little, fighting is never taken seriously. Sometimes, mothers and fathers encourage it! But when boys grow up they fight because it's difficult to control their anger at a time when all their emotions are much stronger than before. Also, a lot of boys fight because it makes them look big — or at least they *think* it does.

GANGS

Most boys want to be in some sort of gang. When they are in a gang, there's a lot of pressure on each individual to behave only in ways which are acceptable to the gang. This might include aggro at football matches, boasting about their sexual experiences, or getting drunk. Most boys won't like doing a lot of the things that the gang says he must, but it takes a really strong character to stand out against it and refuse to take part.

IMMATURITY

Most girls find that boys their own age are a bit immature. This is because girls mature, physically and emotionally, a couple of years earlier than boys. A girl of thirteen or fourteen, for example, will find that boys her own age are not only pretty childish but actually more physically immature than her as well.

Most girls therefore tend to go for older boys, until the late teens, when things tend to even out.

KISSING

Everybody's interested in kissing. In general, though, boys don't have the same kind of approach to it as girls do. A girl's likely to get interested in a boy first and *then* want to kiss him. A boy is more likely to want to kiss a girl — *any* girl — just to see what it's like.

A kiss may mean very different things to the two people involved. You might be crazy about him, but he may be just experimenting. So beware!

BOY FACTS!

LOVE

People need to feel loved to be happy and secure, but boys especially are often scared of admitting this. They feel that if they say they love their girlfriends, they'll be trapped. The last thing they want is for their mates to think that they're under a girl's thumb. So even a boy who does love you may not admit it — even to himself.

OPENNESS

Complete honesty in relationships is worth working for, but with boys you really will have to work for it. For a start, most boys are afraid of hurting girls so they tell them what they think they want to hear, not what's really true.

Your boyfriend might tell you you look great even when you know your new dress doesn't suit you. And he'll tell you he never looks at other girls when you know he does.

Total honesty really is the best basis for a relationship, though — then, you're likely to stay friends whatever happens!

PUBS

Drinking is one thing boys all seem to think is masculine. Lots of boys get drunk at parties and go to pubs when they're under-age just to prove how tough they are. Unfortunately, there's nothing that looks worse or less appealing than a drunk!

If your guy shows signs of thinking that drinking is something big, tell him in no uncertain terms just how stupid you think drunks are — boring and unsexy. Then, maybe he'll think twice before trying to prove himself in such a daft way!

QUESTIONS

He doesn't know much about you and you don't know much about him, right? Well, it makes sense for you to ask each other questions, especially about sex, love and marriage and your attitudes to them.

ROMANCE

Romance is all about the excitement which surrounds getting to know someone of the opposite sex, being attracted to them and becoming fascinated by them.

The thing to remember, though, is that a boy will enjoy things in private with you that he'd never, ever dream of admitting to when he's with his mates. So show some tact and don't remind him of romantic things he's done and said, especially when he's with a gang of his toughest mates!

TENDERNESS

Most girls need tenderness from their boyfriends, but some boys are reluctant to give it. It's not that they don't feel it: they get embarrassed and shy.

You may have to teach your boyfriend to be affectionate, but don't despair — it *can* be done!

UGLY HABITS

Lots of boys act in some pretty terrible (disgusting!) ways when they're with other boys. Some of them think it impresses girls. Things like dirty talk, filthy jokes and constant swearing aren't a sign that your boyfriend is a yob, though.

It might just be that he's trying to impress you. If it doesn't impress you (and it shouldn't!) tell him so.

WOLFS

Sooner or later, you're going to meet a *wolf* — a boy with wandering hands. If he's a stranger and you're enjoying a slow dance with him at the disco when he suddenly starts to grope you, then you should just break away from him. You don't have to make a big scene about it — just be firm.

If your steady boyfriend starts to get a bit much, though, that's different: he's probably getting carried away by his feelings for you as well as seeing how far he can get! Now is the time to have a serious talk about where to draw the line. Make sure you draw the line where *you* want it.

YOUNGER BOYS

Don't write off younger boys (that is, boys of your own age) as possible boyfriends. They may be smaller than you and more immature, but the nice thing about them is that they're likely to be mates with you first, and then, as they grow up, change into something more.

Younger boys are more likely to treat you with the respect you deserve than some older boys who like to prove how grown-up and powerful they are by treating you like a child.

ZZZzzz . . .

A lot of boys are boring and are more likely to send you to sleep than to set your heart racing. Unfortunately, a lot of girls put up with boys like this because they think having a boyfriend (even a boring one) is better than not having a boyfriend at all.

Well, that's rubbish — and one sure way of putting you off other boyfriends for life!

THE OTHER DALLAS STARS...

OK, own up, all you telly addicts out there — you can bring out your stetsons from behind the sofa because it's "Dallas" time!

Don't you ever feel life is boring when you're not engrossed in the Ewing exploits?

Well, wakey, wakey, because here we have the Southfork superstars on this very page, with of course some lesser-known stars as addicted to the series as we are. We asked some of our favourite people who *their* favourite was, and here's what they told us . . . Read on and find out that everybody loves a Ewing . . .

STEVE STRANGE
Sue Ellen must have the most mobile mouth ever. It can go in twenty different directions at once! She's equal with Pam who must have the most mobile **eyes** ever — they can go in twenty different directions at once.

ROB HALFORD — Judas Priest
The best character isn't even in it now, it's Kirstin. She was so scheming and would stop at nothing to get what she wanted. She was one lady with absolutely no scruples.

THERESE BAZAR — Dollar
Miss Ellie drives me up the wall. She's so tolerant and such a martyr . . . I shudder when she gives her all-forgiving smile — and that's about fifteen times a minute!

BOB GELDOF
I don't really have much time to watch "Dallas" now because I'm usually so busy, but for sheer star appeal you can't beat Pam. She wobbles a bit, too. I wonder if you've got to have a wobble to get a part?

PHIL LYNOTT
It's got to be J.R., the evil one himself. It's wonderful that when he does something really nasty, he always manages that sly smile.

SHEENA EASTON
Oh, Sue Ellen's my favourite because it would give me great pleasure to see her get throttled. I'd really enjoy *that* episode.

HOW TO HANDLE HIM...

The first time you meet him, you'll think he's *great*, no faults, no nasty habits — in short, you'll think he's just perfect. Once you get to know him better, and you're seeing him on a regular basis, though, you're bound to uncover a few not so nice things about him. Next time his bossiness, his moodiness or his wandering hands act get too much for you to bear, don't hurl your handbag at him — instead, read on and find out how to handle him!

THE WANDERING HANDS ACT

Every boyfriend from time to time gets carried away by his feelings and this can pose problems for his girlfriend.

There's only one way to react if your boyfriend tries to go too far physically (too far being quite simply what *you* regard as too far) and that's to stop him at once.

The best thing to do is to change the mood abruptly. Break away, say, "Stop that" sharply and get out of his clutches. Make it clear you're annoyed, and make it clear right *then* that you have limits, and tell him exactly what they are. A serious talk will cool him off *wonderfully*.

THE SOULFUL LOOK IN THE EYES ACT

If he's really nuts about you, you might begin to feel pressurised to spend all your time with him and to reassure him constantly that you really care.

If this is the case, it's very important to break away from his clutches *before* you begin to find him a drag and all the good things about your relationship fade into the past.

Tell him straight that you don't want to get too serious too soon.

Make a point of going out without him (with girlfriends maybe) at least a couple of times a week. If he moans and complains about it — well, you might even have to start thinking about ending the relationship.

THE I WANT TO BE FREE ACT

Some boys get attacks of restlessness. He might be fed up with his job or his school, or horror of horrors, he may be feeling a bit cooped up in his relationship with *you*.

His restlessness might show itself in depression, or in attacks of rather weird aggressive behaviour: playing around and doing stupid things, maybe even getting into trouble of some sort. If he's generally restless — that is, he's just fed up with life in general — all you can do is try to get him to talk about it in order to sort out some practical action.

If he's restless about his relationship with you, however, you can do more. Don't cling on for dear life, however panicked you are.

If you desperately want to keep him, the natural reaction is to say how much you love him and to beg and plead with him not to give you up. But the best thing to do is actually the opposite.

Play it *cool*. Go out without him sometimes. Don't keep ringing him up. Give the impression that you're having a great time and that you certainly don't depend on *him*.

That'll give him a chance to feel free and unhassled — and the chances are that he'll then realise how much he does like you!

THE I DON'T CARE ABOUT YOU ACT

Carelessness can show in many ways. Maybe he says he'll phone you at a certain time and then doesn't bother or forgets? Or he borrows money from you and that's the last you hear of it? Or he's careless with things that belong to you?

The best way to treat this nasty situation is to give him a short, sharp talking-to. Tell him you're fed up being taken for granted, that he's getting so don't-care in his attitude that you're sure it's best to pack it all in and finish with each other.

There's just the *chance* that he'll say "OK!" But if he does, he wasn't worth keeping anyway!

More likely, though, he'll realise how important you are to him and start taking care again.

So . . . whatever moods your boyfriend gets into, you ought to be able to handle them now!

Who's A Pretty Boy,

Long, long ago, the last thing on a boy's mind was how to attract a girl. He just dotted her one on the head with his trusty club and hauled her off to his cave.

Today, though, life's a lot more complicated, and relationships are a lot more subtle. The me-Tarzan-you-Jane approach doesn't work now that there are more fellas around than girls (what a nice arrangement!) and boys are thinking more and more about the image they project.

We spoke to some boys and asked them how they saw themselves in the attractiveness stakes and jokingly asked how they'd rate themselves on a scale of 1-10. Here's what we came up with . . .

Steven, who's eighteen, works in a bank.

"I'm pretty average really; average height and build so I'd guess I'd rate a five. I'm just not the sort of bloke who could pull birds by sheer looks alone. If you put me in a shop window, there'd be no queues!

"I've had a couple of nice girl-friends, who were really special, and luckily they got to know the real me first – I can't say it was my looks really. My present girlfriend thinks I'm fantastic, so who am I to argue?

"I'm still living at home, which is a bit restrictive. I suppose I dream of branching out, getting a flat and changing my image completely. I'd love to be someone like Sting. I can't help feeling that I'm missing out on some things. Maybe I should be more outrageous and daring in my life – but even if the chances came along I don't know how I'd react."

Steven sounds like a pretty honest, reliable guy, a boy to trust — but is that the type the girls really go for? Here's Paul, and he's just the opposite. He's good looking *and* he knows it.

"Ten I'd rate – sure, why not! I have no bother attracting girls. I suppose I look the part. I'm pleased with the way I look. Life must be a lot less interesting if you're ugly. Knowing girls fancy you gives you confidence.

"I'm never short of dates but if it's too easy I lose interest and cool off. I enjoy the chatting-up bit. Mind you, I never crawl. But if a girl plays a little bit hard to get, she's got me interested.

"Sometimes I do get the feeling I'm putting on an act all the time, trying to impress. I hear myself trotting out the same old lines with a new girl. Sometimes I don't like myself much and I get fed up playing the scene, but I couldn't see myself sticking to one girl. What a waste!"

Paul certainly knows what he wants, and a lot of girls find that attractive. Bob, on the other hand, hasn't got any confidence at all. He's still at school.

"I don't rate at all. I'm sixteen and I look about thirteen, and I don't know one girl who isn't put off by that. They all go for the big guys, the guys who look older than they do, so that means I'd have to get someone at primary school!

"I think girls go for looks first and foremost. I mean at a disco, if you ask a girl to dance she gives you the once over and if you don't match up she'll turn you down. It's pretty unfair.

"Maybe I'm not meeting the right girls but the ones I meet, especially at school, are pretty hard. Although everyone says it's personality that counts, they want a fella with looks and a bit of cash to spend on them – and I don't have either."

Are we really that bad? Tony is a guy who has the looks but he hasn't got a girlfriend at the moment. He's an assistant in a photographic shop.

"I'd rate five on a good day! I've never gone out with a girl for longer than two months and it's been ages since I asked a girl out because I get more and more scared of being

turned down. It gets worse as you get older, I think. You tend to take things more seriously.

"It's rotten being a bloke, having to be pushy, having to chat up a girl when you're just not sure whether she's interested or not.

"There have been a couple of times I've met a girl and well, kind of backed off at the last minute. Afterwards, I go over what she's said in my head and half the time I realise that it was all my fault. I should have been more positive – asked to see her home, asked her out, at least asked for her phone number, but I always lose my nerve **and** the girl.

"It's just a basic lack of confidence in myself. It even extends to my work – if I was more pushy I'd get a great job as a photographer on a paper maybe, instead of wasting my time here."

Are girls so frightening, then? Are they only after guys with looks? Next, we asked a few of the monsters themselves — the girls — for their opinions of boys, and they weren't shy to tell us what they thought!

Julie is a girl who has strong feelings, and surprisingly, the boys she doesn't like are the nice ones . . .

"Nice guys are boring. I don't even like handsome types – I like interesting types. Somehow I'm always more attracted to boys who treat me badly – who don't phone when they say they

Then?

will, who stand me up, or two-time me. It's much more exciting!

"Sure, I shed a lot of tears but I'd hate to be stuck in the safe 'two nights a week and every weekend' routine some of my friends are in."

That's quite a surprising attitude and one probably not many girls share, but it takes all kinds. Karen is good looking and she freely admits to judging a bloke by his looks.

"I'm lucky because I can pick and choose the type of guy I want. I go weak at the knees for skinny blokes who've got good dress sense. If a guy doesn't make the effort with how he looks then I'm not interested.

"I know I couldn't go out with someone who wasn't good looking, because every time we went out I'd feel embarrassed with him and I'd be wishing I was with someone else."

So what about the ideal imaginary muscle man? The truth is, he just doesn't exist. So next time you feel you've got no chance with a boy just stop and think that he's probably feeling as terrified as you!

The thing to remember is that when you're looking through the eyes of love, *everybody's* gorgeous!

GETTING FRUITY! Something For (Almost) Nothing

Make yourself a bag that's roomy enough to hold schoolbooks, shopping and all your junk — it couldn't be easier! All you need to make the kind of bag shown here is a piece of denim or canvas, any old leftover paint lying around the house and one or two fruits or vegetables.

The sort of material you use to make the bag is really up to you, but it should be strong and fairly light in colour. Off-white denim or canvas is ideal and a piece 50 cms. by 115 cms., which is the amount you need, shouldn't cost much more than £1.

Once you've got hold of the material, the first thing you have to do to make your bag is to print a design on it. Take one of the fruits or vegetables which you've chosen — an apple, for instance — and cut it in half.

Now lay your piece of material out flat on a table, or on the floor. Using a small brush, coat the cut side of your fruit with a thin coat of paint and then print this on to your fabric.

Repeat this procedure all over the material, printing either at random or building up a pattern. You can, of course, use different fruits and print them in various colours. For instance, we used an apple printed in orange, red and black.

You can use any type of household paint to decorate your bag although the easiest to apply is non-drip emulsion — don't try to use water colours as these will wash out.

Most fruits and vegetables will print well as long as they aren't *too* juicy. You can't, for instance, print a plum very easily as it'll squash. If you decide to use an onion, leave it in a warm place for a few hours after cutting it in half, because this will make the rings stand out more and give a better print.

Once you've printed your material, hang it up and leave it to dry for about 12 hours.

WHEN the pattern is dry, cut two strips, each about 8 cms. wide, from one of the shorter edges of the material — these are to make the handles. Take one of these strips and fold it in half lengthways with the pattern inside. Now sew the strip along one short edge and one long edge to make a tube. Using a knitting needle, blunt end first, push the closed edge down the tube, thus turning the handle the right way out and revealing the pattern. Do this with both handles.

Next, take the large piece of material and fold in a strip about 1 cm. wide along each short edge. Stitch these and then attach the handles to them by sewing their

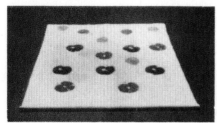

The material with the fruit prints on it.

Cut two strips off the material. These are used to make the handles.

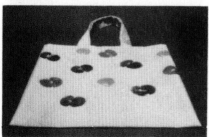

The bag!

ends to these hems, leaving a gap of about 20 cms. between each end.

You should now have a large, flat piece of material with a handle at each end. Now fold this in half, with the pattern on the inside, and sew along the edges, leaving you with an inside out bag. Finally, iron the seams open and turn the bag inside out to reveal the pattern.

With a little care, and about two hours work, you'll have made yourself a shopping bag, one that's pretty unique and totally different from anything you could buy in the shops!

I Saw Him First!

A Jackie short story specially written by Winnie Czulinski.

HIS name was Paul and he was gorgeous. Everyone thought so – especially me. Naturally, I fancied him like mad – everyone did! – but just for once, I seemed to have the advantage over all my giggling rivals.

I had discovered, by means of a great deal of effort and a bit of very unsubtle detective work, that Paul lived just three streets away from me and that we went to the same school, although he was in a different form. There was, however, a Snag.

Martine. Actually, she was (occasionally) my friend, but not so's you'd notice. Not that you could help noticing Martine, with her glossy black hair, glossy red lips and glossy-magazine clothes.

She also lived near Paul and went to the same school, and I lived in constant fear of the moment that he would notice her and be helplessly dazzled.

I would never, ever have wanted Paul to *know* that I was chasing him, of course – a girl has her pride. But I certainly wasn't going to let that female piranha have him without putting up a bit of a fight.

So, on a rather nice, crisp winter morning, I decided to begin "Operation Paul." I knew (because of all the time I'd spent snooping around) exactly when he was due to walk past the end of my street, so I dawdled along as slowly as I could, praying that Martine wouldn't arrive at the same time.

About five minutes later, after I'd looked at everything I could possibly look at, then examined it in minute detail again, Paul appeared.

I pretended to be very interested in

she breathed, "but of course, it was twice as nice meeting you and Ron there . . ."

What you might term a faint glimmer of hope began to flicker through my deepest, darkest despair. She and Paul hadn't met on purpose and they hadn't been alone . . .

". . . he did suggest that we should get Rona to make up a four one night." She paused for effect. "Could be fun," she purred, batting her eyelashes.

Paul looked up, rather enthusiastically, I thought. "I sort of suspected you were quite keen on Ron! And if Rona'll come with me, we can definitely get something organised!"

Paul just gaped after her and I sagged inwardly. I was no competition at all after that little display.

"Well," I said, with a light laugh. "Back to the grind!"

"Mmm . . ," said Paul, in a very absent-minded voice. I gave up. He would never be mine.

BY the end of the day, of course, I had recovered a bit, and decided to make another go. Maybe I wasn't as devastating as Martine, but I wasn't bad. Mum was always telling me I was quite pretty.

It did bother me a bit, though, that mothers tend to say that even if their child has a face that would frighten a horse . . . But I put that disturbing thought to the back of my mind and decided to walk home by way of Paul's house.

He'd be almost bound to catch me up, I thought, so I wandered along quite slowly.

He didn't, of course, and I was back in the dumps again before I got to my own front door. Martine must have caught him, I thought miserably, and he's so besotted, he hasn't the strength to resist.

Next morning, though, he was hanging around on my street corner, just for a change. As I walked towards him, trying to look cool and unconcerned, he smiled straight at me and I felt myself flush scarlet all over.

". . . Adam and the Ants con-

"Thanks," she said, stiffly. "I'll think about it and let you know.."

She smiled as if the effort would kill her and stalked off as soon as we got to the school gates.

Once we were alone, I heard Paul take a deep breath and say, "Great girl, Martine. She must've known that I've been wanting to get to know you for ages. It was nice of her to arrange all this."

"Mind you –" He looked at the ground, and coughed slightly. "She can be a bit overpowering, can't she?"

I choked, and he had to slap me on the back before I recovered enough to walk into class. What a good thing, I thought, as he put his arm round me, that some of us were more – subtle about things . . .

THE world spun round and Martine – seemed to disappear. When the world stopped spinning round, she appeared again, looking red and angry and deflated and blazing mad! She didn't make a fool of herself by explaining that he'd got it all wrong, though.

She was far too sophisticated and cool for that and she wasn't going to ruin her image, even for Paul . . .

I became vaguely aware that Paul was speaking to me. "That is, if you don't mind, Rona?"

I hesitated exactly two seconds. "It sounds smashing to me!" I said, grinning all over my face.

He moved a little closer. Not so close that it made much difference, but still . . .

I turned to Martine and said,

103

I'd fancied Paul for ages — but so had Martine. And what chance did I have against Westdale School's answer to Debbie Harry . . . ?

two horrible little boys having a snow-ball fight on the other side of the road and waited until he called out to me before I looked round.

"Rona! Rona, wait a minute!"

Gratified, I turned and watched him squelch up to me. His voice made my blood run sort of hot and cold at the same time, but, of course, I wasn't going to let him know that.

"Hello," I said, as calmly as I could.

"Hello, Paul," said Martine, appearing as if by magic from a side-street.

PAUL turned. "Oh — Martine! I didn't expect to see you this early!"

"No," I said, gritting my teeth.

"Nor did I!"

She ignored me. "You're looking good this morning, Paul," she murmured, batting her eyelashes. Paul blushed.

"Er — thanks, Martine. Why don't you walk along with us?" he said, like the gentleman he is.

Why he had to choose that particular moment to be a gentleman, I don't know, but we walked along together — in total silence. I thought the sultry looks Martine was casting at Paul would melt the snow and I spent the rest of the walk dreaming up terrible things that could happen to her between here and the school gates.

"Well," she breathed as we reached the playground, "simply must dash to — biology!" She ran her eyes over Paul as if she would have just loved to experiment on him and wiggled off.

cert . . .," he was saying. "I was thinking —."

"Yes?" said Martine, sidling up from somewhere behind him and planting herself very deliberately between us.

I closed my eyes and thought very uncharitable thoughts, about how many years I'd get in jail for strangling someone with their own scarf. When I opened them, she had put her arm through Paul's. She smiled at me, smugly.

"Paul was telling you about the wonderful time we had last night, was he? I can't remember when I enjoyed myself so much!"

I FELT my mouth open and I shut it sharpish, feeling more of a fool than I could bear. What wonderful time? When? Where? I thought desperately. To add insult to injury, I also dropped all my books (from shock) and had to get down on my hands and knees to gather all the bits and pieces together.

I must have looked really awkward, scrambling about in the snow while the immaculate Martine looked on, sneering faintly.

"Here, Rona," Paul was saying. "Let me give you a hand."

I collected my books and what remained of my dignity, thanked Paul as graciously as I could, and the three of us walked along together.

At least, Paul and Martine were together — I was relegated to the iciest area on the outside of the pavement.

Paul was looking a bit pink for some reason and he didn't seem to want to look at Martine. It was so obvious he was really keen on her — boys are like that . . .

She didn't give me a look in, of course — she kept talking all the way along the road.

"I always did like the coffee bar."

innocently. "Where do you think Ron would like to go? All this was your idea, so it's only fair that you should choose!"

We all have to go on first dates at some point in our lives and they're not always successful. But why? Read on to find out how to avoid those first-date disasters!

FIRST DATE PITFALLS

YOU'VE got yourself a brand-new boy and you're about to meet him for your first real date. Everything looks lovely. It'll be wonderful. Nothing can possibly go wrong . . .

Except *First-Date Pitfalls*—and that's the end of another promising romance. They're the mistakes that make the first-date girl clutch her brow and moan, "I shouldn't have done *that*!" as her new guy hares off up the road in a cloud of dust!

Here are just a few:

I SHOULDN'T HAVE . . . got his name wrong. His name's Bill and he reckons he's made such a good impression on you that you'll remember him for ever. Or even longer. But you turn up for that first date and say, "Hi, Sid, . . . er, Frank . . . er, Arthur?" This gives him the impression that he's not quite as memorable as he thought he was and he's likely to go right off you immediately.

But forgetting his name isn't as bad as forgetting what he looks like and walking right past him as he stands at the meeting place with a welcoming smile.

I SHOULDN'T HAVE . . . eaten garlic. Chomping through a garlic-riddled meal before going on that first date isn't a good idea. It'll put him right off the idea of kissing you, and if you've really overdone the garlic flavouring he may even wear a gas mask, which will make conversation difficult. Don't kid yourself that you've had a lucky escape and the garlic has scared him off 'cos he's a vampire. He probably isn't.

I SHOULDN'T HAVE . . . introduced him to my best friend. Not if your best friend is a beautiful man-eater, you shouldn't. It's no fun turning up at the disco to show off your fabulous new boyfriend and then having to walk home on your own, mumbling tearfully, while your dishy best friend waltzes off with him. Keep him to yourself for a while, until you get used to each other. Once he's really got to know you he's not so likely to be snatched. Unless you're incredibly bad-tempered and spotty and horrible. Which you're not, are you? Well, not all three.

I SHOULDN'T HAVE . . . turned up late. Remember the guy doesn't know you all that well. All he knows is that you agreed to a date and you've had a whole night and a day to change your mind. So he's a bit scared of being made a fool of and isn't going to spend too long waiting for a girl who may not turn up at all. If you do turn up late and are lucky enough to find him still standing there like a lemon, have a good excuse. Something to soften him up, like: "I had to stop to rescue a drowning puppy from the lake." Or: "I was caught in a rainstorm and had to go back home to change." If you're very late and he's looking a little tight around the mouth, make it two puppies (or even four), or a freak hurricane.

I SHOULDN'T HAVE . . . taken him home. Dragging the guy home to meet the folks on the first date is a bad idea. The guy has used up most of his available nerve in asking you for a date in the first place. Having to be stared at critically by Mum, Dad, Gran, Aunt Ethel, the budgie and the cat will put him under more strain than the human mind can stand. So don't take him home until he's relaxed enough to cope with it. This could take months, especially if your Aunt Ethel is anything like everybody else's Aunt Ethel.

I SHOULDN'T HAVE . . . arrived for the date in the wrong clothes. It's a good idea to find out roughly what he's got planned for that first date. It won't help much if you turn up in your dolliest dress to find him standing with his greasy motor bike, all dressed up in leathers and ready to bomb off to a grass-track meeting. Or if you arrive in your scruffiest gear expecting to bomb off on his bike while he's immaculate in his best suit and has booked a table for two at the Ritz.

I SHOULDN'T HAVE . . . mentioned my last boyfriend. Keep your last guy out of it. If you say nice things about him, like what a great dancer he was, or how he used to throw his jacket over puddles for you to walk on, your new guy will be worried about how he's going to match up to such a wonderful person. He'll also be wondering how you lost Mr Wonderful. Is there something about you he doesn't know?

And if you try to make the new guy feel good by saying rotten things about your last boy, that won't work either. New guy will have the uneasy feeling that you'll be saying nasty things about him when you move on to your next fella.

. SHOULDN'T HAVE . . . insisted on going to the pictures. He's going to be doing his best to please on that first date, but when he says, "Where do you fancy going?" don't pick on something expensive, just in case he's flat broke. It can be embarrassing watching a poor guy blushing hotly as he sorts through a collection of small change, shirt buttons and dead moths, trying to get enough cash together for two seats in the stalls. Offering to go dutch is fine, but paying the whole lot yourself isn't going to make him feel much better. So settle for a walk on that first date and a couple of Cokes in a café. He'll appreciate it and it'll prove you're not the kind of girl who's trying to rip him off. Of course, once you've discovered that he's *incredibly* rich . . . that's different.

So think hard before going on that first date. Avoid the *First-Date Pitfalls* and have a great time. That way you won't crawl miserably home, minus your new guy, moaning, "*I shouldn't have . . .*"

BOY TALK

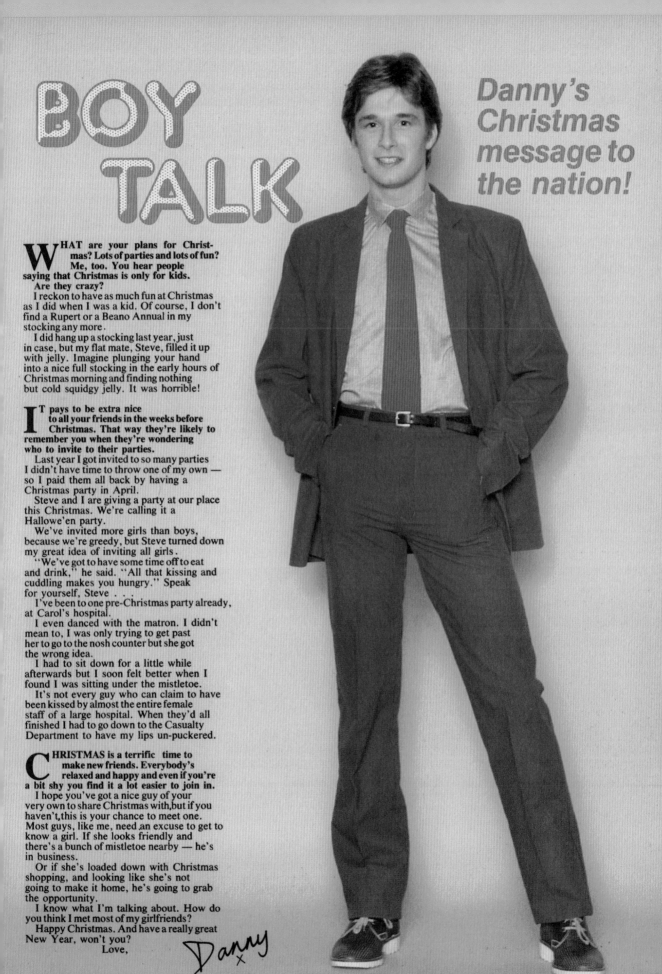

Danny's Christmas message to the nation!

WHAT are your plans for Christmas? Lots of parties and lots of fun? Me, too. You hear people saying that Christmas is only for kids.

Are they crazy?

I reckon to have as much fun at Christmas as I did when I was a kid. Of course, I don't find a Rupert or a Beano Annual in my stocking any more.

I did hang up a stocking last year, just in case, but my flat mate, Steve, filled it up with jelly. Imagine plunging your hand into a nice full stocking in the early hours of Christmas morning and finding nothing but cold squidgy jelly. It was horrible!

IT pays to be extra nice to all your friends in the weeks before Christmas. That way they're likely to remember you when they're wondering who to invite to their parties.

Last year I got invited to so many parties I didn't have time to throw one of my own — so I paid them all back by having a Christmas party in April.

Steve and I are giving a party at our place this Christmas. We're calling it a Hallowe'en party.

We've invited more girls than boys, because we're greedy, but Steve turned down my great idea of inviting all girls.

"We've got to have some time off to eat and drink," he said. "All that kissing and cuddling makes you hungry." Speak for yourself, Steve . . .

I've been to one pre-Christmas party already, at Carol's hospital.

I even danced with the matron. I didn't mean to, I was only trying to get past her to go to the nosh counter but she got the wrong idea.

I had to sit down for a little while afterwards but I soon felt better when I found I was sitting under the mistletoe.

It's not every guy who can claim to have been kissed by almost the entire female staff of a large hospital. When they'd all finished I had to go down to the Casualty Department to have my lips un-puckered.

CHRISTMAS is a terrific time to make new friends. Everybody's relaxed and happy and even if you're a bit shy you find it a lot easier to join in.

I hope you've got a nice guy of your very own to share Christmas with, but if you haven't, this is your chance to meet one. Most guys, like me, need an excuse to get to know a girl. If she looks friendly and there's a bunch of mistletoe nearby — he's in business.

Or if she's loaded down with Christmas shopping, and looking like she's not going to make it home, he's going to grab the opportunity.

I know what I'm talking about. How do you think I met most of my girlfriends?

Happy Christmas. And have a really great New Year, won't you?

Love,

Danny
x

ARIES

At your best, you're full of energy, honest, brave and strong. But at your worst, you can be quick-tempered, impatient, selfish and bossy. You have to be first in everything—the lunch queue, exams, work, relationships. You want everything now and you barge through life making sure you get it. You can be courageous and adventurous, but you can also be just plain aggressive and bad-tempered. You never think before you speak and for this reason you are not the ideal person to trust with secrets!

TAURUS

You can be practical, reliable and warm-hearted. But you can also be stodgy and self-centred and so stuck in a rut that it's difficult to see your way out of it. At your worst, you hate change and are stubborn enough to stick to your opinions no matter what. (You still think there should only be one television channel.) As far as boys are concerned, you're faithful, warm-hearted—and possessive. If your boyfriend so much as glances in another girl's direction, you'll be in a bad mood for a fortnight!

GEMINI

You're so lively, witty and attractive that you just can't help being a two-timing flirt as well! And you get away with it because you're so cunning and convincing. You can be caught entwined with your boyfriend's best mate and still manage to convince them both that you were only testing out your theory that your boyfriend kisses better than any other boy you know. You find it difficult to stick with anything. Once something new appears on the horizon—a new hobby, a new friend, a new boy—you drop all your old interests.

CANCER

Basically, you're kind, sensitive and sympathetic. But if things aren't going right for you, you can be over-emotional, touchy and moody. You're also an expert at harbouring grudges. People can go for months trying to figure out what it is they've done to offend you. You'll never tell them, though, because you think they should instinctively know what's wrong. And it could well be you've taken offence because they've told you you should tidy up your desk/room/handbag, because you do have the reputation for being one of the most untidy signs of the zodiac!

HORROR

Your star sign can tell you a lot about your character and personality—and that means your bad points as well as your good points. Each sign of the zodiac has its nasty side, so if you want to find out what yours is, just read on for some astro facts you <u>don't</u> want to know!

LEO

You're attractive and popular and everybody's sunshine girl—and don't you know it! You just want to spread happiness wherever you go. The trouble is, if other people don't want to fall in with your plans for them, you feel it's your duty to step in and organise their dull, boring little lives for them. You can't help being popular, but you might be a bit more popular if you stopped thinking you were doing people a favour by talking to them. And hard though it might be for you, you <u>could</u> step out of the spotlight once or twice— even if it's only for a few moments!

VIRGO

You're the modest, hard-working, helpful sign of the zodiac. The trouble is, if you're not careful, you can end up being picky, fussy and over-critical. You have to remember that cleaning the cooker and tidying out the hall cupboard isn't everyone's idea of a fun evening. You also tend to worry too much. You worry about your clothes, your hair, your health, other people's health, and if you can't find anything to worry about, you worry about not worrying. You'll never admit to any of this, though, because Virgos love to pretend they're perfect!

LIBRA

You're the nicest, sweetest, most tactful person around. The trouble is, you're so tactful and so anxious not to give offence, you end up being totally ignored. You take so many sides in a quarrel, no-one's got a clue what you actually do think. And after a while, you don't either. You tend to put off making decisions, too, and end up having them made for you. You rely on friends to tell you what to wear, where to go and who to go there with. If you ever do decide you want something, though, you usually end up getting it, one way or another!

SCORPIO

You have powerful feelings and emotions and unfortunately, one of the most powerful is your jealousy. Scorpios are Jealous. You're jealous if your friend gets better exam marks than you; you're jealous if your sister gets a bigger slice of cake than you; you're even jealous if the cat gets to sleep in your chair. And if your boyfriend dares to talk to another girl, they'll both feel the sting of your sharp Scorpio personality. You're stubborn, secretive and suspicious, but you're fascinating and there will always be something exciting going on when you're around!

SAGITTARIUS

You love freedom and adventure and you're in your element striding fearlessly into unknown dangers. Unfortunately, you can end up striding fearlessly into other people's lives. You're one of the most tactless signs of the zodiac and if anyone's going to tell their best friend her new haircut makes her look like Worzel Gummidge, it's going to be you. You tend to exaggerate, too, and you can make deciding between having your chips with or without vinegar seem as difficult as trying to decide which outfit to wear to a Royal Garden party.

CAPRICORN

You see yourself as reliable, careful and self-disciplined. But other people may just think you're being over-practical and disapproving. You can be a bit self-righteous and at your worst, will lecture your friends about what they should be doing with their lives instead of— horrors—enjoying themselves. Just because you think it's your duty to sit at home of an evening sorting out your parents' gas bill, it doesn't mean your friends are complete wastrels because they'd rather go to the movies. It's actually fun to do something mad and daft once in a while. Try it!

AQUARIUS

If there's a cause to be fought for or a wrong to be righted, you'll be the first to lend a hand, so long as there's no emotional commitment. You'd rather be working to Save the Whale than working on your relationships. You also always hate and disapprove of what the majority of people like to do. This means that you can spend many lonely evenings making Save the Whale T-shirts out of recycled string while your frinds are all enjoying themselves at the disco. Of course if everyone were to start making string T-shirts, you'd be off to the disco like a shot!

PISCES

You're sympathetic, sweet and kind. You just hate being nasty to anyone, and this means that you spend your time being nice to the nastiest, weediest people around. You're so busy being nice to other people, in fact, you forget how to run your own life and end up becoming totally dependent. If you don't get total emotional support from friends and boyfriends, you can whine on and on until you do. In fact, at your very worst, you can end up being a real drag. Try being genuinely, honestly, nasty once in a while. You'll be a nicer person for it!

Who Do You View?

Are you crazy about "Coronation Street," daft about "Dallas" and sold on "Superman"? If so, try our special TV and film quiz!

Cop That!

How much do you know about TV cops and robbers? Well, here's your chance to find out!

1. On which island does Jim Bergerac fight crime?

2. OK, so everyone knows they're called Cagney and Lacey. But what're their first names? Are they:
   a. Chris and Maggie,
   b. Maggie and Beth,
   c. Chris and Mary-Beth?

3. Which American police series does Tom Reilly star in?

4. General Lee is a bit of a fast character who is always being chased by the police. What show does he star in?

5. Lee Horsley stars as this Texas millionaire turned private eye. Can you name him?

6. Bodie and Doyle worked for C.I.5. in "The Professionals". What do these letters stand for?

Your Starter For Ten

Find out if you're our special "Mastermind" in this section on TV quizzes.

1. Dusty Bin stars in which quiz show?
2. Mike Read hosts which quiz show?
3. A computer called Mr Babbidge helps in this quiz show. Can you name it?

4. Which show does this describe: "contestants team up with star guests and use their skill to remember where they heard it and who they heard it from"?
5. In which quiz show do contestants shout "Higher" or "Lower"?
6. Willie Carson and Bill Beaumont are team captains in which quiz show?

Series Stuff

See how much you know about your favourite TV series.

1. Where do Petra Taylor, Gordon Collins and Roger Huntingdon all live?
2. Krystle, Fallon and Alexis star in which American series?
3. OK, "Fame" fans – everyone knows this is Carlo Imperato, but can you give us the full name of the character he plays in the series and what career he's aiming for?

4. He left school, where he had a reputation for being a real tearaway, and tried hard to get a job – who are we talking about?

5. Name the high-powered series this gorgeous guy appears in.
6. Name the dishy actor who stars as Brian Tilsley in "Coronation Street."

Music While You Watch

If you're a pop fan — then you're bound to do well with these questions on TV music programmes.

1. D.J. Peter Powell hosted this BBC 2 music show. Can you name it?
2. It began on January 1, 1964, and is Britain's longest-running pop programme. Name that show!
3. Lisa Stansfield jumped for joy when she was asked to present this mad-cap Tyne Tees show. What's it called?
4. This likely-looking lot starred in Channel 4's first Friday evening music show. Do you remember what it was called?
5. Unscramble these letters to discover a BBC 2 arts and music programme. VIREEDRSI
6. Name the show which combines a live pop concert with a simultaneous broadcast on Radio One.

2. This hunky heart-throb starred as Zak Mayo in a romantic movie. Two points if you can tell us the actor's name and also name the movie.
3. Which famous pop star played the lead role in "Merry Christmas, Mr Lawrence"?

4. Can you name Cannon and Ball's crazy comedy film?
5. What's special about "Jaws III"?
6. "Local Hero" was set in what part of Britain?
   a. Scotland.
   b. Wales.
   c. Northern Ireland.
7. OK, all you science-fiction fans. Name the third "Star Wars" movie.

Screen Test

Are you a film fan? Then try these movie questions for size!
1. What's the connection between Michael Jackson and E.T.? (No, it isn't that they're both out of this world!)

A Commercial Break

'Ad enough yet? No? Well try these questions!
1. What's "the best drink of the day"?
2. Barbara Woodhouse tells you to do what?
3. What's "tasty, tasty, very very tasty"?
4. What can you make someone happy with?
5. "If the name fits – wear it." What's the name?
6. "Bite it, crunch it, chew it." What are we talking about?

ANSWERS

Score one point for each correct answer.

Cop That!
1. Jersey 2. (c) 3. "C.H.i.P.s" 4. "The Dukes Of Hazzard" 5. "Matt Houston" 6. "Criminal Intelligence".

Your Starter For Ten
1. "3, 2, 1" 2. "Pop Quiz" 3. "Family Fortunes" 4. "Punchlines" 5. "Play Your Cards Right" 6. "A Question Of Sport".

Series Stuff
1. "Brookside" 2. "Dynasty" 3. Danny Amatullo — a comedian 4. Tucker Jenkins, alias actor Todd Carty 5. "Falcon Crest" 6. Christopher Quinten.

Screen Test
1. Michael collaborated on the "E.T. Storybook" album 2. Richard Gere — "An Officer And A Gentleman" 3. David Bowie 4. "Boys In Blue" 5. It's in 3-D 6. (a) 7. "Return Of The Jedi".

Music While You Watch
1. "The Oxford Road Show" 2. "Top Of The Pops" 3. "Razzmatazz" 4. "The Tube" 5. "Riverside" 6. "Sight And Sound In Concert".

A Commercial Break
1. Tea 2. "Go smash an egg!" 3. Kelloggs Bran Flakes 4. A phone call 5. Levi's 6. Lion Bar.

CONCLUSIONS

30-37 — Award yourself a pat on the back — you're definitely our media mastermind! There's not much you don't know about the world of TV and films. In fact, ignore everyone calling you "Square Eyes." We think they suit you!

20-29 — You're not exactly hooked on television and films but you have quite a good knowledge of them. You'll never threaten Barry Norman on "Film 83" or Barry Took on "Points Of View" but you're a normal Jackie TV and film fan.

19 and under — Mmm! D'you actually know what a TV is? It's that square thing that sits in the corner of your living-room — no, we're not speaking about your dad, stupid! As for the cinema, well, you probably don't even realise that the local flicks is now a bingo hall!

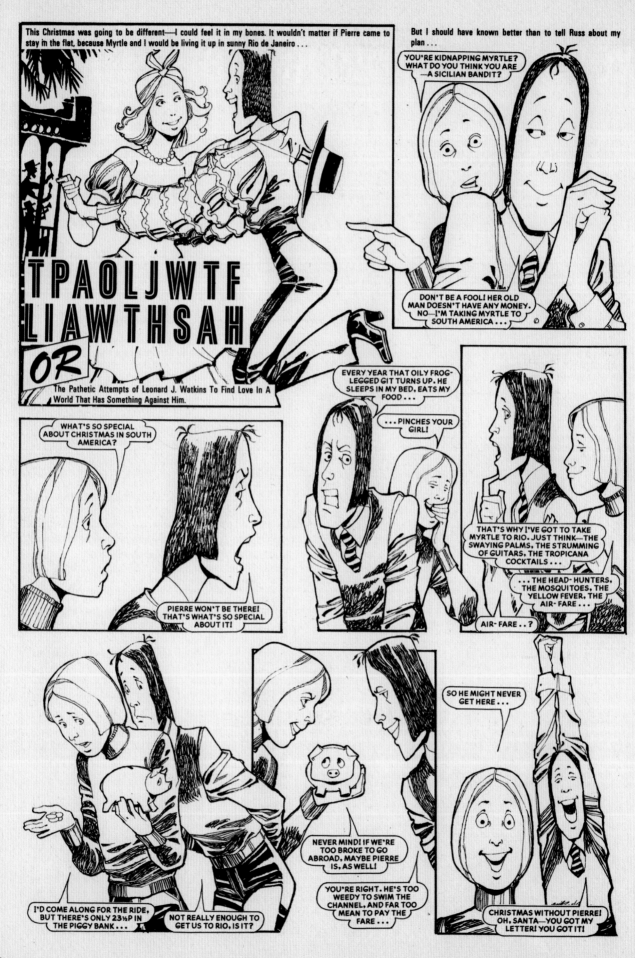

HAIR'S HEALTH!

Here's how to keep your hair happy!

Pic by courtesy of Henara.

● *Hair grows at ½ inch a month and no amount of pulling and stretching will speed this rate up. However, your hair does grow slightly quicker in warm weather so be prepared to visit your hairdresser more in summer.*

● Every day you lose about 50 hairs — so don't panic every time one falls out! If a hair is yanked out instead of falling out naturally, it can take up to 3 months to regrow.

● *Each hair has a lifespan of anything from a few months to several years. The part of the hair we can see is actually dead!*

● To make sure your hair is shiny and healthy, eat the proper things — lean meat, liver, seafood and fresh fruit and vegetables.

● *Brush your hair thoroughly before you wash it. This releases dust and grease, giving a better finished product.*

● Wash your hair in *warm* water. Water that's too hot not only hurts your head — it encourages grease in your hair.

● *You can tell a good shampoo if it goes through your hair easily and rinses out quickly.*

● Normal hair can be washed with most shampoos — but don't let this tempt you into resorting to the very cheap and nasty kind.

● *Dry hair needs a moisturising shampoo, preferably with a built-in conditioner. Special ingredients to look out for include rosemary, camomile and Vitamin C.*

● When blow-drying your hair, don't let the hairdryer touch your hair, and don't concentrate the blast on one spot for very long as the heat will damage your hair.

● If you suffer from dandruff, use a good dandruff shampoo. After the dandruff has cleared up, go back to your normal shampoo.

● Oily hair needs an oil-free shampoo. Don't be tempted by brands which promise to 'cut through the grease' — they'll take away all those essential oils your hair needs along with the grease it could do without.

● *Rinsing your hair should take much longer than the actual shampooing and is just as important.*

● Rinse your hair in *cool* water for the final rinse. You could also add vinegar to the water, if you've got dark hair; or lemon juice, if you're fair haired. This will make your hair really shiny.

● *Don't leave conditioner on for longer than it says on the bottle — it will have stopped working by then.*

● Always rinse conditioner off thoroughly or it will leave a dull covering on your hair.

● *Don't be surprised if your hair seems much longer when it's wet — good condition hair stretches by up to ⅓ of its length after it's been in water.*

● Hair is at its weakest when it's wet so be extra careful with it. *Never* brush wet hair.

● *After washing, wrap your hair in a towel to blot the moisture. Then comb it out very gently with a wide-toothed comb.*

● If you have to wash your hair every day, use a mild shampoo.

● *Never blow dry your hair bone dry. It will stain in much better condition if it's left with a touch of moisture to dry off naturally and be absorbed into the hair.*

● Remember to wash your hair-brush when you wash your hair.

● *If you want a really strong hold on your hair, use gel and hairspray together and then style your hair.*

● Brushing your hair upside down gives it bounce and helps circulation, giving healthy hair.

● *Don't overbrush. Forget all about brushing your hair 100 times before you go to bed. It breaks your hair and make it look greasy. Around 25 strokes is more than enough for even the longest hair.*

● If you back comb your hair, remember to brush it out — carefully.

● *When you are sunbathing put a little conditioner through your hair to protect it from the sun's harmful rays. Remember to rinse it out afterwards, though.*

● And finally . . . standing on your head does wonders for your hair! Try it and see!

Most boys are nice most of the time. No boy is perfect, but some boys are just plain *bad* and if you're unlucky enough to get involved with a bad boy, you're right in line to find out why so many love songs are sad songs.

Think you're too smart to fall for a bad boy? Think again! A bad boy's greatest asset is that he can attract girls the way a spider attracts flies. And he's just as deadly. So don't get caught in his trap. Learn to spot a bad boy before he gets the chance to capture — and break — your heart.

WARNING!
These Boys Are Dangerous !

DANGER!

The Bad Boy who won't take No for an answer.

This bad boy is probably the most dangerous of all. He's charming, tender and romantic, but his one aim with girls is to go a lot further than just kissing and cuddling. And if you say "No," he's got a whole arsenal of speeches already prepared and all guaranteed to break down your defences.

He'll tell you you're not a couple of kids any more . . . he'll tell you that for him this is the real thing . . . he'll let you know there have been other girls in his life — girls who weren't afraid like you . . .

And if you like him, which you most probably will, since this type of boy is usually popular and attractive, you'll listen to him.

Even though you know all about his reputation, you'll persuade yourself, with a little help from him, that you're different from all those other girls. You'll think this really is the real thing for him and that he really is in love with you, so what harm can it do?

The answer is an awful lot.

And if you think he really does love you, ask yourself why he's trying to push you to take decisions you feel are wrong for you.

Any boy who tries to cash in on emotional blackmail like this is bad news. If he won't listen to your opinions, respect your ideas and trust you to know what's right for *you*, he's a candidate for our bad boys line-up.

Beware of the boy who pushes you too far, who threatens to drop you "unless." A boy who cares about you will want decisions about the physical side of your relationship to be mutual ones.

But the bad boy doesn't care about you at all. He's out to get his own way and he'll threaten to walk out on you if he doesn't. And if, against your better judgment, you're silly enough to give in to him, he'll walk out on you anyway.

To a bad boy like this, a relationship means proving himself. Proving he can get any girl he wants. And once the challenge is gone — he is, too.

DANGER!

The Bad Boy who'll two, three and even four-time you.

This particular bad boy finds it easy — too easy — to attract girls, and he finds them impossible to resist. He just adores being adored.

And the trouble is, he's just so easy to fall in love with. He'll tell you he really loves you back, too, and while he's saying it he probably means it. And he probably means it when he whispers exactly the same thing to Karen, Lucy, Annette or Hazel . . .

The two-timer is superb. When you eventually catch him out, it's more likely to be because he wanted you to. Then, you see, he doesn't have to go through all the trouble involved in breaking off a relationship when he's tired of it.

All he has to do is let himself be caught out a few times and, what do you know, *you* do all the work for him! You send him packing.

Then, of course, you spend the next few weeks wondering why it was you packed up a boy you were crazy about. Maybe you should have forgiven him . . . maybe there's still time . . . maybe you should be more broad minded about these things . . . maybe he's really nice underneath it all . . .

Well, he's not! He's attractive and fun and great to be with, but he's also a grade one Bad Boy.

DANGER!

The Bad Boy who wants to take over your life.

He walks into your life and everything is suddenly beautiful. He really loves you. He's fascinated by everything about you — your hair, your clothes, the new shoes you bought . . .

He takes so much interest in you, in fact, that pretty soon he's suggesting what you ought to wear when he takes you out. He's also considerate enough to point out all the little faults you have.

So you wear the clothes he likes you to wear, you go to the places he wants you to go, you think the way he wants you to think, and you end up being completely dominated by him.

And when the dominating bad boy

does tell you it's over, you spend a long time wondering why. Didn't you try to be everything he wanted in a girl? Didn't you dress the way he liked and talk the way he liked and think the way he liked?

Yes, you did — and that was your mistake.

Beware of the boy who tries to do all your thinking for you and tries to turn you into someone else. If a relationship founders on the colour of a dress or the kind of records you like listening to, it isn't much of a relationship. And if a boy is attracted enough to ask you out in the first place why would he want to change you?

The boy who does is more than likely a little bit selfish and insecure and isn't ready for a relationship based on mutual give and take.

So don't make the mistake of allowing some boy to tell you what to think and how to dress. Nice boys will accept you as you are and won't try to change you. Bad boys won't.

DANGER!

The Bad Boy who pretends you don't exist.

Unlike the two-timer, this bad boy needs, and wants, just one steady girlfriend. He likes having a steady girlfriend in the background. The trouble is, in the background is strictly where you'll stay.

When he takes you out, he'll be attentive, concerned about you, and generally a pretty nice person to be with. Then you meet one or two of his friends and suddenly your nice boyfriend becomes a prime candidate for the bad boy stakes.

He doesn't introduce you to anyone, he completely ignores you, he leaves you sitting on your own while he chats to his mates and he generally behaves as if you just don't exist.

He likes to feel free to chat up other girls at parties, to talk to his mates and generally to feel that he can do as he likes. At the same time, though, he likes the security of having a steady girlfriend. It's a classic case of the person who wants the best of both worlds.

The one thing in this bad boy's favour is that he won't actually two-time you and he'll be attentive and loving when

you're on your own. It's when other people are around that you'll suddenly become part of the wallpaper as far as he's concerned.

The last thing this boy wants is to be free. But he likes to play at being free. It's all a game, you see, and if you get entangled with this bad boy, you could end up the loser.

> Falling for a genuine bad boy can be a heartbreaking experience and it can take a long time to recover.
>
> Remember, though, the good guys really do outnumber the bad guys and chances are you'll be a whole lot luckier second time around!

DON'T LOOK NOW—IT'S
SUPERYAWN!

You know the feeling — you're halfway through a detailed description of Granny's birthday party when suddenly you notice your mate's glazed expression as her eyelids begin to droop. In other words, she's BORED — and you're BORING! So how d'you beat the boring blues? Read on, discover your own brand of bore, and you'll never have to face another yawn!

CONDITION: THE GRUMBLE-BORE
REMEDY:

Only the boring are bored, as the saying goes, and it's true, too! It stands to reason that those among us who slither out of bed amid grumbles and groans, slouch to school with a face of thunder and fester the evening away in front of the telly aren't the most dynamic or exciting of people. If life bores you, it's impossible to summon up the slightest scrap of enthusiasm for any goings-on, and with a sullen expression, you'll spend life with a constant chip on your shoulder. In other words, you're a Grumble-Bore — of the very worst kind!

Think about it, and if you suspect you're boring, analyse your attitude to life in general. There's nothing more irritating than having a Grumble-Bore around — someone who's totally fed-up and lives under a huge, grey cloud, constantly reminding everyone of the fact. The first step in breaking out of the super-yawn trap is to banish your boredom, so work up a little more enthusiasm for life — whether it's the countryside you love or a gorgeous sunrise — and you'll be a whole lot more fun to have around!

CONDITION: THE SELF-BORE
REMEDY:

We're all guilty of looking after number one, flattering ourselves and guarding our own interests. It's when this feeling of self-importance gets out of hand that you're well on the way to becoming a self-bore!

You'll have heard people rambling on about their talents and achievements — boring all in sight — and the tragedy is that Self-Bores just don't seem to notice their audience of stifled yawns. Are *you* a Self-Bore? If you suspect that, yes, you do ramble on about number one, take stock of yourself and resolve to keep your tongue under control in future.

Self-Bores, surprisingly, aren't as confident as they may seem. In fact, as well as trying to convince everyone in sight that they're amazingly talented and interesting, they're trying just as hard to prove to *themselves* that they're worthwhile. Perhaps you've admitted that you do go on rather a lot and you've realised that although people are interested in your new fella — and are dying to hear about your first date — they only want to hear about the man of your dreams once. By the third telling, the tale's lost its attraction — so instead of boosting your ego and boring all around you, show an interest in your friends. Ask questions, be willing to listen as well as chatter, and when you hear yourself begin, "You know what I did at the weekend . . ." — bite your tongue!

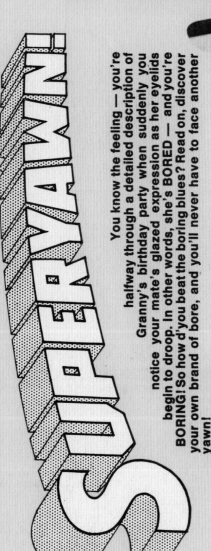

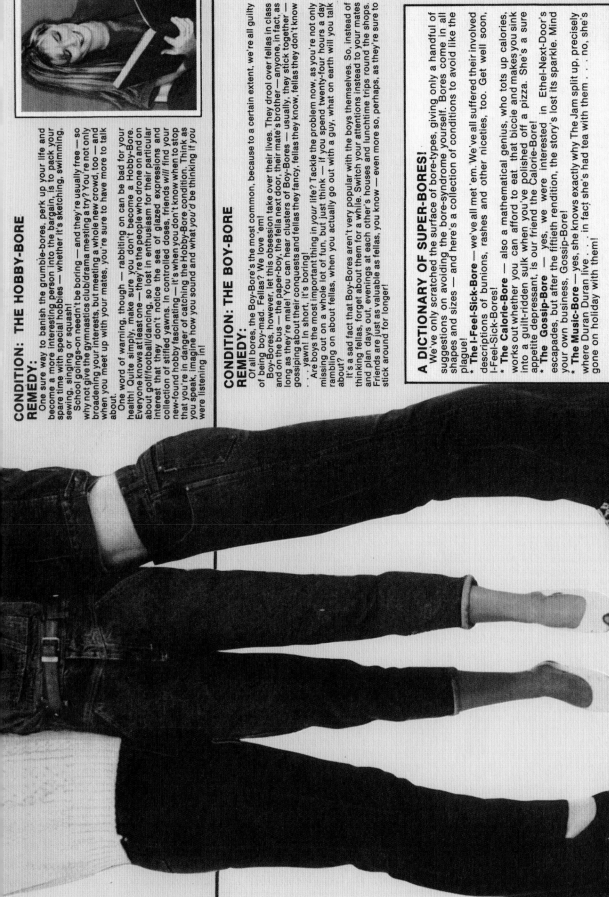

CONDITION: THE HOBBY-BORE
REMEDY:

One sure way to banish the grumbie-bores, perk up your life and become a more interesting person into the bargain, is to pack your spare time with special hobbies — whether it's sketching, swimming, sewing, singing or squash!

School goings-on needn't be boring — and they're usually free — so why not give the gymnastics club/drama meeting a try? You're not only broadening your interests, but meeting a whole new crowd, too — and when you meet up with your mates, you're sure to have more to talk about.

One word of warning, though — rabbiting on can be bad for your health! Quite simply, make sure you don't become a Hobby-Bore. Everyone knows at least one — they're the people who drone on and on about golf/football/dancing, so lost in enthusiasm for their particular interest that they don't notice the sea of glazed expressions and collection of stifled yawns. In controlled doses, friends will find your new-found hobby fascinating — it's when you don't know when to stop that you're in danger of catching the Hobby-Bore condition. Think as you speak, imagine how you sound and what you'd be thinking if you were listening in!

CONDITION: THE BOY-BORE
REMEDY:

Of all bores, the Boy-Bore's the most common, because to a certain extent, we're all guilty of being boy-mad. Fellas? We love 'em!

Boy-Bores, however, let this obsession take over their lives. They drool over fellas in class and on the bus — the paper-boy, the fella next door, their mate's brother — anyone, in fact, as long as they're male! You can hear clusters of Boy-Bores — usually, they stick together — gossiping about their conquests and fellas they fancy, fellas they know, fellas they don't know . . . yawn! In short, it's boring!

Are boys the most important thing in your life? Tackle the problem now, as you're not only missing out on a whole lot of fun, but just think — if you spend twenty-four hours a day rambling on about fellas, when you actually go out with a guy, what on earth will you talk about?

It's a sad fact that Boy-Bores aren't very popular with the boys themselves. So, instead of thinking fellas, forget about them for a while. Switch your attentions instead to your mates and plan days out, evenings at each other's houses and lunchtime trips round the shops. Friends are just as valuable as fellas, you know — even more so, perhaps, as they're sure to stick around for longer!

A DICTIONARY OF SUPER-BORES!

We've only scratched the surface of bore-types, giving only a handful of suggestions on avoiding the bore-syndrome yourself. Bores come in all shapes and sizes — and here's a collection of conditions to avoid like the plague!

* **The I-Feel-Sick-Bore** — we've all suffered their involved descriptions of bunions, rashes and other niceties, too. Get well soon, I-Feel-Sick-Bores!

* **The Calorie-Bore** — also a mathematical genius, who tots up calories, works out whether you can afford to eat that biccie and makes you sink into a guilt-ridden sulk when you've polished off a pizza. She's a sure appetite depressant, is our friend the Calorie-Bore!

* **The Gossip-Bore** — yes, we were interested in Ethel-Next-Door's escapades, but after the fiftieth rendition, the story's lost its sparkle. Mind your own business, Gossip-Bore!

* **The Music-Bore** — yes, she knows exactly why The Jam split up, precisely where Duran Duran live . . . in fact she's had tea with them . . . no, she's gone on holiday with them!

Let's hope we've helped you beat the boring blues and become more interesting, popular and fun . . . let's hope we've helped you beat the boredom blues, too, with our Jackie Annual! You can't possibly be boring after our fun features, beauty and fashion hints, super stories, great quizzes . . . yawn . . . zzzzzz.

WHAT DO BOYS

Your reaction to each of the scenes below can tell you an awful lot about your attitude to boys—and can also reveal what *they* think about *you*. Just pick which sentence you think best fits each scene, add up your score and then turn to the conclusions to find out just what you and boys think about each other!

1. *This couple have just met at a lively, fun party. Is he saying to her—*
a) " OK, I give up. If that's not a jelly-baby hanging from your ear, then what is it?"
b) " Just a bit higher and you'll feel my heart beating."
c) " You must go to the same dentist as me. I can tell by your fillings."

3. *She's just opened the door to this boy. What do you think he's saying to her?*
a) " Is your sister in?"
b) " Remember me? We got engaged last night!"
c) " If your mum's in, I've come about the gas leak. If she's not, what are you doing tonight?"

4. *This couple have just finished a fun game of tennis. Is he saying to her—*
a) " I don't care who won. As far as I'm concerned, it's love all."
b) " Never mind. You might win next time."
c) " You may not be very good at tennis, but at least you're game for a laugh!"

2. *These two are on their first date and he's just given her flowers. Is she saying to him—*
a) " Very nice. Why have you given them to me?"
b) " They're lovely. No-one's ever given me flowers before."
c) " Thanks very much. But just *what* am I going to do with flowers in a *disco?*"

THINK OF YOU?

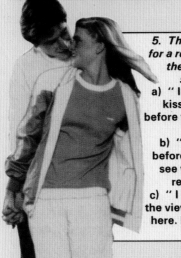

5. These two are out for a romantic walk in the country. Is she saying to him—
a) "If youre going to kiss me, do it quick before this wind blows us both away!"
b) "I never noticed before, but now I can see your eyes aren't really blue at all."
c) "I don't care what the view's like from up here. I only have eyes for you."

6. This couple are out for a walk in the park. Is he saying to her—
a) "Look! There goes Concorde!"
b) "We'll have a place like this one day."
c) "You and that duck have a lot in common. Neither of you are very good swimmers!"

7. These two are fooling about with a camera. Is she saying to him—
a) "Make sure you get in *all* my fillings, won't you!"
b) "Do you know we'll get cramp standing like this?"
c) "This photo will always remind you of me."

8. This couple are in a disco and for a dare, she's just ripped his shirt off. Is he now saying to her—
a) "Careful! My mum wahed that this morning!"
b) "Thanks! I neeed that! It's really hot in here!"
c) "Hey! Don't be daft! That girl *was* my cousin, you know!"

Now count up your score and turn to the conclusions.

1. a)11	b)9	c)7.	5. a)11	b)7	c)9.
2. a)7	b)9	c)11.	6. a)7	b)9	c)11.
3. a)7	b)9	c)11.	7. a)11	b)7	c)9.
4. a)9	b)7	c)11.	8. a)7	b)11	c)9.

CONCLUSIONS

IF YOU SCORED: BETWEEN 72 AND 88

You're warm, friendly and a bundle of laughs and you refuse to take anyone, far less boys, seriously. At the moment, you don't want to be tied down to one particular person. Boys like you because they feel they can talk to you easily and have a few laughs without it all getting too heavy. When you do find your particular person, though, it'll be a case of " 'till death us do part'' because underneath all that bouncy humour, you're very loyal and sincere. Watch you don't miss out on the right boy for you, though, by being too jokey. If you are, he may think you don't care enough about him. You can be romantic and serious about want, so give it a try sometimes!

IF YOU SCORED: BETWEEN 64 and 72

Aah! You're nothing but a big soppy romantic who wants everybody to take care of her. You're ready to fall for any boy who says two nice words to you (like, " Hi there!") and after three dates you're dreaming about engagement rings and wedding bells. Fortunately, you've got a good sense of humour which saves you taking yourself too seriously. Boys find you warm and easy to get on with, and you'll never be short of dates and admirers. Try not to see every boy you meet as the Great love of Your Life, though. If you do, boys will get scared off by your attitude and the next time you mention weddings or engagements, you won't see them for dust!

IF YOU SCORED: BETWEEN 56 AND 64

You're extremely practical and down-to-earth, but as far as boys are concerned, you're inclined to take everything they say with two pinches of salt! Maybe you've been badly hurt in the past, which would account for you being almost deliberately unromantic most of the time. This attitude does tend to scare boys off a bit because they think you don't like them. The truth is, though, you do like them—it's just that you're scared to show your feelings in case you get hurt. Maybe you should try relaxing more. Not all boys are as bad as you think. In fact, quite a few of them are very nice, if only you'll give them the chance to prove it!

KNIT WITS!

Clever little extras to knit up in a night!

Knit yourself these matching accessories with a difference and look good and keep warm at the same time. Designed by Alan Dart, these unusual fingerless mittens and ankle warmers take just two balls of wool but are so easy, even the no-nonsense kind can make the quickly look one evening to knit them up!

LEGWARMERS AND MITTENS

YARN — Two x 100 g balls of Sirdar Gemini Brushed Chunky.

NEEDLES — A pair each of 5½ mm and 6½ mm, and a stitch holder.

TENSION — 13½ sts and 19 rows to 10 cm square, measured over stocking-stitch on 6½ mm needles.

ABBREVIATIONS — K — knit, P — purl, st(s) — stitch(es), cont — continue, comm — commencing, st-st — stocking-stitch, one row knit, one row purl, inc — increase, beg — beginning.

LEGWARMERS

With 5½ mm needles cast on 32 sts and work 14 rows K1, P1 rib.
Change to 6½ mm needles and cont in st-st comm with a K row.

Work 5 rows.
Inc (by working into front and back of st) 1 st at beg and end of next and every following 5th row until there are 46 sts on the needle.
Cont without shaping for 10 rows, ending with a P row.
Change to 5½ mm needles and work 8 rows K1, P1 rib.
Cast off in rib.

MITTENS

With 5½ mm needles cast on 26 sts and work 10 rows K1, P1 rib.
Change to 6½ mm needles and cont in st-st comm with a K row.
Row 1 — K.
Row 2 and all alternate rows — P.
Row 3 — K13, inc (by working into horizontal thread before next st), K13.
Row 5 — K13, inc, K1, inc, K13.
Row 7 — K13, inc, K3, inc, K13.

Row 9 — K13, inc, K5, inc, K13.
Row 11 — K13, inc, K7, inc, K13.
Row 12 — P.
Next row — K13, slip these sts on to a stitch holder, with 5½ mm needles work 9 sts in K1, P1 rib, slip remaining 13 sts on to a stitch holder.
Work 3 rows P1, K1 rib on these 9 sts.
Cast off loosely in rib.
Slip the first set of held sts on to a 6½ mm needle, rejoin yarn to the remaining held sts, and with 6½ mm needles K to end (26 sts).
Next row — P.
Change to 5½ mm needles and work 4 rows K1, P1 rib.
Cast off loosely in rib.

TO MAKE UP

Do not press work. Join seams on legwarmers. Darn in yarn at base of thumbs. Join thumb seams. Join seams of mittens.

What did he mean by that?

When it comes to dealing with boys, one of the things to remember is that they don't always say what they mean. It can take a lot of time and practice to break through the language barrier and find out what they're really thinking, so to speed things up a bit, here's our fun look at some of the things a boy might say to you—and what he really means . . .

YOUR FIRST DATE

What he says

" It's a great evening. Fancy walking to the disco?"

What he means

" I know it's freezing and about to rain, but I could only get £5 off my dad and the bus fare's 50p each into town."

Or he could say

" Aren't you taking a bag or something?"

And what he means is

" If you're not taking a bag, that means you're not taking a purse and that means you're not taking any money. And I've only got a fiver."

AT THE DISCO

He says

" Let's sit in the corner. It's far quieter over there."

What he means is

" It's really dark in the corner. Let's go and have a necking session." Or, if you're very unlucky, he could mean

" It's really dark in the corner. With any luck my mates won't see me with you over there."

When he wants to impress, he'll say

" Great record, huh? I know that group pretty well."

What he means is

" I once sent them a song I'd written and they sent it back asking me to try again in five years' time."

WHEN YOU'VE BEEN SEEING EACH OTHER FOR A WHILE

He'll say

" I phoned you last night and you weren't in."

What he means is,

" Someone told me you went out with Steve Smith last night. Did you?"

Or he'll say

" Me? Go out with Brenda Jones? Don't be silly! Who told you that?"

What he means is

" How did you find out about me and Brenda? I bet it was that so-called mate of mine. Was it him?"

WHEN HE WANTS TO DROP YOU IN FAVOUR OF BRENDA JONES

He'll say

" I think we should stop seeing each other for a week or two. That'll give us a chance to find out what we really feel about each other."

What he means is

" I want to go out with Brenda Jones. But just in case things don't work out, I want to make sure you'll still be around."

Or he'll say

" I like you too much to lie to you."

What he means is

" I'm too much of a coward to tell you the truth, so there's no way I'm going to mention Brenda Jones. I wonder if you'll believe me if I tell you I'm going to join the Foreign Legion?"

Or he could say

" I think we're getting too involved, too soon."

And what he'll mean is,

" I want to go out with Brenda Jones."

WHEN HE WANTS YOU TO BE HIS GIRL

He'll say

" My brother's coming home in four months. You'll like him."

What he means is

" I want you to know I'd still like to be going out with you in four months. And besides that, I want you to meet my family."

Or he'll say

" I really like you a lot. More than I've ever liked any girl."

What he means is

" I think I love you."

Or he could say,

" I love you."

And what he'll more than likely mean is

" I love you!"

125

How To Cope When He Says Goodbye

IT'S finally happened. He's told you he doesn't want to see you any more. Your whole world's collapsed and you can't imagine how you're going to get through life without him. But you can — and you will. What's more, you can almost chart your progress through a break-up. Your timing and your speed will depend on you as an individual, but you can be sure you'll go through all the normal stages of crying over him, missing him, remembering all the good times and, unbelievable as it seems at the moment, getting over him.

The first thing you'll do is cry for him

So go ahead and cry. Lock your bedroom door and cry all you want to. Stare at his picture. Torture yourself with the thought that you'll never see him again. Imagine him kissing his new girl. And cry some more.

Then you'll think it was all your fault

This is when that awful phrase, *"If only"* creeps into your thoughts. You think, *"If only I'd been more understanding about that other girl,"* or, *"If only I'd been more interested in snooker,"* or you could even think, if you've got it badly enough, *"If only I was prettier he wouldn't have chucked me."* Well — forget it!

Chuck out all the if-onlys and might-have-beens and start to shift the blame a little. Instead of feeling it's all your fault, think about how awful **he** was. Think about how creepy he was to go out with that other girl; think about how selfish he was to expect you to put up with him playing snooker five nights a week; think about how you're actually **too** pretty for a toad like him.

Think anything you like so long as you start to feel good and **angry** with him.

Then it's time to face the truth

Now you finally admit it's over. You stop hoping, stop waiting for the phone to ring and stop dreaming about the big reunion scene.

Now's the time to keep your tears for when you're alone. Now's the time to resist the temptation to blurt everything out to anyone who'll listen.

And while you're facing the truth, ring all your mutual friends and tell them you've split. It's easier to get this out of the way quickly and you'll be relieved once everyone knows.

You'll find that quite a few mutual friends will prove to be less mutual, so be prepared for this.

Be prepared, too, for everyone to ask, "Where's Bert/Steve/Harry?" as if you were permanently glued together — which you were, of course.

Trouble is, you've been two

for so long, you've forgotten how to be alone. But it can be fun!

Now's the time to go crazy and be adventurous. Make yourself over, take up new interests. Don't play safe with flower-pressing or cookery classes — try tap-dancing, self-defence classes or a drama group.

Now's the time to face up to yourself

Use the break-up positively. Take decisions you've always put off and do things you've always wanted to do. If you've always wanted to go Youth Hostelling, or take dance classes, or try your hand at motor cycle maintenance but always put it off because of him, now's the time to strike out.

You've no-one else to think about now, so you can be as selfish and independent as you like.

You're almost cured now

It won't all be plain sailing, of course. Just when you think you're beginning to get over him, some little incident will set you off again. This is when you start to think you'd give it all up, if only

you could have those times back.

But that feeling doesn't last long and you're now halfway towards being able to remember the special things about your relationship without pain. Now, too, you're well on the way to remembering what you loved about him without necessarily wanting him back.

Now you can start again

Now you're ready to face the world again. Your cousin's twenty-first party may not sound like fun — but go anyway. You'll be meeting people, and that's what counts.

Try not to compare new experiences with the way things used to be. What you had was very special — and that kind of relationship doesn't happen every day, or with every boy.

Complete recovery — The test

You see him again — and everything you've worked for hangs in the balance. Resist the temptation to ignore him.

Face him. Smile at him. The sheer satisfaction of knowing you look good, knowing you've survived,

will be worth the willpower it takes to smile and chat to him for a minute or two.

Chances are you'll think he's changed and you may wonder how you could have spent so much time and trouble getting over someone who's so — well — *ordinary*.

Getting over a break up, starting all over again, isn't a case of slamming a door on one part of your life and opening a new one. It's much slower than that and a much more complicated process. It's a bit like wandering along corridors when you're not too sure of the way.

The most important factor in your recovery is time. Gradually, instead of only acting as if you're over the heartbreak, you'll find it's true.

You'll admit you wouldn't have missed out on the relationship, even though it made you more miserable than you've ever been. You've been in love — and out of love. It's a crazy merry-go-round and you're getting ready to jump on all over again . . .

Curls, Curls, Curls!

Try out the following ideas and you'll never be bored with your hair again!

PIPE DREAMS!

To achieve a wrinkly, pre-Raphaelite cascade of curls, try this pipe cleaner method. You'll need about two packets of pipe cleaners if your hair is fairly long; they're quite cheap and available from newsagents and tobacconists or your dad, if he's a pipe smoker. (He won't need them once you've nagged him into giving up his pipe on account of his health!)

Bend each pipe cleaner in half, like a hoop, and plait two strands of hair round it, one strand to each leg of the loop (see photo). Twist the pipe cleaner round to secure the hair and repeat until you've plaited your whole head of hair. Leave to dry for a few hours or overnight before unpleating each pipe cleaner again. If you want your curls to last, spray them with a fine mist of hair spray and don't comb or brush your hair.

You'll achieve a similar effect without pipe cleaners if you make lots of little plaits all over your hair. Tie the ends of the plaits with wool to keep them in, but don't use elastic bands as they damage your hair. However, you'll probably find the pipe cleaner method is less fiddly.

RAG DOLLY!

Binding up damp hair with rags has been done by generations of girls — ask your mum or granny! It takes several attempts before you discover the best way to wrap and tie your own particular hair for the end result you want, so practise plenty before you attempt to stun at a special occasion!

The way the girl in the photo has bound her hair will result in a full, bouncy head of hair rather than tight curls, because she's only tied up about half the length of each strand. So, if your shoulder-length or even jaw-length hair is looking rather lank and droopy, try this idea to put back its natural bounce.

First rip up some old soft cotton items of clothing to make your rags. You can sleep quite comfortably with your hair in rags but, if you tied your hair with attractive patterned cotton or rags, you could actually keep them in as you go about your business in the daytime — at weekends or holiday time, anyway!

To give the end result extra body, grab a section of wet hair and pull it in the opposite direction to the way you want it to lie and tie one knot or two in your rag as you tie it round. Carry on until all your hair is wrapped up.

Wait until your hair is dry then untie the rags and brush or comb your hair into the style you want.

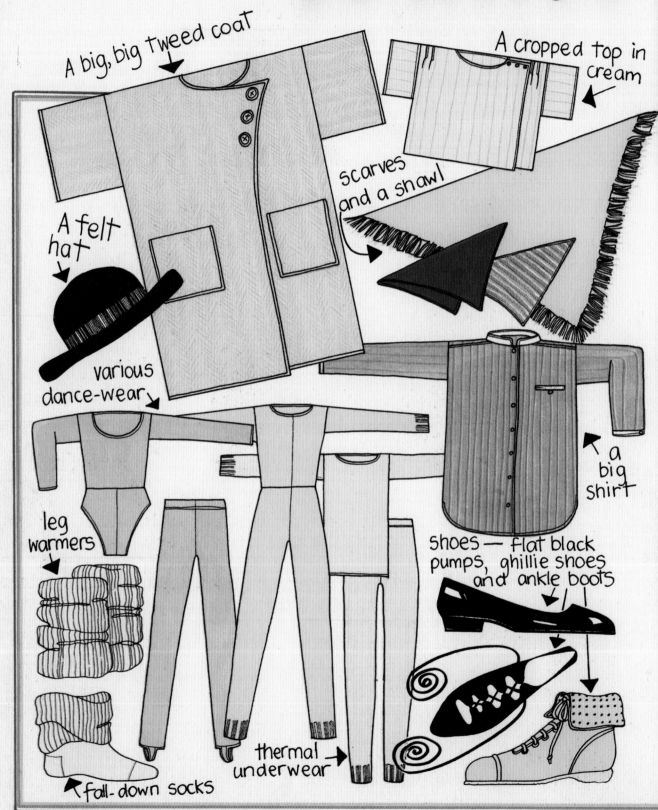

Swap skirts for shawls for trousers for tops — and come up with a look that's all your own!

Winter

A big, big tweed coat

A cropped top in cream

A felt hat

Scarves and a shawl

various dance-wear

a big shirt

leg warmers

shoes — flat black pumps, ghillie shoes and ankle boots

thermal underwear

fall-down socks

Wardrobe!

A cropped jacket in a natural fabric

A big dress—maybe linen or cord or fine wool

A big hand-knitted jumper

diamante jewellery

A frilly petticoat

belts

A full flannel skirt

A pleated skirt

A classic saddle-bag

cropped trousers

cropped jeans

Putting the look together ——

The coat is big – wear it over everything – don't worry about skirts hanging below the coat – it's a nice look!

The dress can be belted and worn over the skirts or trousers and dance-wear.

Wear fall-down socks and the hat and the petticoat – pile on the layers.

The cropped jacket goes over everything too.

Don't forget your diamante!

The cropped top with the skirt and the shawl as a belt on the hips — roll a scarf for your neck.

YOU SAID IT!

YOU SAID IT!
YOU SAID IT!
YOU SAID IT!
YOU SAID IT!

Boy George has said some daft things, some funny things and some downright weird things in his time. Here's just a few he's come out with in the past couple of years. And remember — he said it . . .

Boy George on Beauty:

"I used to go out with a green face, or a blue face and a red neck. I used to look like one of the ugly sisters."

"I make the best of what I've got. Anyway, I'm not interested in that 'isn't he pretty' crowd."

"I don't care if people think I'm a girl."

"I don't want to be a sex symbol, I don't want to be a freak or a clown. I want to be a bit more interesting."

Boy George on Hong Kong:

"It was weird going 17,000 miles and still getting mobbed when I got off the plane. It was 7.30 in the morning and I had no make-up on. I looked like a potato. And the papers said I was heavily made-up. I looked like a pig. In fact I looked like two pigs."

Boy George on Himself:

"My mum and dad know that underneath all this make-up I'm pretty normal. Well, I think I am."

"I'm game for anything really."

"When I first started experimenting with clothes, my mum tried to keep me indoors."

"I think I look better if I don't smile. I'd look like a clown if I did."

"It's easy to get attention."

"Sometimes I look at myself in the mirror and think — you prat. It does you good to laugh at yourself."

"I've got a lot more in common with Norman Wisdom than Simon le Bon."

"I think I've got a really good voice, I'm really pleased with it."

"I don't think I'm any better than anyone else just because I dress up."

Boy George on The Band:

"I think one of the good things about this band is that we really don't know what we are."

Boy George on other people:

"I hate people who think they're really risqúe and daring."

"I like reality, old women with Mr Spock eyebrows. I like character . . . that's art."

Boy George on Marilyn:

"Marilyn was a little soul boy when I met him, I remember I thought he was a right wally."

Let your bedroom reflect your personality, with some of these great ideas for giving it style!

PRETTY FEMININE

So you're the romantic type? In that case, how about a very pretty feminine style like the one shown here? Our reversible quilt has clouds on one side and hearts on the other. It costs £16.99 and the pillow cases are £7.50. This look depends on lots of little knick-knacks like the little wooden boxes (shown on the floor), the heart shaped cushion, framed photographs on the dressing-table and pretty pot plants.

The fans shown here can be found at various small gift stores. The two paper ones left and right were only 59p and the feather one 69p. The pink lamp shade costs around £4.99 (available from Debenhams stores).

PRIMARY POINTS

If you want to completely transform your room and you're lucky enough to be getting a helping hand from Mum and Dad money-wise, here's a style you may like.

Everything is in primary colours, which keeps the room bright and cheerful and makes it look more like a bedsit than a bedroom!

The quilt cover is a design called Shooting Star and it's shown here with matching reversible pillow cases. The single quilt costs £16.99 and pillow cases are £7.50 per pair. The red cotton piped cushion is £3.99. Copy our idea and hang belts and beads on a bright coathanger. You can get a pack of 3 coathangers in yellow, green, red or white for 75p. All of these items are available from Lifestyle departments in branches of House of Fraser stores.

Plastic kitchenware comes in great colours and is very useful for holding clothes rather than vegetables and kitchen tools as intended. Shown here are a large yellow Spacemaker bin (£2.99), a small red bin (£1.99), and a yellow vegetable rack by Addis (£2.85). On the small table (smallest of a set of three from MFI stores, price £10.99) are a red Crayonne kitchen utensil holder, (£1.69), a small racing car jelly mould (49p), and a red lampshade (£4.99). All these items are available from Debenhams stores. The blue curly lead and plug are available from electrical stores at approximately £3.49 in various colours.

50 ways to

1. COME ALIVE AT NIGHT! Make up that's perfect in daylight can look pallid at night so use twice as much blusher, dark brown or black mascara and eye-liner, rich coloured lipsticks and plenty of gloss and iridescent highlighters!

Night is the right time to experiment, too — try wearing gold apricot eyeshadow on your eye-lids and cheeks, or colour your eyebrows the same shade as your eyeliner pencil, even if it's green!

2. MORE LUCK WHEN YOU PLUCK! Plucking your eyebrows into shape can make quite a difference to your appearance, so make the process painless by holding a hot flannel over your eyebrows for a few minutes before you begin and always pluck in the direction of growth with a close-headed pair of tweezers.

3. OPEN UP YOUR EYES by brushing your eyebrows upwards after you've plucked them — keep them up with a little Vaseline!

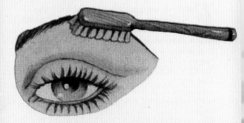

4. BALANCE A BIG NOSE OR WIDE MOUTH by sweeping and shaping your eyebrows upwards and outwards — this also helps space out narrow eyes.

5. FOR A ROUND FACE pluck your eyebrows into an angular shape.

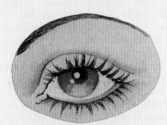

6. SHOW OFF YOUR EYES and a good forehead with nicely rounded brows.

7. OVERPLUCKED? Use a sharp eyebrow pencil to sketch in individual lashes.

8. FOR A QUICK REFRESH in the middle of the day make your own face-cleansing pads by soaking squares of cottonwool or lint in your favourite cleanser or toner and packing them in a small tin or soap box.

9. POWDER should go on after foundation but before any other make-up.

10. UNEVEN LIPS can be balanced up if you cover your lips with foundation, blot with a powder puff then draw in the correct shape with a lip pencil and fill in with lipstick.

11. MAKE LIPSTICK LAST LONGER by applying, blotting with a tissue and reapplying.

12. CONTROL GREASY SKIN with a water-based foundation like Rimmel's Oil Free Foundation for greasy skin.

13. MATCH FOUNDATION TO YOUR SKIN TONE by trying some on your face. Don't go by the shade it looks in the bottle!

14. IF YOU'VE PICKED THE WRONG SHADE don't panic, buy your next supply now but in a shade lighter or darker so you can mix the two together till you get the exact shade. The darker colour will also come in useful as shader.

15. WARM FOUNDATION in your hand first for smoother application.

16. APPLY FOUNDATION ANY WAY YOU LIKE — in dots all over face and blended on with fingertips or on a damp sponge — but try to apply it as quickly as possible.

17. LIGHTEN THE TEXTURE of your foundation in summer by mixing it with equal quantities of moisturiser.

18. FRESHEN UP YOUR MAKE-UP by patting a pad of damp cotton wool all over your face.

19. USE EVERY LAST DROP OF FOUNDATION by leaving the bottle upside down between uses, dropping some moisturiser into the bottle and mixing it up, or using a long-handled brush, or a cotton bud, to get every last drop out.

20. DISGUISE RED CHEEKS with green tinted moisturiser (Boots No. 7) or colour corrective powder like Bourjois' Jade.

21. DUST OFF EXCESS POWDER in a downward and outward direction using a big, babysoft face brush or a ball of cotton wool.

22. IN AN EMERGENCY use talcum powder lightly dusted over face instead of face powder.

23. FOR A PERFECT EYESHADOW BASE cover your entire eyelid with foundation.

24. BLUE EYESHADOW and eye pencils accentuate the whites of the eyes.

25. BEFORE YOU THROW AWAY any finished make-up in tubes cut open the tubes to extract the last few dregs.

26. IF YOU'VE GOT A FULL FACE avoid wearing pure white near the face as it throws up the light and places extra emphasis on the jaw and chin area.

27. AVOID IRRITATING EYES when removing make-up with cotton wool by slightly dampening it first.

28. ALWAYS REMOVE EYE MAKE-UP wiping from inner corner of eyes outwards.

29. ALWAYS USE ELECTRIC TONGS and curlers on dry hair. If the hair's wet or damp the high heat produced can scald.

30. INVENT HIGH CHEEKBONES, if you haven't got them, by using shader in a sideways low triangle at edge of cheeks (see drawing) and lots of glossy, cream-coloured highlighter above, where cheekbones should be. Blend both shader and highlighter well in and apply on top of foundation.

31. PLACE BLUSHER in the right position for your face shape. If your cheeks are slightly sunken apply blusher high on cheek. Widen a narrow face by applying blusher towards the edge of the face and if your face is plump put it more towards the centre of the face (see illustration).

32. PICK SHADE OF BLUSHER by matching it to the colour of your cheeks when you pinch them.

33. USE BLUSHER WITH MORE IMPACT by blending it with your eyeshadow and merging the two colours between cheek and eye area. Or use your lipstick as blusher for a perfect colour match.

34. GLOW ALL OVER YOUR FACE by adding touches of blusher to brow-bone, chin and earlobes.

35. BE DIFFERENT! Line around eyes with two different colours, or one colour along the top lid and another along the bottom.

36. IF YOU'VE GOT SMALL EYES, never line the inside of lids with dark kohl eyeliner — it makes them look smaller.

37. LINE DROOPY EYES with a line that grows thicker towards outer edges of eyes.

38. LINE INSIDE OF LIDS more easily by gently pulling eyelid down (or up) a bit first. If eyes are at all sensitive line with eye pencil outside lashes and smudge a little for a subtle effect.

39. NO EYELINER? Use a wet brush and powder eyeshadow.

40. CREATE NEW COLOURS by mixing different eyeshadows together in a tin lid.

41. ALWAYS CURL LASHES before applying mascara.

42. IF LASHES ARE VERY PALE consider dyeing them with a home kit (about £3) or at a salon (£4-£5) — it won't last for ever but you'll save on mascara.

43. IF LASHES ARE VERY SHORT add to them with extra single false lashes just stuck on at the outer edge of the eyes. Dab eyelash adhesive onto eyelid with an orange stick for a neater finish.

44. CHANGE CHARACTER entirely for special occasions by trying a stark, no-colour make-up as here. Create a pale, matte base by blocking out all natural colour with green powder under very pale foundation or even white theatrical powder. Hollow cheeks with brown shader (don't use blusher or highlighter). Leave lips just foundation covered but outline with a brown eye pencil. Use black eyeliner only on eyes, swinging it upwards at outer edges to create a slightly Oriental-eyed look.

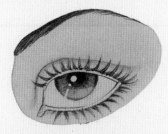

45. MAKE SMALL EYES BIG by outlining with white or pale-coloured eye pencils.

46. WHEN APPLYING MASCARA to bottom lashes hold a folded tissue underneath lashes to prevent mascara marking cheeks.

47. STOP CLOGGED LASHES by wiping mascara wand on the side of the container before applying, or by combing through lashes with an old, washed mascara wand immediately after applying mascara. Or use Maybelline's Dial A Lash mascara which allows you to control the amount of mascara that gets onto the brush.

48. SPACE OUT CLOSE-SET EYES by using highlighter on the whole area from the side of the nose up to the centre of the eyelid. Keep brows light and wing them outwards and upwards. Smudge eyeshadow on the outer area of the eyelid only. Also only mascara lashes at the outer edges of the eyes.

49. DISGUISE A DOUBLE CHIN by covering the whole area with a darker foundation than that used on your face but be sure to blend the edges well in.

50. SHOW OFF CUPID LIPS with a dot of highlighter just under the centre of your nose.

HOW LIBERATED ARE YOU?

How liberated are YOU? Come on now . . .think about it! When was the last time you chained yourself to the school railings? Can't remember . . .eh? Well, there was that time you arranged a ' sit-in ' in the common room when they wouldn't let you play football for the school team! JUST COZ YOU WERE A GIRL! What a cheek!

So if you want to find out how you stand as a defender of female rights . . .eyes down, and complete our quiz below.

1. You've managed to get yourself a little Saturday job at the local supermarket, but you discover that a boy working with you is getting a whole 10p. an hour more than you. Do you . . .

a) Keep giving him evil looks and try to trip him up every time he walks by carrying a pile of cans?

b) Immediately march off to the manager and demand equal pay?

c) Think nothing of it! After all, he's got to lift those heavy crisp packets all day . . . which is really man's work, isn't it?

2. Your favourite football team is playing in your home town. You try to persuade your big brother to take you with him, but he declines, saying it's no place for a girl. What do you do?

a) Puncture his best football?

b) Go, with a mate! Who needs brothers anyway?

c) Stay at home and watch the match on the telly?

3. You've fancied that gorgeous guy in the sixth form for ages. And he must like you too, coz he always smiles, but he never gets round to asking you out. Drat it! What are you going to do?

a) Try bumping into him at every opportunity, murmuring . . ." We can't go on meeting like this . . ." and hoping he'll take the hint?

b) Ask him out yourself! Well, why not? What have you got to lose? Go on . . . the shock won't kill him!

c) Worship him . . . from a distance?

4. If you went away to stay with friends for the weekend, and forgot your make-up, what would you do when you found out?

a) Panic? Not even the cat's allowed to see you without your mascara!

b) You couldn't care less! It's what's underneath that counts as far as you're concerned. And your hosts will just have to like it or lump it!

c) Wear dark glasses all weekend, and keep apologising to everyone for looking so hideous?

5. Your latest fella is getting a bit on the possessive side. And he detests you going out with your mates without him. Do you . . .

a) Get crafty? Tell him you're going to see your Maths teacher about extra lessons; and then sneak out to meet your friends?

b) Make no bones about the fact that you're not his personal property, and you think it's good for both of you to have your own friends, as well as each other?

c) Put up with it? You'd sooner be with him than your mates anyway!

6. You'd love to see that latest David Bowie film, but you don't want to go on your own. And you know your fella can't afford it. Do you . . .

a) Keep dropping massive hints, until the poor guy's driven either to cadging the money off his Dad, or robbing his little brother's piggy bank?

b) Tell him you've been dying to see the film, and you want to treat him for Christmas/Easter/his birthday/ passing his ' O ' Levels . . . whichever applies?

c) Say nothing, and wait till the video's released?

7. And finally: Do you think that fellas should still open doors and give up their seat on the bus for you?

a) Absolutely . . . Yes! You'd expect to be given preferential treatment all the time.

b) Not really. You think people should be considered more by age and circumstance, than by their sex?

c) You'd be flattered if they did, but you wouldn't really expect it.

Right now . . . let's see how you scored! Score 2 points for every a) you ticked. 3 points for a b). And 1 point for a c).

17-21 points

What a truly liberated female you are! And being a girl's never going to stop YOU getting where you want to go. But in spite of your feminist point of view, you're fair minded and considerate, and smart enough to know the right way to tackle a problem. Fellas will admire your independent ways, and appreciate your willingness to share responsibilities and not look on them as a free meal ticket!

10-16 points

Well, you've certainly got some strong views on the subject, but we can't help feeling it's the boys that need liberating in your case! You want it all your own way, and you're not averse to using all the feminine tricks at your disposal to get what you want! Come on . . . play by the rules. Don't sneak about making catty comments—come out in the open and say what you think. Not all guys are budding chauvinists . . . at least give them a chance to prove it!

Under 10 points

Oh dear, you really don't want to be liberated, do you? You're quite happy letting him play Tarzan, while you just stay at home and play Jane. You'd cook his meals and wash his socks until you were worn to a shadow. Come on . . . get wise! Don't be pushed around. Stand up for what you want, and fellas will respect you more for it!

Happy with your score? Or feeling a bit peeved coz you always fancied yourself as an ardent women's libber and you've just found out you're not? Well, it's all up to you really! If you're happy playing second fiddle to the guy in your life, who are we to tell you you're wrong! At least now you have a choice . . . and that's something that's entirely up to you!

BODY TALK!

You may not be able to read his mind, but his body is a different matter. We all give away feelings we think we've hidden by the way we sit, stand, walk and react to others – so to find out how receptive you are, see if you can read the story behind the pictures!

Q. WHICH GIRL REALLY TURNS HIM ON?

A. The girl in the blue top. The other girl has spoken to him, so he's turned towards her to reply. But look at his body – his legs remain crossed towards the girl he likes better, and his hands, pointing in the same direction, underline his feelings.

Q. DOES HE LIKE HER?

A. He is unsettled and bored. His hands are already making the first move to get up. They're clutching the edge of his chair, and he's full of tension – not at all relaxed. His head is also turned slightly away. The girl hasn't really noticed his situation – she's outstretched and relaxed, but she's not making much effort to interest him.

Q. IS HE TELLING THE TRUTH?

A. What he's telling you may be what you want to hear, but look closely and his body will give him away. We each have our own tell-tale movements, and as well as not being able to look you in the eye, he's shuffling his feet, playing with his hands, and looking very awkward.

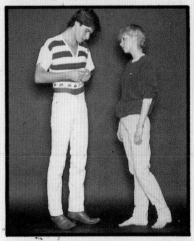

Q. IS HE REALLY A TOUGH GUY?

A. He's only acting big, though he may even have fooled himself that he can take anyone on. But the real character inside feels threatened. He uses the wall for moral as well as physical support, and the way he's crossed his arms and legs shows that he's really shut in against others.

Try watching yourself for a day or so, and you'll become aware of how you sit, stand, and move when you're with your friends. You can learn from the signs and movements you make when you're feeling shy or interested in someone, and then you'll know what to look for in your friends' behaviour.

YOU'RE IN HIS THOUGHTS WHEN:

1. You're across the room talking to someone else and you catch him looking at you – he's keen to know what you're doing.
2. He sees you walk into the room and tells a "big" story that bit louder than he needs to – he's trying to impress you.
3. He takes up the "big guy" pose against a handy wall or chair whenever other boys come to speak to you when you're with him – he feels threatened.

START LOOKING FOR SOME-ONE ELSE WHEN:

1. You meet him and his mouth smiles but his eyes don't – he's not being honest.
2. You suggest a date and he starts combing his hair and looking the other way – he's trying to get out of it.
3. He talks to you with his arms folded, legs crossed, and his gaze fixed firmly on the floor – he's already built a barrier between you.

GIANT POP

Well here it is at last, just what you've all been waiting for — a giant, month-by-month quiz of the point for each correct answer, then add up your score and turn to the conclusions to find out if

JANUARY

1. "Imagine" by John Lennon reached number one in January '81. In what year was it first released as a single?

2. Bucks Fizz were number one in January '82 with "Land Of Make Believe," but what was the name of the song they won the Eurovision song contest with?

3. David Soul had a hit with "Don't Give Up On Us" in January '77. What was the name of the famous police show he starred in on television?

4. The Pretenders had a January hit with "Brass In Pocket." What were the names of the original Pretenders?

5. What was Shakin' Stevens' real name, which he adopted by deed poll, when he had a hit with "Oh Julie" in January '82.

6. Can you identify this song by the lyrics? —
    "I light a candle to our love
    In love our problems
    *   disappear*
    But all in all we soon discover
    That one and one is all we
    *   long to hear."*

7. In January 1979 Village People had a number one hit with YMCA. Which "village" did the group represent?

FEBRUARY

1. "Don't Cry For Me; Argentina" was a number one hit for Julie Covington in February 1977. Which successful musical was it taken from?

2. The Chrysalis label scored their first number one hit with "When I Need You." Who sang it?

3. Joe Dolce had a hit with "Shaddup You Face" in February '81, but do you know what he called the "character" he played while singing it?

4. The Jam's second single to go straight in at number one was "A Town Called Malice/Precious" in February '82. What was their first single to do this?

5. What was the name of the album that John Lennon's "Woman" came from?

6. Michael Jackson had a hit in February '83 with "Billie-Jean." Lydia Murdock sang a follow up single — what was it called?

7. Kajagoogoo had a hit with "Too Shy" before they sacked their lead singer. What was his name?

MARCH

1. Kate Bush had a smash hit with "Wuthering Heights," but who wrote the classic novel by the same name?

2. In March '79 the Bee Gees had a hit single called "Tragedy." Shortly before this they made a smash with the soundtrack of a film. This was the best selling album of all time until it was knocked off its pedestal by Thriller. What was it called?

3. In March 1981, Roxy Music were number one with "Jealous Guy." The only words printed on the sleeve of this single were the title, the artist, and the phrase "a tribute." Who was it a tribute to?

4. Tight Fit had a hit in March '82 with a cover version. It is the only number one to have as many as six names on the writing credits. What is it called?

5. The Goombay Dance Band had a hit with "Seven Tears," in '82. What, apart from singing, is their front man Oliver Brendt famous for?

6. Which album did the Thompson Twins' single "Love On Your Side" come from?

TRIVIA QUIZ

hits from the past few years. Answer the questions (they're dead easy — honest), award yourself one
you're a pop egghead, Miss Average, or just plain dumb . . .

APRIL

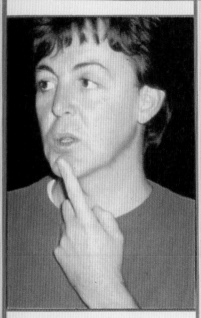

1. In April 1982 Paul McCartney had a hit single with Stevie Wonder. What was it called?

2. The Detroit Spinners had a number one with "Working My Way Back To You" in April '82. What were they originally called?

3. Mike Batt wrote Art Garfunkel's "Bright Eyes." Who had he previously written songs for?

4. Which famous person was the song "Matchstalk Men And Matchstalk Cats And Dogs" written about?

5. The Bay City Rollers had a number one hit in April '74 with "Bye Bye Baby." Can you name the only other number one hit they had?

MAY

1. Boney M had a hit in May '78 with "Rivers Of Babylon." What was the name of the B side of this record which was also a big hit for them?

2. This song was a major hit in May '83. Can you recognise it and the singer by these lyrics?
   "If you say run I'll run with you,
   And if you say hide we'll hide.
   Because my love for you
   would break my heart in two,
   If you should fall into my arms
   and tremble like a flower."

3. The first ever number one to include a day of the week in the title was by Blondie in May '79. Can you name it?

4. Dexy's Midnight Runners had their first hit with "Geno." Who was this song a tribute to?

5. Adam and The Ants had a hit in May' 81 with "Stand and Deliver" but do you know what Adam Ant's real name is?

JUNE

1. In June '83 Big Country announced the dates for their tour. Can you name their lead singer and the band he was formerly in?

2. In June '83 "The Tube" did a five-hour summer spectacular. Paula Yates was then a co-presenter of the programme. She once brought out a book of photographs called —
   a) Rock Stars In Their Underpants,
   b) Rock Stars In Their Socks,
   c) Rock Stars In The Flesh.

3. "Are Friends Electric?" was a hit for Tubeway Army in June '79. What is odd about this?

4. What was the name of the group who had a hit with "Candy Girl"?

5. The Wurzels had a hit with "Combine Harvester (Brand New Key)."What year was it released in?

141

GIANT POP TRIVIA QUIZ

JULY

1. John Travolta and Olivia Newton-John had a hit with "You're The One That I Want." What other track sung by them from the film "Grease" reached number one?

2. A bizarre story heard over the radio prompted a young man to write a song. A teenage Californian had shot at her playground playmates causing death and injury. What is the name of the song and what band sang it?

3. The Specials reached number one in July '81 with "Ghost Town." Subsequently they split up. What band was formed by three member of the Specials?

4. Can you name the band and its members who had a hit with "Bad Boys" in July '83.

5. *"Every move you make,*
   Every step you take,
   Every claim you stake,
   I'll be watching you."
Can you name this song and who sang it?

AUGUST

1. A Scottish folk singer, Mary Sandeman, had a one-off hit in August '81 with "Japanese Boy." What was the name she used instead of her own when she recorded the record?

2. David Bowie continued the story of Major Tom in August 1980 with "Ashes To Ashes." It was not a great hit in the U.S., however, but Bowie scored an even more important triumph when he took over the title role in what Broadway production?

3. Twenty years and 25 days after his first number one hit, Cliff Richard did it again in August '79. What was the name of the record?

4. Can you name the singer and song by these lyrics. It was a hit in August '83.
   "By the look in your eyes
   I can tell you're gonna cry,
   Is it over me?
   If it is save your tears,
   'Cos I'm not worth it,
   you'll see."

5. This one's the same — name the group, the song and the album it came from.
   "I was thirty-seven,
   You were seventeen,
   You were half my age,
   The youth I'd never seen.
   Unlikely strangers meeting in
   a dream,
   Heaven only knows the way
   it should have been."

SEPTEMBER

1. In September '78 there was another hit in the charts from the film "Grease." But do you know which characters Olivia Newton-John and John Travolta played?

2. Which single by The Police followed up their "Message In A Bottle" hit?

3. A young girl from Paisley in Scotland went to number one with her first single, "Feels Like I'm In Love" in September 1980. What was she called?

4. Soft Cell reached number one in September '83 with "Tainted Love." Which record label did they record it with?

5. Who was the "fairy godmother" in the video for Adam And The Ants' "Prince Charming" single?

OCTOBER

1. Lesley Gore sang "It's My Party" in 1963. Who was it a hit for in October '81?

2. Can you name the L.P. which Culture Club's "Karma Chameleon" came from?

NOVEMBER (questions continued)

3. Unravel this hit by the Police in October 1980. Me cons sold toes to Dan.

4. Rod Stewart had his biggest ever hit in October '71. It sold even more than "Sailing" — what was it called?

5. "Video Killed The Radio Star" was a hit for which group in 1979?

NOVEMBER

1. Name the song and the group from these lyrics:

*"I wanna be your number one, number one.
I'm not the kind of girl who gives up just like that."*

2. Which band did David Bowie have a number one hit with in November '81 called "Under Pressure"?

3. Dr Hook had a number one with "When You're In Love With A Beautiful Woman" one November but in what year?

4. What nationality were the band who had a hit with "Rat Trap" in November '78 and who are they?

5. What kind of girl did Billy Joel sing about in November '83?

DECEMBER

1. Which well-known heavy metal group had a Christmas number one in 1973 with "Merry Christmas Everybody"?

2. The Flying Pickets had a Christmas hit with a cover version of "Only You." Which band first sang this?

---

3. Tina Turner made an amazing comeback in December '83. Who was the other half of the famous duo she sang with several years before that?

4. What was the name of Showaddywaddy's smash hit in December '76?

5. Paul Young re-released his single "Love Of The Common People" at Christmas time in 1983. It reached number 3. What were his backing singers called?

6. Who had a hit with "There's No-One Quite Like Grandma"?

7. The Police had their second chart topper with "Walking On The Moon" in December '79. Which album was it taken from?

8. Pink Floyd had a huge hit with an anti-education anthem. What was it called?

9. The only single that sold a million copies in '81 was by the Human League. What was it?

10. "Mull Of Kintyre" was number one during December '77. What was the single on the other side called?

CONCLUSIONS

55-70: All right, Smarty-Pants, you might as well admit it now — you cheated, didn't you?

30-54: Not bad, not bad at all, but we bet you had to look up your book of hit singles for half the answers.

15-29: This isn't so hot, is it? How often do you listen to the radio? Once a month? Once a year? Oh, I see — never.

Under15: Aw, c'mon. Where have you been hiding for the past few years? Oh sorry, didn't realise you were still into Barry Manilow . . .

ANSWERS

JANUARY
1 1975, 2 Making Your Mind Up, 3 Starsky And Hutch, 4 Chrissie Hynde, James Honeyman-Scott, Pete Farnon and Martin Chambers, 5 Clark Kent, 6 Pipes Of Peace by Paul McCartney, 7 Greenwich Village in New York.

FEBRUARY
1 Evita, 2 Leo Sayer, 3 Giuseppi, 4 Going Underground, 5 Double Fantasy, 6 Superstar, 7 Limahl.

MARCH
1 Emily Bronte, 2 Saturday Night Fever, 3 John Lennon, 4 The Lion Sleeps Tonight, 5 Fire-eating, 6 Quick Step And Side Kick.

APRIL
1 Ebony And Ivory, 2 The Motown Spinners, 3 The Wombles, 4 L. S. Lowry, 5 Give A Little Love.

MAY
1 Brown Girl In The Ring, 2 Let's Dance, David Bowie, 3 Sunday Girl, 4 Geno Washington and his Ram Jam Band, 5 Stuart Goddard.

JUNE
1 Stuart Adams, The Skids, 2 a, 3 It was Gary Numan who sang it — The Tubeway Army was a thing of the past and he simply retained the name, 4 New Edition, 5 1976.

JULY
1 Summer Nights, 2 I Don't Like Mondays, The Boomtown Rats, 3 The Funboy Three, 4 Wham, Andrew Ridgely and George Michael, 5 Every Breath You Take, The Police.

AUGUST
1 Aneka, 2 The Elephant Man, 3 We Don't Talk Anymore, 4 Paul Young, Wherever I Lay My Hat (That's My Home), 5 Heaven 17, Come Live With Me, The Luxury Gap.

SEPTEMBER
1 Danny and Sandy, 2 Roxanne, 3 Kelly Marie, 4 Some Bizarre, 5 Diana Dors.

OCTOBER
1 Dave Stewart with Barbara Gaskin, 2 Colour By Numbers, 3 Don't Stand So Close To Me, 4 Maggie May, 5 Buggles.

NOVEMBER
1 The Tide Is High, Blondie, 2 Queen, 3 1979, 4 Irish, Boomtown Rats, 5 Uptown Girl.

DECEMBER
1 Slade, 2 Yazoo, 3 Ike Turner, 4 Under The Moon Of Love, 6 St Winifred's School Choir, 7 Regatta de Blanc, 8 Another Brick In The Wall (Part 11), 9 Don't You Want Me? 10 Girls School.

We have some clothes encounters with Kim Wilde
as she shows us her own . . .

STAR STYLES

1. "I must admit I've been wearing some rather weird and wonderful designs on T.V. recently," laughed Kim Wilde when we spoke to her, "but I think when you appear on the television, you have to be very much larger than life! However, when I'm out socialising, I don't wear things that do so much damage to the eyeballs!"

Has Kim got fed up with the simpler jeans and jacket look she wore at the beginning of her career?

"Before I became a singer, I was an

Art-school student, and my friends and I used to experiment with some pretty outrageous outfits and colour combinations. We'd phone up each other the night before and plan our colour schemes for the next day! I think though that you have to be in the right mood to wear certain clothes, and I often felt great in just a simple T-shirt and jeans, so I suppose it was just natural for me to carry that through when I started singing. It wasn't a planned image really, it was just what I liked to wear at the time. At the moment I suppose I'm getting interested in bolder colours, like this gypsy blouse, which is definitely one of my current faves!"

2. "Another thing people are always asking me about are these gloves," giggled Kim, "they were a birthday present from a good friend, so I can truthfully say, I have no idea where they came from, but I tell you one thing — they really do come in handy!" (Groan!)

3. "I really like diamante jewellery because it is cheap to buy and adds a bit of sparkle to your outfits. The brooch came from Miss Selfridge and I picked up the necklace at a funny little Market Stall at Camden Lock in London. I've always liked things that

shine . . . I think in a previous life I must have been a magpie!"

4. "I also love men's waistcoats, in fact any men's clothes! When I was young I was a bit of a tomboy. I was always borrowing my father's and brother's clothes, much to their annoyance, but these days they make me go out and buy my own!"

5. "This leather jacket is absolutely the favourite item of clothing I possess. It is an old friend that's travelled all over the world with me. I picked it up at a flea-market in Carnaby Street for £18. Once again, it's a man's jacket, but because it was such a small size, they couldn't sell it, hence the cheap price-tag!"

6. "I only possess two badges, but they are both very special to me. One is of Billy Fury, who was a great singer and a friend of my father. The other badge is of Elvis Costello. He's got a reputation for being very hard to get on with, although I found him to be very charming as well as being a great singer and song-writer.

"And finally my message to Jackie readers is to keep your peepers peeled, because you never know what bargain you may find . . . just around the corner."

Pic 1 "Just sit down while I put the kettle on," Paul said. "There's some newspapers on the coffee table, if you want to read them."

What a choice — reading about world affairs or watching Paul Young make you a cup of coffee!

Pic 2 Yes — this is what we looked at over our cornflakes!

Pic 3 After breakfast, Paul went for a quick work out in his mini-gym.

"It's what keeps me fit," Paul explained. "I need to be really

breakfast at PAUL's

An invitation to breakfast with Paul Young isn't something to turn down without a second thought . . . we didn't even need ½ a second to say 'Yes.'

strong and healthy in order to go on tour — and survive!"

Pic 4 Another cup of coffee. I need to recover from my exercise before I do anything else.

"The pictures on the wall? Oh, they're all my heroes — and heroines. Isn't Marilyn Monroe beautiful?"
P.S. If you're really eagle-eyed you'll be able to spot the Gold Disc lurking in this photo.

Pic 5 On the way to work.
Oh well, all good things have to come to an end!

Jackie

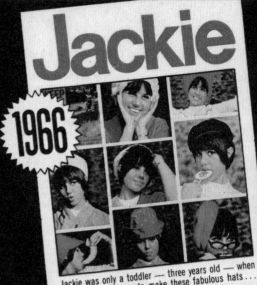

1966

Jackie was only a toddler — three years old — when you had the chance to make these fabulous hats... (what, *sarcasm* from *our* Ed?)

Jackie

FREE GIFT FOR YOU *inside*

...but who car

about that wh

SPRIN IS JU: AROUN

1967

I want a pair of wellies and a potty to wear on my head just like hers!

Jac

UFO

1968

Peace, love and pop— time John Lennon, B were on the cover of J

Jackie

1971

The ethereal look — or how to look a million dollars in your mum's old net curtain.

Jackie

I'd be a happy person too if I had legs that long. Don't think much of the hat, though.

1972

Jac

1975

David Essex is still p

Jackie

EYES RIGHT! How To Make Great Big Beautiful Eyes

Find Out About Your Feelings From Our Fantastic Quiz

STAR WARS EXCLUSIVE Mark Hamill tells all

MAKING HIS MARK!

SPECIAL SUPER SIZE DAVID SOUL PIN-UP

Part One This Week

1978

David Soul was a pop star when this was on the streets... and green was the ultimate in up-to-the-minute beauty...

Jackie

WHAT SECRETS ARE YOU GIVING AWAY? Find out on page 30...

WE TALK TO BLONDIE see page 16

DELICIOUS DAVID ESSEX PIN-UP

1980

What — David Essex again? And fashion was bordering on the fringe...

Jac

YOUR JACKIE POP CALENDAR! art One This Week

LOW TO 1981

Our Special Feature Te You How!

ARY NUM AST CONC

Picture Special

And Gary Numan one